PRINCIPLES AND PRACTICE IN RECORDS
MANAGEMENT AND ARCHIVES
Series Editor: Geoffrey Yeo

Community Archives
the shaping of memory

Other titles in the Principles and Practice in Records Management and Archives series (Series Editor: Geoffrey Yeo)

Archives: principles and practice
Laura A. Millar
ISBN 978-1-85604-596-4

Managing Records in Global Financial Markets
Lynn Coleman, Victoria L. Lemieux, Road Stone and Geoffrey Yeo, editors
ISBN 978-1-85604-663-3 (paperback); 978-1-85604-917-7 (e-book)

Preserving Archives Second edition
Helen Forde and Jonathan Rhys-Lewis
ISBN 978-1-85604-673-2

PRINCIPLES AND PRACTICE IN RECORDS
MANAGEMENT AND ARCHIVES
Series Editor: Geoffrey Yeo

Community Archives
the shaping of memory

edited by
**Jeannette A. Bastian
and Ben Alexander**

facet publishing

© This compilation: Jeannette Bastian and Ben Alexander 2009
The chapters: the contributors 2009

Published by Facet Publishing,
7 Ridgmount Street, London WC1E 7AE
www.facetpublishing.co.uk

Facet Publishing is wholly owned by CILIP: the Chartered Institute of Library and
Information Professionals.

British Library Cataloguing in Publication Data
A catalogue record for this book is available from the British Library.

ISBN 978-1-85604-639-8

First published 2009

Text printed on FSC accredited material.

Typeset from editors' disks by Facet Publishing in 10.5/13 pt Bergamo and MicroSquare.
Printed and made in Great Britain by CPI Group (UK Ltd, Croydon, CR0 4YY.

Contents

**PRINCIPLES AND PRACTICE IN RECORDS
MANAGEMENT AND ARCHIVES**
Series Editor: Geoffrey Yeo

Introduction to the series

ECORDS AND ARCHIVES are important resources for individuals, organizations and the wider community. Records are created in the course of
the functions and activities of organizations and the personal lives of
individuals, and are preserved and maintained to support business and
accountability and for cultural use. They provide evidence of, and information
about, the actions of their creators and the environment in which those actions
occurred. They extend and corroborate human and corporate memory and play
a critical role in maintaining awareness of how the present is shaped by the past.
Records are kept by almost everyone, but their management (and especially their
medium-term and long-term management) is a professional discipline with its
own distinctive body of knowledge. Within the discipline, 'records' and
'archives' are sometimes used as synonyms, but in English-speaking countries
'archives' usually denotes records which have been recognized as having long-
term value. The term 'archives' can also be used more widely, to refer to
collections of historical materials maintained by organizations, individuals,
families or community groups, or to the locations where such materials are held.

The series Principles and Practice in Records Management and Archives aims
both to disseminate and to add to the body of professional knowledge and
understanding. Each text in the series is intended to offer a detailed overview
of one or more key topics. The archives and records management discipline is
experiencing rapid changes - not least as a result of the digital revolution - and
the series will fully reflect the new technological context as well as the societal

changes and governmental initiatives in many countries that are placing new emphases on compliance, accountability, access to information and community relations. Some volumes in the series will address theoretical and strategic issues relating to the creation, management and interpretation of records and archives or their role in society; others will give practical guidance for those seeking successful and effective ways of managing them and presenting them to users. The authors come from many countries worldwide and are recognized experts in the field.

Community Archives: the shaping of memory

The fourteen essays in this book offer a range of perspectives on archives and communities, and on the interactions and interrelations between them. The editors, Jeannette Bastian and Ben Alexander, have assembled a team of contributors from a variety of backgrounds – academics, consultants, archivists, librarians, cultural heritage specialists – and from many different parts of the world. In their Introduction, the editors suggest that communities, and human needs for community, often find expression through archives and records; and that acts of record making, keeping and using may themselves be pivotal to the construction of communities. Other contributors explore how records and archives might form a basis for community identity, how they can promote justice or reconciliation, how they can empower those on the margins of society, and above all how they build and reinforce community memory. *Community Archives: the shaping of memory* also examines the role of archives and records professionals in supporting communities and the relationships of archivists to community records. Intentionally or inadvertently, established professional approaches may often privilege the value systems of powerful governments, corporate businesses and organizations or individuals with influence in the world. As the editors affirm, communitarian perspectives may oblige archivists to revisit traditional perceptions and extend their understanding of records to encompass new forms of evidence and more fluid manifestations of human memory.

Geoffrey Yeo, Series Editor

Acknowledgements

A COLLECTION OF ESSAYS such as this one that emanates from no particular conference, seminar or other imperative is entirely dependent upon the generosity of its authors. The editors wish to acknowledge the dedication and extraordinary efforts of the 14 authors who wrote essays solely out of personal conviction and because experience had taught them the value of communicating their own vision of community.

The editors also wish to acknowledge the efforts of Geoffrey Yeo, lecturer in the Department of Information Studies, University College London, for helping to bring the publisher and the editors together, Helen Carley at Facet Publishing who guided our efforts and Richard J. Cox who provided his usual good measure of common and archival sense.

Producing publications often requires significant support and tolerance on the part of the writers' or editors' families. This publication is no different. Ben wishes to thank Peggy and Molly, whose love is a constant inspiration, and Joy, Fran, Donna and Spencer whose endless support defines family. Jeannette would like to thank her family and in particular her husband Calvin whose wise advice, generosity and caring make all things possible.

Jeannette A. Bastian, Simmons College
Ben Alexander, Queens College

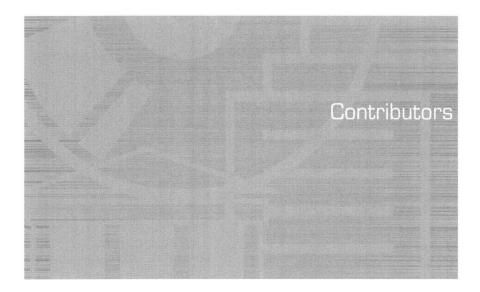

Contributors

Opeta Alefaio has been an archivist with the National Archives of Fiji for the last five years, coming to the field from a journalism background. He attained his BA majoring in journalism and history/politics at the University of the South Pacific. Prior to his current position Opeta worked in the Information Services section of the Ministry of Information and before that in the private sector as a journalist and radio announcer.

Ben Alexander (co-editor) is an Assistant Professor at the Graduate School of Library and Information Studies, Queens College, City University of New York. Before holding his current position he completed a two-year appointment as a post-doctoral scholar and the Associate Director of the Center for Information as Evidence in the Department of Information Studies at the University of California Los Angeles. Alexander received his Master's degree in British and American literature from Columbia University and his PhD in American literature from the City University of New York. He combines his academic training with ten years' experience in Special Collections at the New York Public Library (NYPL). For much of his tenure at NYPL he worked as a manuscript specialist (archivist) in the Manuscripts and Archives Division and served as Project Archivist for the Yaddo Records (the archival record of the artists' community located in Saratoga Springs, New York). He also administered an oral history project designed to complement Yaddo's material record. Alexander has lectured across the USA and throughout Europe on issues relating to archival theory and practice. Recent articles have appeared in *The New England Quarterly*, *English Studies Canada*, *American Archivist* and *Archival Science*. He is currently at work on a monograph entitled 'Yaddo: a creative history' forthcoming from the University of Georgia Press.

Marcel Barriault was born and raised in Moncton, New Brunswick, Canada. He holds a Bachelor of Education degree from the Université de Moncton (1992) and a Master's degree in English literature from the University of New Brunswick (1995). In 1999 he began his career at the National Archives of Canada, now Library and Archives Canada, first as a reference archivist, then as an archivist in the Political Archives section, where he is currently serving as Acting Manager. His interest in Acadian archives and genealogy stems from his research and work experience at the Centre d'études acadiennes while working on his Master's thesis. He has presented several papers on this topic at various conferences, including the Association of Canadian Archivists (ACA) Conference in Winnipeg (2001) and in Fredericton (2008), and he has published his findings in such journals as *Archivaria* and *Les Cahiers de la Société historique acadienne*. His other main research interest is the emerging field of queer archives. He has presented papers on this topic at the ACA Conference in Montréal (2004) and in Kingston (2007), as well as at the GLBT Archives Libraries Museums and Special Collections (ALMS) Conference in New York City (2008). An article on the preservation of gay male erotica and pornography in Canada is forthcoming. He is presently conducting research to produce a biography of the pioneering Acadian genealogist and archivist, Placide Gaudet (1850–1930), and he is currently the French language editor of *Archivaria*.

Jeannette A. Bastian (co-editor) is an Associate Professor at the Graduate School of Library and Information Science, Simmons College, Boston, Massachusetts, where she directs their Archives Management programme. From 1987 to 1998 she was the Territorial Librarian and Archivist of the United States Virgin Islands and she received her PhD from the University of Pittsburgh in 1999. Her research interests and writings are in the areas of post-colonialism, collective memory and archival education. Her publications include *West Indian Literature: an index to criticism, 1930–1975* (1981), *Owning Memory: how a Caribbean community lost its archives and found its history* (2003) and (with Donna Webber) *Archival Internships: a guide for faculty, supervisors, and students* (2008).

Joel A. Blanco-Rivera has an MSI with specialization in archives and records management from the University of Michigan School of Information (2003). From 2004 to 2005 he was a lecturer at the University of Puerto Rico, where he taught courses for the certification in archives and records management. He is currently pursuing a PhD at the University of Pittsburgh School of Information Sciences. His research interests include archival implications of records of truth commissions and human rights documentation in Latin America, archives and social memory, government secrecy, and accountability.

Richard J. Cox, Professor in Library and Information Science at the University of Pittsburgh, School of Information Sciences, is responsible for their archives concentration in the MS and the PhD programmes, and also chairs the LIS programme and the Doctoral Studies programme in LIS. He was a member of the Society of American Archivists Council from 1986 to 1989. He served as editor of the *American Archivist* from 1991 to 1995 and editor of *Records & Information Management Report* from 2001 to 2007. He has written extensively on archival and records management topics, publishing 13 books in this area including *American Archival Analysis: the recent development of the archival profession in the United States* (1990), winner of the Waldo Gifford Leland Award given by the Society of American Archivists; *Documenting Localities* (1996); *Managing Records as Evidence and Information* (2001), winner of the Waldo Gifford Leland Award in 2002; co-editor, *Archives and the Public Good: records and accountability in modern society* (2002); *No Innocent Deposits: forming archives by rethinking appraisal* (2004), winner of the Waldo Gifford Leland Award in 2005; *Lester J. Cappon and Historical Scholarship in the Golden Age of Archival Theory* (2004); *Understanding Archives and Manuscripts* (2006) with James M. O'Toole; *Ethics, Accountability, and Recordkeeping in a Dangerous World* (2006); and *Personal Archives and a New Archival Calling* (2009). He is completing an extended essay on war, memory and archives, and research on the diaries of Lester J. Cappon, 1954–1981. Dr Cox was elected a Fellow of the Society of American Archivists in 1989.

Andrew Flinn is Director of the Archives and Records Management MA programme in the Department of Information Studies at University College London. He is also the current chair of the Forum for Archives and Records Management Education and Research (FARMER) and a member of the Community Archives and Heritage Group. He is the principal investigator on the Arts and Humanities Research Council funded 'Community archives and identities' project (2008–9) which examines community archive and heritage initiatives among black and minority ethnic groups in the UK. Among other professional positions, Andrew was previously archivist at the National Museum of Labour History in Manchester. As a social historian and archival educator, his interests include documenting grassroots community organization and activism, collective and social memory, and the relationship between archives, heritage and identities. Recent publications include 'Community Histories,

Community Archives: some opportunities and challenges' in the *Journal of the Society of Archivists*, 2007, and 'Other Ways of Thinking, Other Ways of Being: documenting the margins and the transitory: what to preserve, how to collect' in *What are Archives?*, ed. L. Craven, 2008.

Steven G. Fullwood is the founder and project director of the Black Gay and Lesbian Archive at the Schomburg Center for Research in Black Culture, New York Public Library. He is also the founder and publisher of Vintage Entity Press, and the author of *Funny*, a book of humorous essays. In 2005 Fullwood was honoured with a New York Times Librarian Award.

Patricia Galloway has a BA in French from Millsaps College (1966), MA (1968) and PhD (1973) in comparative literature from the University of North Carolina at Chapel Hill (UNC-CH), and a PhD in anthropology (2004), also from UNC-CH. She worked as a medieval archaeologist in Europe in the 1970s and then became involved with humanities-oriented computing, which she supported in the Computer Unit of Westfield College of the University of London 1977–9. From 1979 to 2000 she worked at the Mississippi Department of Archives and History (MDAH), where she was a documentary editor, archaeological editor, historian, museum exhibit developer and manager of information systems. From 1997 to 2000 she directed a National Historical Publications and Records Commission-funded project at MDAH to create an electronic records program for the state of Mississippi. In 2000 she went to the School of Information, University of Texas-Austin, where she is Associate Professor in Archival Enterprise and teaches courses in digital archives, archival appraisal and historical museums. Her recent publications include *Choctaw Genesis 1500–1700* (1995), *The Hernando de Soto Expedition* (1997) and a book of essays entitled *Practicing Ethnohistory*. She has also published book chapters in *Historical Archaeology* (2006) and the forthcoming *Mapping the Mississippian Shatter Zone* (2009); and articles in *American Archivist*, *D-Lib* and *Ethnohistory*. She supervises and participates on the committees of MA and PhD students involved with digital preservation, history of scholarly communication, digital preservation and access policy, archival appraisal theory and practice, and qualitative methods in information science research.

Glen Kelly is Chief Executive Officer of the South West Aboriginal Land and Sea Council in Perth, Australia. SWALSC is a native title representative body that works in the interests of the Noongar People.

Eric Ketelaar is Emeritus Professor at the University of Amsterdam. From 1997 to 2009 he was Professor of Archivistics in the Department of Media Studies of the Faculty of Humanities of the University of Amsterdam. Since 1997 he has been involved in research on social and collective memories. At the request of the UN International Criminal Tribunal for the former Yugoslavia (ICTY) Ketelaar scrutinized ICTY's records and archives management, writing a report (2005) with recommendations on the legacy of the ICTY and its use in justice and reconciliation. In 2007–8 he was a member of an expert group providing ICTY and its sister tribunal for Rwanda with an independent analysis of how to ensure future preservation and accessibility of their archives. Ketelaar was General State Archivist (National Archivist) of The Netherlands from 1989 to 1997 and held the archivistics chair in the Department of History, University of Leiden, 1992–2002. In 2000–1 he was Netherlands Visiting Professor at the University of Michigan (School of Information) and Honorary Professor at Monash University, Melbourne, 2003–8, where he continues involvement as Adjunct Senior Research Fellow. He served the International Council on Archives in different capacities, and in 2000 was elected Honorary President. He is President of the Records Management Convention of The Netherlands. He has written over 300 articles mainly in Dutch, English, French and German and several books, including two general introductions on archival research and a handbook on Dutch archives and records management law. He is one of three editors-in-chief of *Archival Science*.

David Mander has worked in British archives for over 30 years. He has been active in London, serving as archivist for two London boroughs from 1977 to 2005, and now works across Britain as a partner in Creative Cultures, a heritage and arts consultancy. In his capacity as Head of Hackney Archives, David was active in the Linking Arms project launched by The National Archives, which included proposals for the development of community archives. Hackney served as one of two English pilot areas. Subsequently David went on to become involved in the group that emerged from this project, the Community Archives Development Group. He has formed a range of London-wide bodies for archivists and users, including the Greater London Archives Network (1982–2005), the London Archives Users Forum (1987–2005) and the London Archives Regional Council (1999–2005). These three bodies were succeeded by Archives for London Ltd in 2005, which David currently chairs. He was also active in the formation of MLA London, part of the strategic partnership for museums, libraries and archives in England, and served as a board member from 2004–6. David is active in a number of UK professional bodies, including the Public Services Quality Group, and edited a new edition of *A Standard for Access to Archives* in 2008. David has written on a range of local history topics. His services to UK archives were recognized by the award of an OBE in the Queen's honours list in 2007.

Stephen Naron, born and raised outside Kansas City, has a BA in history from the University of Kansas (1998), and an MSIS from the School of Information in Austin, Texas (2003). Stephen also studied abroad at Tel Aviv University as an undergraduate, and pursued a Magister in Jewish Studies/History at the Freie Universität Berlin, and the Zentrum für Antisemitismusforschung, Berlin. In 2003 he began his career at Yale University's Fortunoff Video Archive for Holocaust Testimonies (FVAHT), where he worked for nearly five years as an archivist. In addition to cataloguing hundreds of survivor testimonies, he also participated in the archive's long-term preservation efforts. He now resides in Stockholm, Sweden, where he works as a translator, and continues to consult for the FVAHT. He is a member of the Association of Moving Image Archives.

Victoria Borg O'Flaherty is the Director of Archives at the National Archives of St Kitts-Nevis. She has a degree in history from the University of Malta and an MLitt in archives and records management from the University of Dundee. She was the secretary of the Caribbean Branch of the International Congress on Archives (CARBICA) from 2003 to 2005 and has served on several advisory committees dealing with education and culture. She has published and lectured on labour history in St Kitts and has in recent years extended her interest to resistance to enslavement.

Ricardo L. Punzalan is an assistant professor at the School of Library and Information Studies at the University of the Philippines. He is currently pursuing his doctoral studies at the School of Information at the University of Michigan. His current research explores how archives figure in the propagation of stigma associated with leprosy and the formation of collective memory of the disease in a former leprosarium in the Philippines. Aside from a PhD in information, he is also pursuing graduate certificates in science, technology and society, and museum studies.

András Riedlmayer, a native of Budapest, Hungary, and educated in Germany and the USA, holds degrees from the University of Chicago (BA, history), Princeton University (MA, near Eastern studies) and Simmons College (MS, library and information science). Since 1985 he has directed the Documentation Center of the Aga Khan Program for Islamic Architecture at Harvard University's Fine Arts Library. A specialist in the history and culture of the Balkans, he has spent over a decade documenting the destruction of architecture, archives, libraries and other cultural heritage during the wars in Bosnia–Herzegovina (1992–5) and Kosovo (1998–9). He has testified as an expert witness before the International Criminal Tribunal for the former Yugoslavia in The Hague in several cases, including the war crimes trial of former Serbian president Slobodan

Milošević and also before the International Court of Justice, in the case brought by Bosnia–Herzegovina against Serbia and Montenegro, concerning the application of the Convention on the Prevention and Punishment of the Crime of Genocide (2006). Author of numerous articles in professional journals and edited volumes, published in five languages, he has served as president of the Turkish Studies Association (2006–8) and chair of the Middle East Librarians' Association's Committee on Iraqi Libraries (2003–7). He is co-founder of the Bosnian Manuscript Ingathering Project, an innovative effort to trace and recover extant microfilms and photocopies of some of the thousands of archival documents and manuscripts destroyed when archives and libraries in Bosnia–Herzegovina were burned by nationalist extremists during the 1990s.

Mary Stevens is a post-doctoral research associate in the Department of Information Studies at University College London (UCL). She is working with Andrew Flinn and Elizabeth Shepherd on the Arts and Humanities Research Council funded 'Community archives and identities' project (2008–9) which examines community archive and heritage initiatives among black and minority ethnic groups in the UK. Mary's PhD, also from UCL, was jointly supervised in the departments of French and Anthropology and explored the reworking of national identity discourses in the project for a national museum of immigration in France, which opened in 2007. Her research interests include the politics of memory, particularly in France, and the way these are mediated through heritage practices and institutions. Recent publications include 'Museums, Minorities and Recognition: memories of North Africa in contemporary France' in *Museum and Society* (2007) and she has articles forthcoming in 2009 in *The Public Historian* and *African and Black Diaspora*.

Setareki Tale is the head of the National Archives of Fiji where he has contributed to the acquisition, safekeeping and access of Fiji's documentary heritage for the last 23 years, 10 of which have been as Government Archivist. Seta, as he prefers to be called, received his Master of Information Management – Archives/Records from the University of New South Wales. He is currently the President of the Pacific Regional Branch of the International Council on Archives, is on the executive board of the International Council on Archives as the Vice President, Regional Branches, and is a professional member of, and involved in, other national, regional and international organizations.

David A. Wallace is Lecturer IV and Research Investigator at the School of Information, University of Michigan, where he teaches in the Archives and Records Management specialization. He received his BA from the State University of New York, Binghamton; MLS from the State University of

New York, Albany, and PhD from the University of Pittsburgh. Wallace's major areas of research include investigations into the connections between archiving and the shaping of the present and the past; the role of archives in enabling and denying accountability and justice; and computerization of government records. Since 1994 he has authored more than 45 professional publications and given over 50 presentations at professional forums on record keeping and accountability, freedom of information, government secrecy, professional ethics, electronic records management, graduate archival education, information infrastructures and cultural heritage on the web. He is co-editor of *Archives and the Public Good: accountability and records in modern society* (2002) and served as the series technical editor to the National Security Archive's *The Making of US Policy* series (Chadwyck-Healy and National Security Archive, 1989–92). In 2001 he received ARMA International's Britt Literary Award for best article in the peer-reviewed *Information Management Journal*. Wallace's consultations include associations with the Nelson Mandela Foundation's Memory Programme, the South Africa History Archive and Computer Professionals for Social Responsibility.

Introduction

Communities and archives – a symbiotic relationship

JEANNETTE A. BASTIAN
BEN ALEXANDER

S EEKING, BUILDING OR dwelling within the close kinship of community
is both an acute desire and a pressing need for many citizens of our global,
unbounded and networked 21st century society. These desires and
needs often find expression through records. Through their formation,
collection, maintenance, diffusion and use, records in all their manifestations
are pivotal to constructing a community, consolidating its identity and shaping
its memories. Archivists have significant roles to play in this process. Sustaining
a community – whether digitally or physically – depends not only on a practical
and theoretical understanding of its records but also on the knowledge and ability
to preserve and value them. The collection of essays in this volume addresses
both the ability of archivists to assist in the community-building process and
the responsibilities that archivists have in fostering and furthering all aspects of
that development. For while records may fulfil beneficial and legitimating
roles in our search for community, they also have other often prescriptive, less
benign, but no less critical parts to play. As they demonstrate the many different
ways in which communities and records interact with one another, these essays
call our attention to both the salutary and the controversial acts of record
making and record keeping, illustrating how these activities in themselves may
create community.

Every volume presents its own intellectual and professional challenges. This
volume is no different. The central challenge is the idea of 'community' itself.
How do you ask authors to write essays about community when the concept

is so ambiguous, so difficult to define? How do you construct a collected volume around ideas that are generally 'understood' but not well articulated, that essentially are agreed upon to be fundamentally subjective? While the subjectivity of 'community' initially lay at the heart of the editors' concerns it also proved to be the glue, binding all definitions together and resulting in rewarding analyses as well as inspired and unexpected insights. The authors in this volume, an eclectic group of archivists, librarians and lawyers, approach questions of community from a range of national, cultural and individual perspectives that highlight both the versatility of 'community' and its close connection to memory and identity.

The 14 essays in this book make immediately clear that there is no one definition of 'community' or even of 'archives' and that both of these concepts assume widely disparate meanings in different contexts. Similarly the relationships between records and the communities that create or use them vary in accordance with the conditions, traditions and situations of creation and use. The activity of community archiving in the UK, for example, is a recent rapidly evolving phenomenon focusing primarily on minority social and ethnic groups, while special collections and historical societies in the USA and Canada have been sites of regional and group expressions since the 19th century. But these are only a few of the ways that communities express themselves through records in these chapters. Records feature prominently as weapons of justice in international criminal tribunals and truth and reconciliation commissions, records become instruments of power for marginalized groups seeking a place in society, records become the memory glue that binds people seeking to recall and share similar experiences, and for postcolonial countries, records are a complex and painful mixture of narratives that both deny and offer historical possibilities. The essays in this volume are an attempt to come to grips with these multiplicities of communities as well with the myriad ways that communities relate to their records as both expressions and promoters of common identities.

Each essay is one chapter and these are arranged in four groups of case studies, each group illustrating a different aspect of the communities/archives relationship. The essays were not selected with any specific geographic dimensions in mind, nor as orderly representations of any particular groups or proponents of any cause, rather, the editors cast a wide international net in their request for material and were eager to portray a variety of different perspectives. The volume begins with a model of community archives from the UK, moves to communities creating non-traditional records, considers issues around records loss, destruction and recovery and looks at online communities constructed around records. The final section offers practical examples of the construction of the archives of three very different communities. The concluding essay considers the responsibility of the archivist in relationship to the community.

The wide-ranging perspectives on community reflected in these essays also reflect great variety in tone. The reader should bear several caveats in mind. The diversity of these essays is not the diversity of content and location alone but also of voice, format and style. Each essay offers a highly individual lens through which concepts of community are examined, each author writing from a discrete philosophical space. While many of the authors are academics, several are practicing archivists and librarians, consultants and lawyers living both in metropolitan countries and small post-colonial islands. Their visions of community may be national as well as local, societal as well as personal. The tones and voices of these essays reflect community on a variety of levels and through many interpretations.

As a group, the essays generally express several common themes. Primary among these is an expanding and expandable view of a record, illustrating how defining archives becomes increasingly complex in a global society. Records can be the traditional textual evidence-bearing documents described so well by Ketelaar, or the more elusive and difficult to capture oral expressions discussed by Galloway, Tale and Alefaio. Perhaps records are the artificially created and reconstructed collections illustrated by Riedlmeyer and Naron, the assorted formats and artifacts characterized by Barriault, Kelly, and Fullwood, the electronic traces analysed by Flinn and Stevens, the performances and music examined by Wallace, or the monuments and locations described by Punzalen. Records may even include commemorations and cultural activities such as community festivals and parades, as many of these essays imply. Clearly records are all of these things and more.

What also seems clear is that the dynamic structures of communities and their complex cultural expressions challenge archivists to look beyond traditional practice and embrace new ways of seeing and understanding records. Today it is the minor narratives, the untold stories, the traces, the whispers and the expressions of marginalized identities that people yearn to find in the archives. Their success may depend on the availability of evidence, but their success may also depend on the ability of archivists to recognize and accept this evidence into the archives, for the stuff of minor narratives may not always be perceived as archival. If the archive is to be a place where all stories can be found, then archivists must expand their own horizons, extending traditional boundaries of recordness to embrace a larger and more inclusive vision of the records that communities create. Cox in his concluding essay recognizes the power of the many kinds of records that support communities but at the same time cautions archivists against the potential dangers inherent in the exclusiveness of the community itself.

An additional pervasive theme is the relationship between records and memory. Whether the memory is being sought, reconstructed or preserved, the ability of a community to conceptualize itself, now and into the future depends to a great extent on its capacity for remembrance and its ability to express that remembrance communally. Amnesia is not a viable option for any group that wishes to continue to exist, as the essay on reconstructing Bosnian villages (Riedlmeyer and Naron) distressingly reminds us. Records are not only the path to our history and identity (O'Flaherty) but even the records of a painful past can over time mellow into common memory (Punzalen). Memory through records can also bring justice (Ketelaar; Kelly), allow communities to come to terms with their pasts (Blanco-Rivera), enable marginalized groups to express themselves (Barriault; Galloway; Fullwood) and give communities a presence and a stake in the future (Flinn and Stevens; Mander).

One the one hand these essays describe communities on the margins, out of the mainstream, not part of the master narratives. On the other, they demonstrate that all communities are in various ways woven into an international social fabric. As major and minor narratives conflate and become interdependent, these essays illustrate above all that 'marginal' is no longer a concept that makes sense in our world.

Part 1

A community archives model

'It is noh mistri, wi mekin histri.'[1] Telling our own story: independent and community archives in the UK, challenging and subverting the mainstream

ANDREW FLINN AND MARY STEVENS

And it is that history that I want to retrieve – the history that we made in this country, the history that Claudia Jones inspired. The history of us as black settlers, not coloured immigrants, the history that black workers contributed to the working-class struggle, which has been ignored by white historians, the history of the struggles of black women to overcome the particular racisms visited upon them . . . the history of black youth rebellion . . . It is that history I want to talk about . . .

Sivanandan, 2004

. . . the strongest reason for creating the archives was to end the silence of patriarchal history about us – women who loved women . . . we wanted our story to be told by us, shared by us and preserved by us.   Nestle, 1990, 87

Introduction

As the quotations opening this chapter suggest, the act of recovering, telling and then preserving one's own history is not merely one of intellectual vanity; nor can it be dismissed – as some still seek to do – as a mildly diverting leisure activity with some socially desirable outcomes. Instead the endeavour by individuals and social groups to document their history, particularly if that history has been generally subordinated or marginalized, is political and subversive. These 'recast' histories and their making challenge and seek to undermine both the distortions and omissions of orthodox historical narratives, as well as the archive and heritage collections that sustain them (Hall, 2005, 28). Archivists and others concerned with exploring archives and their power are beginning to examine the significance that engaging with archival materials – and the history created from them – can have for individuals. Rather less has been written, in the UK at least, on the impact that creating archives and 'making histories' can have on the development of subversive and counter-hegemonic social or public memories (Johnston, 2001; Flinn, 2007; Hopkins, 2008).

This chapter seeks to add to the literature by examining independent community archives as social movements (or as elements of social movements) and by identifying individuals involved in community archives as political and cultural activists campaigning for equality and cultural recognition and against racism and discrimination. Research that the authors are currently conducting into independent and community archival activity amongst communities of predominantly African and Asian heritage in the UK seeks to explore the motivations, challenges and impacts of community history initiatives by working closely with a number of such organizations over a sustained period of several months each.[2] This chapter will not present the final findings of this research, nor deal explicitly with our four main cases, but it will draw on interviews with individuals who are active in independent community archives and on the readings and understandings which have informed our work thus far.

To introduce and explicate the motivations behind the community archiving endeavour, this chapter will first sketch something of the social, intellectual and political context in which some independent archives have arisen and to which they have responded. It will then examine in more detail some of the variety, history, aims and ideologies underlying such initiatives with reference to some specific examples of independent community archives and activists. Although the main focus will be on archives that document the experiences of communities of African and Asian heritage in Britain, we will also indicate parallel developments in working-class, women's, and gay and lesbian archives as well as acknowledging the existence and influence of similar initiatives internationally. The final section will attempt to identify the significance of community history activism in transforming narratives of British history and, ultimately, the impact of such initiatives on the complex area of the construction and articulation of identity, particularly when viewed through the frame of shifting public policy agendas for archives and heritage more generally.

Language and terminology shift and evolve, often describing varied and multiple identities imperfectly and imprecisely. In the context of this chapter, and some of the organizations on which we are concentrating, at times we use 'black' in a broader, political sense ('Black was the colour of our politics, not the colour of our skins', Sivanandan, 2009, 96), embracing individuals of African, Asian and other heritages. In the words of one leading activist, Linda Bellos (2006), 'black' was an inclusive, political term, 'we progressives called ourselves black . . . because we knew that we shared a common experience of racism because of our skin colour'. However, it is important to acknowledge that while such usage was common in the debates of the 1970s, 1980s and 1990s, it is less frequent and current today, when generally 'black' is taken to refer to people of African and African-Caribbean heritage. Throughout this chapter we will seek to be aware of such important distinctions and use of language.

In addition, given the enormous variety of activities and forms of organizations that might be referred to as community archives, it is instructive to try to clarify what it is we are referring to. In general our research adheres to broad and inclusive definitions of what community archives or community history activity might comprise – the (often) grassroots activities of creating and collecting, processing and curating, preserving and making accessible collections relating to a particular community or specified subject (Flinn, 2007, 152–4). The term 'community' is capable of many interpretations (Crooke, 2007, 27–40), including being used as a reductive euphemism for an ethnic or faith minority (Terracciano, 2006, 24). The sociologist Brian Alleyne, among others, has warned of the dangers of using such an ill-defined term, especially when the idea of 'community' is employed simply to denote 'human collectivities' rather than seeking to better understand the formation of such collectivities (2002b, 608). 'Independent archives' or the qualified form 'independent community archives' might be a more appropriate nomenclature; however, we use 'community archives' in this context as a term which is already widely used and generally understood. The emphasis is on the community or group's own self-definition and self-identification by locality, ethnicity, faith, sexuality, occupation, ideology, shared interest or any combination of the above.

Further variety is to be found in the form that these archives take, whether operating largely in the physical world or the virtual world as well as in the type of archives collected. Most community archives collect many materials (including objects, all manner of recordings, works of art, ephemeral items such as leaflets, posters and badges, and a range of other printed materials and grey literature) that do not conform to traditional notions of what is a record or an archive. In practice distinctions between community archives and those 'community-based exhibitions' and museums described by museum and heritage scholar Elizabeth Crooke (2007, 3) as being established entirely independently of the formal museum sector, or indeed between community libraries, resource centres and even community bookshops, are not at all precise nor necessarily very useful.

The politics of community archives

In all this broad variety and definitional vagueness, there are two areas of commonality to most if not all independent community archive initiatives. First, while many community archives are willing to work in partnership with a range of mainstream heritage and other bodies, experience has made them often cautious about such relationships and they frequently maintain a strong sense of independence and autonomy in their decision-making and governance. It is possible that over time the aspiration or the ability to sustain such independence may decline. Some archives may eventually entrust their collections to a mainstream institution with custody shared or even relinquished. Others may be less concerned with custody and retaining the material they collect, preferring instead to be independent actors in the heritage field in other ways.[3] However, at source a strong desire for autonomy may be inspired by either a distrust of or antagonism towards mainstream institutions. In the case of those groups whose origins and motivations are rooted in new left, anti-racist or identity politics of the 1960s onwards, the autonomy imperative may be driven by a political and ideological commitment to ideas of independent grassroots organizations, self-help and self-determination. For Stephen Small, independent black institutions such as 'schools, cultural centres, bookshops or museums . . . are safe spaces in which we can decide our priorities and work towards them without hindrance by those hostile to our goals or by those with good intentions who don't share our priorities' (1997, 61).

The second point of commonality, and perhaps an even more universal one, follows on from the above. Most, if not all, community archivists are motivated and prompted to act by the (real or perceived) failure of mainstream heritage organizations to collect, preserve and make accessible collections and histories that properly reflect and accurately represent the stories of all of society. As cultural theorist Stuart Hall noted in the case of the African and Asian Visual Artists' Archive, 'the absence of any sustained attention or critical dialogue within the dominant institutions of the art world, and given a systematic marginalisation over the years' of work from African-Caribbean and Asian diasporas, meant that the artists were themselves 'obliged to act first as curators, and now as archivists' (2001, 91).

The collection, creation and ownership of resources that challenge, correct and re-balance these absences and partial narratives were and are often viewed explicitly as counter-hegemonic tools for education and weapons in the struggle against discrimination and injustice (Alleyne, 2007, 463–4). The lessons of the past, and the ways in which these lessons inform different (but similar) contemporary struggles, is frequently stressed by influential writers such as historian, former librarian and director of the Institute of Race Relations (IRR), Ambalavaner Sivanandan. In one passage for instance he writes, 'You see the connections – between Third World struggles and anti-racist struggles, between Africans, West Indians and Asians, between the class and the community? If I am at pains to draw these out it is because they are unique to the history of black people in Britain – and it is a history we must recall if we are to contest the racist imperialism of the global era' (Sivanandan, 2004).

It is this close identification between the production of history, education and political struggle that leads to an understanding of independent community archives as, or as a part of, new social movements.

New social movements tend to embrace a model of grassroots and local organization that focuses on campaigning in their local environment or community (as opposed to, for instance, the workplace). This organizational model and campaign focus is allied to broad, often trans-national transformative aims and objectives, which seek fundamentally to challenge contemporary norms and social organization (Alleyne, 2002a, 2–3; Crooke, 2007, 36–7, 110). The role of culture within the new urban social movements of the post-war period has also been widely acknowledged; in sociologist Paul Gilroy's words, what defines these movements is their 'common struggle for the social control over historicity', that is their attempts to present an alternative way of understanding the current development and functioning of society (1995, 225). Elizabeth Crooke notes the importance of the presentation of counter-hegemonic histories and heritage for binding and sustaining social movements, 'through telling the history of the community, group leadership evolves and the history and heritage becomes a springboard for further action' (2007, 37), and identifies certain community museums (such as the District Six Museum in Cape Town) as part of transformatory social movements.

Brian Alleyne takes a slightly different position – rather than historical and educational initiatives being social movements themselves, he sees activists and intellectuals like John La Rose and others in the New Beacon circle and the George Padmore Institute as engaging with and supporting a variety of social and grassroots campaigns without necessarily being characterized as a social movement themselves (2002a, 179–82). This distinction, while significant, is perhaps not as important as a shared view that alternative histories and education about these histories are powerful tools in challenging dominant narratives and the societies that these narratives help sustain.

Within this framework, it should be clear that community archives are not 'constituted' on impulse. The moment when the archive is created and named as such is a moment of reflection and often a response to other societal conditions. It is an act of resistance against subordination and discrimination, 'always a critical one, always a historically located one, always a contestatory one' (Hall, 2001, 89). When a history is denied or made invisible, a group or a community may sustain or recover that history by combining powerful (yet sometimes destructive) mythic memory with communal memory that through activities like community archives is strengthened and reinforced by being made visible and shared (Josipovici, 1998). It is in this context, of challenging and resisting historic and ongoing discrimination in society and subordination in national narratives, that independent histories and community archives are perhaps best understood.

Three independent community archives
The George Padmore Institute

> . . . we all had other lives to live as well, we weren't being paid as formal archivists.
>
> White, 2008

An examination of the lineage of independent community archives suggests that there are close associations between many of these organizations and initiatives and a range of political struggles and social campaigns. It also indicates the interdependency between these struggles and the archives. Centres and archives are not seen as alternatives to struggles but as part of them, a resource for continuing and renewing the fight. Sometimes this has developed into a more definitively historical project but even in these cases the history represented by the archive and created by those who research in the archives is frequently connected to an agenda of education for social change – either as a resource to inform present and future actions, or as a corrective to the absences and misrepresentations of mainstream and dominant accounts.

The London-based George Padmore Institute (GPI) was founded in 1991 as an archive, library, educational resource and research centre by John La Rose, his partner Sarah White and others associated with New Beacon Books.[4] Named after George Padmore, the radical anti-imperialist, the institute seeks to honour his legacy by 'continuing the traditions which shaped his life', Marxism, internationalism, anti-imperialism and anti-racism (Alleyne, 2002a, 99–100). The key influence behind the establishment of the GPI was John La Rose (1927–2006), who like fellow Trinidadian Padmore was active in international, anti-racist and anti-imperialist activity in several countries. An 'activist-organiser-intellectual' (Alleyne, 2002a, 23), La Rose had been actively involved in trade union organizing in Trinidad and Venezuela before coming to Britain in 1961. Thereafter he was at the centre of a group of political and cultural activists who founded or supported a range of campaigns and organizations including the Caribbean Artists Movement, the New Beacon bookshop and publisher, the George Padmore Supplementary School, the Black Parents Movement, the New Cross Massacre Action Committee and the International Book Fair of Radical Black and Third World Books. The latter, a (near) annual festival running between 1982 and 1995, was particularly significant in providing a space that brought together currents of radical black thought from across the world for discussion and the sharing of ideas. All these campaigns and organizations were strongly informed by an ethos of radical self-help and empowerment, in which alliances were sought that articulated both race and class but also stressed the necessity of black political and cultural self-organization and self-determination (Alleyne, 2002a, 27–30, 162; Johnson, 2006b; Alleyne, 2007).

The GPI and its archive were and are seen as continuing and sustaining the work of the Book Fair and the supplementary schools into the future. In the same way as the supplementary school movement (community schools established and run in evenings and at weekends by concerned parents and other volunteers) acted to redress imbalances and absences in the British state education system, the GPI and archive were to act as resources for education and information about black history, struggle and achievement, not only in Britain and the Caribbean but across the world. This internationalist, diasporic dimension was an essential part of La Rose's political and cultural approach and continues to underpin what the GPI archive stands for. As one of his obituaries described, 'Making a home in Britain while carrying a living sense of the Caribbean was a creative tension he [La Rose] achieved and helped others achieve' (Scott, 2006).

The collections within the GPI, which are steadily being made accessible as the cataloguing continues, reflect the activities and concerns of La Rose and the others in the New Beacon circle in the UK and elsewhere. So papers from the Caribbean Artists Movement, the Black Parents Movement, and the International Book Fair of Radical Black and Third World Books among others are complemented by La Rose's personal collections of papers and political ephemera as well as significant runs of otherwise rare journals and publications.

Although these are the papers of political organizations and campaigns (their contents frequently reflecting the urgency of their creation and use) their preservation demonstrates that like many political activists La Rose and his colleagues had 'an eye for the future', a keen awareness of the importance of historical records and the utility of history in informing future struggles (Garrod, 2008). According to White this awareness had always been there, 'the collecting started in the sixties' and allied with a strong sense of the importance of sharing the historic 'experience of campaigning, on issues and cultural activities' with new generations. As a charitable body, the GPI itself cannot be a campaigning organization but it can provide the resources for others 'to understand what happened' (White, 2008). One example of the way in which the GPI would like to see its archive being used as a resource is a booklet aimed at schools for the teaching of history and citizenship produced in partnership with Museums, Libraries and Archives (MLA) London. Entitled *Exploring Archives: the George Padmore Institute*, it uses the archives to probe issues of protest and struggle, specifically 'about the intellectual, political and creative culture that people from Britain's former colonies brought with them' (Naidoo, 2006).

Despite being established in 1991, the archive has only gradually become publicly accessible. Working as 'slow builders and consolidators' is one of the key principles of the GPI and the New Beacon circle who believe that if independent, grassroots organizations are to be built they need to develop in ways that are measured and sustainable and which do not threaten the independence and control of the organization (White, 2008). Initially hoping to take on the work of archivists themselves, the GPI sought advice and guidance from a variety of archival institutions and consultants, but more recently, with funding from the Heritage Lottery Fund, they have appointed a professional archivist to catalogue the collections. However, 'skills transfer' and building capacity to enable the organization to sustain itself over the long term remains a significant objective. In addition to the archivist's drawing on the knowledge and expertise of the volunteers and the trustees to add detail and value to her descriptions of photographs, campaigning ephemera and other material, she is also training the volunteers in archival practices, including basic conservation and cataloguing (Alleyne, 2002a, 100–5; Garrod, 2008). As a consequence, if the GPI were unable to continue to employ a professional archivist, 'the whole place isn't going to collapse. It will carry on. But carry on obviously at a much slower pace' (White, 2008).

The Institute of Race Relations

The writings of Sivanandan (2008), like those of John La Rose and others involved with the GPI, frequently emphasize the importance of under-standing the relationship between history and contemporary struggles: 'History tells us where we come from and where we are at. But it also should tell us where we should be going' (Sivanandan, 2009, 94). In 1972, the staff of the Institute of Race Relations (IRR) including Sivanandan and other radicals wrested control of the Institute from its Council of Management and in the process transformed a liberal establishment research institute concerned with commercial relations with former colonies and race relations in the UK into an anti-racist and anti-imperialist think-tank and radical publishing house, notably of the journal *Race and Class* but also of many other publications. The IRR dedicated itself to providing research and resources for those involved in anti-imperialist activity. Essays such as 'From Resistance to Rebellion: Asian and Afro-Caribbean struggles in Britain' (1986, reprinted in Sivanandan, 2008) documented the history of black struggles that had been noticeably absent even from Labour and other histories 'from below'. A series of anti-racist educational books aimed at young people included *The Fight Against Racism* (IRR, 1986). Sivanandan writes that, 'Hoping that these would provide community organisations with the ammunition they needed to mount their own fights and win their own battles. We were aware that we were neither grassroots nor establishment – merely a servicing station for oppressed peoples on their way to liberation. We'd put gas in their tanks' (Sivanandan, 2008, 28).

For over 50 years, the IRR's library, particularly after Sivanandan's appointment as librarian in 1964, has been an important resource for academics and activists on the subject of racism and resistance in Britain. In 2006 the bulk of the library collection (government and other official publications, academic journals and books) was transferred to the University of Warwick but the IRR retained the Institute's own archive and a large collection called the Black History Collection.[5] This is an extensive and relatively unique collection of publications and political ephemera produced by black groups in Britain, and others who supported their struggles. The collection includes newspapers, journals, letters, leaflets and flyers from a range of organizations and on a wide range of subjects covering black struggles over the past 50 years and represents the traces of campaigns and organizations that in some cases have not been preserved anywhere else. According to Jenny Bourne, project manager and long-time IRR employee, the decision to retain, catalogue and make this material accessible (with the support of a Heritage Lottery Fund grant) was made because 'it was political in the way it had been collected and how it was seen and it was about the struggles, very much, that people had gone through or were going through or wanted to learn from each other' (Wild and Bourne, 2008). The cataloguing and the arrangement of the collection has been led not by a professionally-trained archivist but by a subject specialist and a team of volunteers, drawing upon the advice, training and support supplied by archival institutions including London Metropolitan Archives.

The IRR wishes to ensure that their collections continue to be available as a resource for new generations to learn about past struggles and to inform present and future campaigns. Like the GPI, the IRR recognizes the power of education and wants their collections to be used for teaching, creating a set of free, downloadable teaching resources, *Struggles for Justice*, aimed at the citizenship curriculum in secondary schools so that students 'See what ordinary people, who often had not spent long in Britain, achieved by getting involved in their communities and tenaciously refusing to submit to injustice will, we hope, fire the curiosity and imaginations of a new younger audience' (Bourne, 2008, 38).

Something of the importance and emotional impact of the Black History Collection can be gauged by the reactions of volunteers who have been working on the cataloguing of the collection. At a seminar organized as part of the cataloguing project, volunteers revealed how much they were learning from the experience and how much it meant to them to engage with this material and with these histories: 'it was an opportunity for me to learn more and to carry on what I have been doing most of my life which was reading black history, accessing the hidden story of black people all over' (IRR, 2008; Wild and Bourne, 2008).

The Black Cultural Archives

Although not as explicitly related to a political organization as the IRR or indeed the GPI, and employing a more cultural, pan-Africanist definition of 'black' focusing on the heritage of those of African and African-Caribbean descent, the Black Cultural Archives (BCA) were nonetheless founded and based in the same social, economic and political context.[6] Whereas those involved in GPI and IRR ultimately built up their collections as part of ongoing political, anti-racist campaigning, the BCA was explicitly founded as a museum and an archive which sought to challenge the systematic failure of formal museums and histories to represent black history to a black (and indeed a white) audience by 'replacing the myths, ignorance and denigration of the African people's past' (Garrison, 1994, 241).

Specifically, the BCA grew out of general dissatisfaction with and anxiety about the way that the history taught in schools made little or no mention of black history, marginalizing 'black people's contribution to the development of British society and Western civilization' (Walker, 1997, 45). As previously mentioned with reference to John La Rose and the New Beacon circle, from the 1960s and 1970s onwards, a key concern for communities of African and Asian heritage in Britain was the treatment of their children in state schools. The persistent classification or 'banding' of black children as 'under-achieving' led to the establishment of supplementary schools and organizations such as the Black Parents' Movement. The content of the teaching in the schools was also the focus of campaigns. Len Garrison (1943–2003), the founder and inspiration behind the BCA, set up the African and Caribbean Educational Resource (ACER) in the late 1970s to provide materials on black history that teachers could use in the classroom.

By 1981, two years into Margaret Thatcher's first term of office as Conservative party Prime Minister, mass unemployment, institutionalized discrimination and oppressive policing culminated in a series of major disturbances in Brixton and elsewhere in inner-city Britain (Gilroy, 1995, 102–5; Sivanandan, 2008, 134–9). That same year Garrison and other parents and teachers, concerned about the seriously alienating effect that being deprived of their history was having on black children, formed the African People's Historical Monument Foundation. Key to the thinking behind the foundation was the establishment of a physical black cultural archive and museum 'to collect, document and disseminate the culture and history of peoples of African and African-Caribbean descent living in Britain' (Walker, 1997, 45–8; BCA, 2007). Garrison argued that, denied their history and reference points, many black children were experiencing an 'identity crisis', writing that, 'Young Black people have faced the forces of racism and its contradictions and have been ashamed to identify their Blackness as a positive attribute. Victims of the assimilation process, their lack of recognized history has rendered them invisible, thereby disinheriting and undermining their sense of a Black British heritage' (1994, 238).

Drawing inspiration from the Schomburg Center for Research in Black Culture in New York, Garrison and others felt that the material collected and made physically available in the Black Cultural Archives in Brixton could eventually make a significant difference by offering a black child 'a positive notion of his or her history, identity and self-image, and have that reflected in the wider society' (Garrison, 1994, 238–9; Hopkins, 2008, 94–5).

> We do not assume that historical data and artefacts by themselves are going to change a child's self-image. They will however, provide the environment and structure within which the Afro-Caribbean child can extend and build positive frames of reference, and a basis for White children to understand the Black presence in an anti-racist context.   Garrison, 1994, 239

The archive's initial collections were based heavily on Garrison's personal collection. According to one writer 'Len had been assembling the BCA since he was a student' (Phillips, 2003, 296). In common with other community archives, not only did the collecting impetus lie with one or two individuals, but as with the GPI and IRR, what was collected might sometimes have been considered ephemeral and of little 'archival' value by a formal archive.

However, in a context where few collections or institutions adequately documented the black experience, Garrison's personal collection (and others like it) represented 'a unique record of black migrant life'. As Phillips further described it,

> The handbills, flyers, posters, programmes for a wide range of events, including political meetings, art exhibitions, concerts, plays, community meetings about education, welfare and politics . . . may be not only the only surviving record of transient organizations, but the only way of understanding whole movements and trends, like the 'self-help' movement, or the rise of African nationalism in the black community.   Phillips, 2003, 297

Despite the importance of its core collections and some significant public access activities, the BCA was inhibited in making the same kind of impact and extending its collections as the Schomburg did in America. The not uncommon problems for independent community archives of the lack of suitable premises and scarce physical and financial resources meant that the BCA struggled to meet its own aspirations and full potential. Notwithstanding a series of noteworthy exhibitions and collaborations with other local bodies, BCA's existing collections were sometimes difficult to access and some potential depositors were wary of donating their papers because of the organization's uncertain future. Since the very beginning BCA has sought to overcome these problems by concentrating on capital projects aimed at establishing a sustainable, physical location (Hopkins, 2008, 96, 106).

After a number of setbacks over the years, and in partnership with the local council (Lambeth) and grants from the Heritage Lottery Fund and the London Development Agency, BCA has identified a future permanent home. Raleigh Hall will be renovated and redeveloped as a state of the art heritage and cultural centre with archive, library, exhibition and meeting space in the rejuvenated Central Square in Brixton (Kennedy and Manzi, 2008). Further funding is still required to ensure that this can all happen, but BCA is set to open in 2011 as a professionally staffed and pre-eminent archive and museum of the experience of those of African and African-Caribbean heritage and their contribution to Britain. The acquisition and development of this physical presence will constitute a major, symbolic statement about the equal and permanent place of black history and culture with British heritage (Hopkins, 2008, 96). For Sam Walker, one of the founders of the archive and its long-time director, the prospect of 'a specially built museum which is run by black professionals who will devise a selection and display policy from an African perspective . . . will help in destroying racist imagery which is so commonly perpetuated by mainstream institutions' (Walker, 1997, 43).

Although some tensions and compromises in managing the shift from a small, community-led organization to a larger and perhaps more mainstream heritage body are somewhat inevitable, those running the BCA envision meeting these challenges by taking on a future role as a 'hub for Black heritage in the UK', supporting smaller, independent community organizations and encouraging the training of black heritage workers (BCA, 2008; Hopkins, 2008, 95–6, 98; Newman, 2008).

Other independent archives, parallel questions

Questions of independence, sustaining resources, keeping archives open, achieving organizational aspirations and navigating the possible compromises required in partnerships with formal heritage organizations are common to many independent archives all over the world, and often grow in significance over time. A commitment to complete autonomy is not and was never universal among all independent community archives. But, for example, the librarians and archivists who established the Working Class Movement Library in Salford, the Lesbian Herstory Archive in New York or the Australian Lesbian & Gay Archives[7] as well as those who founded and continue to take forward the IRR, GPI or BCA were all informed by 'community' attitudes and critical political ideologies that were at best ambivalent (if not outright hostile) to the state and profoundly mistrustful of those mainstream public heritage organizations that for the most part had been implicated in the 'conspiracy of silence' about working-class, black, lesbian, gay, bisexual and trans (LGBT) and many other histories (Carbery, 1995, 34; Small, 1997, 50–63).

For the founders of the rukus! Black LGBT Archive Project,[8] the impetus to found or in Stuart Hall's words to 'constitute' the archive was an act of reclamation and a 'political intervention' designed to challenge the lack of visibility and representation which made it possible for others to deny a black and gay experience. While not averse to engaging with and taking their archive into all sorts of formal heritage (and other) spaces, rukus! is also very much in control of its agenda and future, embodying an almost punk-inspired, 'abrasive' and disruptive do-it-yourself ethos (Ajamu and Campbell, 2008).

In all these examples, the value of the archive (and of creating or 'constituting' the archive) to contemporary social movements and concerns is evident and explicit, 'our goal is to connect the present struggles . . . to the past, to show the legacy of resistance and to give the keys needed to unlock the sometimes coded language of liberation battles of another time' (Nestle, 1990, 91). Seen within the context of challenging invisibilities and documenting often difficult or traumatic histories, the archival act can be highly charged and loaded with emotional as well as political significance – especially when those acts of recovery rescue personal and social, collective histories from deliberate and physical erasure. As Joan Nestle, a founding member of the Lesbian Herstory Archives, has written, 'one of our battles was to change secrecy into disclosure, shame into memory. We spoke of how families burned letters and diaries, how our cultural artefacts were often found in piles of garbage or on bargain tables' (1990, 90). Similarly for rukus!, some of the power of its endeavours comes from the fact that the archive reclaims and acknowledges the collective and individual memories of those who have lost their lives, often unremarked and ignored. Through the archive, these lives and their achievements can be both mourned and celebrated (Ajamu and Campbell, 2008).

If resources remain scarce and the energy of key figures begins to wane, maintaining independence from the state and its institutions may become increasingly difficult for many independent community archives to sustain. Some may look for partnerships out of necessity. Others may wish to actively engage with the mainstream, on their own terms, as part of their transformative and counter-hegemonic mission. In either case, although the compromises those kind of relationships entail may have to be negotiated carefully, progressive and mutually beneficial partnerships can be established without the independent community archives necessarily surrendering their autonomy. Of course this in part depends on the commitment of mainstream organizations to approaching such relationships equitably and with integrity.

After over four decades of history from below, acts of historical recovery and independent activity, one would like to be able to say that our local and national histories and narratives no longer exclude and subordinate the stories of many in society, that the idea of a democratized heritage which so inspired Stuart Hall has become a reality. Unfortunately – as Gilroy's (2008, 51) acute identification of a national post-imperial 'melancholic attachment' to the imagined whiteness of the World War Two era British society and the revived promotion of a dialogue about Englishness and Britishness, which is more exclusive than it is inclusive illustrate – much of a transforming and demo-cratizing historical project remains profoundly contested. The continued frustration on the part of historians and activists in the Black and Asian Studies Association (BASA) about histories and school curricula, which still often exclude rather than include evidence of the black presence in many aspects of British life, indicate that UK national histories in the classroom, on the television and in archives and museums still have a long way to go before they can be described as representative or inclusive. For example, a letter written to the BBC's family history magazine *Who Do You Think You Are?* by

BASA chair Cliff Pereira in 2009 criticized the magazine's failure to acknowledge the thousands of Black and Asian servicemen in an issue on the First World War. A recent lecture by the historical geographer Caroline Bressey argued that there is 'Still no Black in the Union Jack' (2009). Nevertheless while there is much still to be done, it is difficult to imagine any systematic subordination of these stories going unchallenged or even being justified – not least because of the continued efforts of those who have created and sustained independent community archives.

Independent community archives and identity

Taken individually and as a whole, the initiatives described above as well as many others have made a significant impact on dominant understandings of heritage, not least in terms of the recognition of the need for societies to develop more inclusive narratives of their pasts where a range of stories are equally valued. The very existence of these independent archives provides evidence of just how much has been excluded and the professional practice that has been responsible for such exclusions (Hopkins, 2008, 99). This challenge has coincided with what might be characterized as a reflexive turn in archival science, a shift from an understanding of the archive as the ' "natural" residue or passive by-product of administrative activity to the consciously constructed and actively mediated "archivalisation" of social memory', or discursive construction (Cook, 2001, 4). As political scientist Achille Mbembe has suggested, the archive is a point of origin for the dissemination of a powerful imaginary; through a common affective investment in the archive we become members of a 'community of time', membership of which is characterized by a feeling of ownership over a past to which we are all heirs (Mbembe, 2002, 21). Similarly Eric Ketelaar (2005) has written of the way 'communities of memory' are sustained by a relationship to 'memory texts . . . through which th[e common] past is mediated'. Jeannette Bastian's (2003) discussion of 'communities of records' suggests that the intimate and emotional connection to the archive and the events it reflects goes beyond those immediately involved in its creation and touches all those it describes. These feelings of connectedness, ownership and community are fundamental components of a sense of belonging to contemporary society which might be fostered by a more democratic collective memory; and support for the development of independent and community archives by heritage professionals is increasingly seen as one way of filling those gaps in the official record that perpetuate the exclusion of marginalized communities with potentially deleterious effects.

The idea that community archives are a valuable tool in the

democratization of heritage, and consequently in developing feelings of belonging in society have been increasingly widely accepted by policy-makers over the last ten years. In 1999 the Black and Asian Studies Association (BASA) organized a conference on archives which focused attention on the absences and hidden stories within local and national collections, the MacPherson report (into the investigation of the 1993 murder of the black teenager Stephen Lawrence) (1999, Chapter 6) turned the spotlight on institutional racism in the police force and in British society more generally, and Stuart Hall made a provocative and influential speech to the 'Whose Heritage?' conference, jointly supported by the Arts Council, the Heritage Lottery Fund, the Museums Association and the North West Arts Board (Hall, 2005, 23–35). Since then, the Heritage Lottery Fund for example has transformed itself from being not just the guardian of Britain's elite spaces but also the primary funder of grassroots community-based initiatives.[9] The opening in late 2007 of Rivington Place, the 'first permanent public space dedicated to the education of the public in culturally diverse visual arts and photography in the UK' and including a photographic archive ('the UK's first print and digital resource for a collection of photographs documenting the emergence of post-war Britain as a multicultural society'), is a powerful testament to the influence of Stuart Hall's thinking, not least because as vice-chair of the organization he was instrumental in driving the vision forward.[10] The Mayor of London's Commission on African and Asian Heritage (MCAAH, 2005, 9 and 81–2) was clear about the continuing disabling effect of institutional racism in the heritage sector and the need to ensure that better and more substantial support was directed towards independent heritage projects. The announcement in 2008 of the award of £4 million to support the opening of the Black Cultural Archives (Kennedy and Manzi, 2008) was a further indication of how far community archives have come.

The preliminary findings from our own research strongly support the idea that involvement with community archives enhances self-esteem and a sense of belonging in minority communities of African, Asian and other heritage. Some activists have talked explicitly about 'giving people a sense of belonging' but perhaps more significantly, by observing the relationships between community archivists, heritage sector professionals and other peers we have begun to develop evidence of strong positive regard and understandings of a particular group's experience, history and position in society developed by and through contact with an archive. As well as providing an intellectual resource in support of contemporary struggles and interventions, such understanding works to generate civic and social engagement within and beyond a given community (for example, in support of young people who share the same self-categorization).

It is important at this point to sound a note of caution, however. The growth in official recognition and support for independent community archives rests on two principal assumptions: that community archives and related heritage projects deliver a strong sense of belonging or of identity, and that such feelings or identities are socially productive. However, on closer inspection the evidence base for both claims remains for the most part extremely slim. To date, most studies of community archive initiatives have been reports commissioned by funders rather than academic studies; concerns have been rightly expressed about 'the quality of "evidence" put forward by the profession in policy documents in the form of personal expressions of conviction or practitioner studies that lack the explicit rigour shown in quality academic research' (Wavell et al., 2002, 9). Indeed, many claims about the value of community archives are arguably either inadequately supported by the data or insufficiently generalizable. For example, a recent study, *Black and Minority Ethnic Community Archives*, for the London region of the MLA identified developing 'a sense of pride' as an outcome of engaging with community archives (Ander, 2007, 9). However true we may feel this to be, the claim rests solely on the testimony of the community archivists in whose interest it might be to celebrate the value of their work when talking to funders, rather than on any rigorous evaluation of reception or engagement by volunteers or users. Moreover, since only one person from each project was interviewed in this study, such assertions could not be confirmed via other data sources.

Even where claims do appear to be evidence-based the data often remains anecdotal. Judith Etherton's fascinating study (2006) of archival research as part of the therapeutic process for people coming to terms with histories of adoption and other family ruptures suggests the strong potential of archives to contribute to individual wellbeing. However, as Etherton openly acknowledges, her evidence is based on her observations in the course of her work as a local archivist and as a consequence the findings may not be generalizable. There is nothing wrong with this – case study research is often used 'to develop the conceptual underpinnings of future social scientific inquiry' (Schrank, 2006, 23) – but we are at the beginning of understanding what impacts are being identified here. What is an exciting agenda for future research should not be mistaken for conclusive findings.

Even more fundamentally, community archives are frequently celebrated in policy documents and elsewhere for their role in delivering 'a sense of identity' but the under-theorizing and uncritical use of identity as a category in both the academic and the policy literature on cultural heritage calls the whole premise – that the identities delivered by community archives are socially valuable – into question. The under-theorizing of the buzz word 'identity' has been an issue across the social sciences. As Brubaker and Cooper have pointed out, as a category of analysis, 'identity' has been used by social scientists to describe a range of phenomena from the idea of a core unchanging aspect of group or self-hood to its obverse, the process of purely relational positioning that defines postmodern understandings of the self and contextualist accounts of ethnicity (Brubaker and Cooper, 2000, 6–10).[11]

The slipperiness of the term limits its usefulness to archivists and activists alike and makes organizations that espouse it, particularly when attempting to obtain public funding, highly vulnerable to realignments of high-level policy. For instance a sense of 'identity' – if taken to mean in this case a high level of 'self-understanding' (Brubaker and Cooper, 2000, 17) – may well provide the 'ontological security' seen by Anthony Giddens as a precondition for effective individual action in the social world (1986, 50). Community archives arguably can help generate this security (and thereby empower people) by enhancing individuals' awareness of their social location (in Hall's terms 'the different ways we are positioned by, and position ourselves within, the narratives of the past' (1998, 225)). In a supportive policy climate they might use the language of identity to make their case and have a reasonable expectation of support and perhaps funding.[12]

However, when the definitions are so fluid and poorly understood the ground can quickly shift. So a sense of 'identity' can just as readily be characterized as a threat to social cohesion if it becomes politic to use a contrasting definition: a 'strongly binding, vehemently felt groupness' for example (Brubaker and Cooper, 2000, 21). There are good grounds for being wary of this form of 'identity' and the role that heritage activity might play in fostering and reinforcing it. As Elizabeth Kaplan has noted, 'History constantly reminds us that the reification of ethnic identity does not foster tolerance or acceptance; it constructs communities and then draws hard, arbitrary lines between them, creating differences and making them fixed' (2000, 151). Different community archives may be ideologically opposed to supporting just such narrow and reified identity constructions but the problem is that policy-makers are not obliged to clearly define their terms when talking about 'identity'. As soon as government policy shifts, for example from a broadly multiculturalist to a more assertively assimilationist approach to the management of cultural difference, then independent community archives may find that their own discourse, which previously aligned them with government policy, can now be turned against them, even if their understanding of identity – as 'self-understanding' rather than exclusive 'groupness' – has not changed.

Indeed, in the UK there is ample evidence of precisely such a shift taking place and this is one reason why we should proceed with caution when celebrating the impact of community archives on 'identities'. Key moments in this shift include the riots in north-west England in 2001 and the terrorist incidents in London and Glasgow in 2005 and 2007. These events have been seized upon by opponents of policies championing cultural diversity and the emergence of a 'new identity politics', which places the emphasis on 'shared identities' (Muir, 2007). The thinking underlying this shift was exemplified by the speech given in 2005 by the chair of the then Commission for Racial Equality in which he argued that Britain was 'sleepwalking into segregation' (Phillips, 2005).

These changes are having a growing impact on cultural and heritage policy. In 2008, the then Minister for Culture, Creative Industries and Tourism, Margaret Hodge, talked about the potential divisiveness of diversity (2008) and in London, Boris Johnson, the Conservative mayor since May 2008, appointed a culture adviser, Munira Mirza, who has publicly argued the same case (Mirza, 2006). Although the work of the Heritage Diversity Task Force – set up under Johnson's predecessor to implement the recommendations of *Delivering Shared Heritage*, the report of the Mayor's Commission on African and Asian Heritage (MCAAH, 2005), which strongly recommended increased support for independent community archives (Archives Divers-ification Sub-committee, 2007) – continues, its profile is much reduced. The change in emphasis and language from *Delivering Shared Heritage* is quite pronounced. In a new culture policy document, Mirza wrote: 'We will support events and projects that show off the internationalism and diversity of this city. However, we must also listen to debates within London's differ-ent communities about how they are changing. People want to celebrate their identities but they also want to transcend them and not be pigeon-holed' (Mayor of London, 2008, 10).

In this context independent and community archives of African and Asian heritage that champion their contribution to bolstering feelings of belonging are looking increasingly vulnerable, just at the very moment when they were also beginning to achieve recognition for their work from heritage policy-makers and funders.

Conclusion

In this rapidly shifting political landscape, there is an urgent need for archivists, activists and researchers to collaborate on research projects that aim to fill this evidential gap and build a more detailed picture of the work that independent community archives do and the impacts they may have on the lives of those who volunteer in them or who encounter their work through exhibitions, performances and workshops. Our University College London research project, which uses ethnographic methods in a case study design to collect the necessary thick qualitative data, is one such attempt. The findings of this research should not be a foregone conclusion – it may be that in certain contexts community archive initiatives can reawaken old wounds or foster suspicion towards a specific out-group. We do not expect this to be the case in our research – the community archivists and social movement activists with whom we have worked are in many cases acutely aware of these issues and have developed sophisticated readings of the relationship between collective memory, identity and the materiality of the archive – but nothing should be ruled out.

Furthermore, researchers need to draw on more sophisticated, composite models of 'identity' that will rescue it from those nostalgic for the cultural dominance of a narrow elite or who use criticisms of 'identity politics' (such as Amartya Sen's warnings about the 'miniaturization' of society (2006)) to dismiss any initiative that helps members of under-represented or marginalized groups enhance their self-understanding and develop self-representations that may in fact challenge the simplistic categorizations often associated with identity discourse. This may entail looking further afield and drawing on literature from sociology and social psychology, rather than solely from cultural studies, which has opened itself up to criticism by failing to advance its thinking in this area, while nevertheless remaining dominated by identity as a research theme (Grossberg, 1996).

Stuart Hall's powerful articulation of the relationship between heritage and identity, histories encompassing both the possibility of a sense of belonging and alternatively the alienation of not being represented, drew attention to 'the heritage' as a terrain of struggle for marginalized groups in the UK (Hall, 2005, 23–35).[13] But now that identity has become the explicit subject of policy[14] there is a need to introduce greater clarity into Hall's 'sophisticated but opaque discussion' (Brubaker and Cooper, 2000, 9). For independent community archivists, those who articulate narratives with an outward-looking, transformatory counter-hegemonic interplay between multiple identities including class, race, gender and sexuality may be better placed ideologically to weather the changes in policy and funding that others may find it more difficult to withstand.

Notes

1   'Mekin Histri' by L. K. Johnson (2006) *Selected Poems*, London, Penguin, 64.

2   UK Arts and Humanities Research Council funded project, 'Community archives and identities: documenting and sustaining community heritage', 2008–9. The research team comprises Andrew Flinn, Elizabeth Shepherd and Mary Stevens. This

research would not have been possible without the help and partnership provided by all our case studies (Future Histories, rukus!, Moroccan Memories and Eastside Community Heritage) and all the other participants and interviewees. For further details see www.ucl.ac.uk/infostudies/research/icarus/community-archives/.

3   The possibilities of the digital environment make a difference here as well. Both rukus!, the Black Lesbian, Gay, Bisexual and Trans (LGBT) archive and Eastside Community Heritage are clear about the benefits of ensuring the preservation of their physical collections in professional archives or heritage organizations, while continuing to explore the more flexible, less restricting possibilities of engaging with and using their collections via digital environments.

4   For more details about GPI see www.georgepadmoreinstitute.org/.

5   Details of the IRR and its collections can be found at www.irr.org.uk/information/index.html.

6   Details about the Black Cultural Archives and its work can be found at www.bcaheritage.org.uk/.

7   See Working Class Movement Archives at www.wcml.org.uk/; Lesbian Herstory Archive at www.lesbianherstoryarchives.org/; and Australian Lesbian and Gay Archives at http://home.vicnet.net.au/~alga/.

8   See rukus! at www.rukus.co.uk/content/view/12/27/.

9   This shift can be traced in part through its strategic plans. Whereas the first plan (1998–2002) prioritized 'conservation, access and education' the second (2002–7) sought to emphasize 'involvement' and the expansion of the 'boundaries of heritage' to include 'a richer mix' (HLF, 2002, 2–3). The third and most recent plan (2008–13) again emphasized preservation and participation but also gave priority to enabling 'people to learn about their own and others' heritage' (HLF, 2007, 14).

10   See www.rivingtonplace.org/facilities/photographicArchive.

11   The 'contextualist' account of ethnicity could be seen as epitomized by Stuart Hall's thinking.

12   Sociology and social psychology offer some empirical evidence to support these claims, often in the specific context of educational achievement. For example, Chatman et al. (2001) found in their study of patterns of ethnic identity among African American youths that adolescents who displayed high levels of positive personal regard (judgements made by people about their own identities), 'explicit importance' (the individual's subjective appraisal of the degree to which collective identity is important to her or his overall sense of self) and 'cultural connectedness' (roughly, awareness of a group's history, experience and position in society, or collective social location) were the most 'well adjusted', as long as this was not also combined with a strong perception of 'ethnically based social challenges' – the idea that they might suffer discrimination as a consequence of their 'race' (cited in Ashmore, Deaux and McLauglin-Volpe, 2004, 108). The multi-dimensionality of their study – identity is broken down into inter-related components – illustrates the

extent to which 'identity' is far too complex a term to be correlated simply to wellbeing or social cohesion.

13   The idea that the struggle for history is part of any liberation struggle has of course been around since Fanon and before, but what was new in Hall's discourse was the idea that this battle needed to be fought on the protected turf of the UK heritage sector, given up by its critics in the 1980s and early 1990s as an inherently elitist construct (e.g. Wright, 1985; Lowenthal, 1998).

14   For example in the context of the MLA's 'Generic Social Outcomes'.

References

Ajamu, X. and Campbell, T. (2008) Project interview.

Alleyne, B. (2002a) *Radicals Against Race: black activism and cultural politics*, Berg.

Alleyne, B. (2002b) An Idea of Community and its Discontents: towards a more reflexive sense of belonging in multicultural Britain, *Ethnic and Racial Studies*, **25** (4), 607–727.

Alleyne, B. (2007) Obituary: John La Rose (1927–2006), *History Workshop*, **64**, 460–4.

Ander, E. (2007) *Black and Minority Ethnic Community Archives in London*, MLA London, www.mlalondon.org.uk/uploads/documents/Black_and_Ethnic_Minority_Community_Archives_in_London_final.doc.

Archives Diversification Subcommittee (2007) *Archives Diversification Subcommittee Report*, Heritage Diversity Task Force, Greater London Authority.

Ashmore, R. D., Deaux, K. and McLauglin-Volpe, T. (2004) An Organizing Framework for Collective Identity: articulation and significance of multidimensionality, *Psychological Bulletin*, **130** (1), 80–114.

Bastian, J. (2003) *Owning Memory: how a Caribbean community lost its archives and found its history*, Libraries Unlimited.

Bellos, L. (2006) Black v Asian?, *Catalyst*, 25 May, http://83.137.212.42/siteArchive/catalystmagazine/Default.aspx.LocID-0hgnew0ex.RefLocID-0hg01b001006009.Lang-EN.htm.

Black Cultural Archives (2007) Black Cultural Archives: 2011, www.bcaheritage.org.uk/BCA_2011.pdf.

Black Cultural Archives (2008) About the Black Cultural Archives, unpublished.

Bourne, J. (2008) IRR: the story continues, *Race and Class*, **50** (2), 31–9.

Bressey, C. (2009) Still no Black in the Union Jack, lunchtime lecture, UCL, 12 February, available to listen to at http://podcast.steeple.org.uk/component/option,com_mediadb/task,view/idstr,UCL-podcast-rss_feeds_public_lectures_lhl/Itemid,98.

Brubaker, R. and Cooper, F. (2000) Beyond 'Identity', *Theory and Society*, **29** (1), 1–47.

Carbery, G. (1995) Australian Lesbian & Gay Archives, *Archives and Manuscripts*, **23** (1), 30–7.

Cook, T. (2001) Archival Science and Postmodernism: new formulations for old concepts, *Archival Science*, **1**, 3–24.

Chatman, C. M., Taylor, E. D. and Eccles, J. S. (2001) *'Acting White' and 'Acting Black':
ethnic identity and academic achievement among African American high school students*; poster
presented at the biennial meeting of the Society for Research in Child
Development, Minneapolis, MN, April 2001.

Crooke, E. (2007) *Museums and Community: ideas, issues and challenges*, Routledge.

Etherton, J. (2006) The Role of Archives in the Perception of Self, *Journal of the Society of
Archivists*, **27** (2), 227–46.

Flinn, A. (2007) Community Histories, Community Archives: some opportunities and
challenges, *Journal of the Society of Archivists*, **28** (2), 151–76.

Garrison, L. (1994) The Black Historical Past in British Education. In Stone, P. G. and
MacKenzie, R. (eds), *The Excluded Past: archaeology and education*, 2nd edn,
Routledge, 231–44.

Garrod, S. (2008) Project interview, 15 April.

Giddens, A. (1986) *The Constitution of Society: outline of the theory of structuration*, Polity.

Gilroy, P. (1995) *There Ain't No Black in the Union Jack*, Routledge.

Gilroy, P. (2008) Melancholia or Conviviality: the politics of belonging in Britain. In
Shire, G. (ed.), *Race, Identity & Belonging*, Lawrence and Wishart.

Grossberg, L. (1996) Identity and Cultural Studies: is that all there is? In Hall, S. and Du
Gay, P. (eds), *Questions of Cultural Identity*, Sage.

Hall, S. (1998) Cultural Identity and Diaspora. In Rutherford, J. (ed.), *Identity:
community, culture, difference*, Lawrence & Wishart.

Hall, S. (2001) Constituting an Archive, *Third Text*, **54**, 89–92.

Hall, S. (2005) Whose Heritage? Un-settling 'The Heritage', re-imagining the post-
nation. In Littler, J. and Naidoo, R. (eds), *The Politics of Heritage: the legacies of 'race'*,
Routledge.

Heritage Lottery Fund (2002) *Broadening the Horizons of Heritage: The Heritage Lottery
Fund strategic plan 2002–2007*.

Heritage Lottery Fund (2007) *Our Heritage, Our Future: towards the HLF's third strategic
plan 2008–2013*.

Hodge, M. (2008) 'Britishness, Heritage and the Arts: should cultural institutions
promote shared values and a common national identity?' Speech at the National
Portrait Gallery.

Hopkins, I. (2008) Places From Which to Speak, *Journal of the Society of Archivists*, **29** (1),
83–109.

Institute for Race Relations (1986) *The Fight Against Racism: a pictorial history of Asians and
Afro-Caribbeans in Britain*, Institute for Race Relations.

Institute for Race Relations (2008) Black History Collection Seminar, 8 July.

Johnson, L. K. (2006a) *Selected Poems*, Penguin.

Johnson, L. K.(2006b) John La Rose, obituary, *Guardian*, 4 March,
www.guardian.co.uk/news/2006/mar/04/guardianobituaries.socialexclusion.

Johnston, I. (2001) Whose History is it Anyway?, *Journal of the Society of Archivists*, **22** (2), 214–29.

Josipovici, G. (1998) Rethinking Memory: too much/too little, *Judaism: A Quarterly Journal of Jewish Life and Thought*, **47** (2), 232–40.

Kaplan, E. (2000) We Are What We Collect, We Collect What We Are: archives and the construction of identity, *American Archivist*, **63** (1), 126–51.

Kennedy, M. and Manzi, E. (2008) After 30 Years, Black Archive Gets a Permanent Home, *Guardian*, 9 May, www.guardian.co.uk/uk/2008/may/09/britishidentity.

Ketelaar, E. (2005) Sharing: collected memories in communities of records, *Archives & Manuscripts*, **33**, 44–61.

Lowenthal, D. (1998) *The Heritage Crusade and the Spoils of History*, Cambridge University Press.

MacPherson, W. (1999) *The Stephen Lawrence Inquiry: report of an inquiry, by Sir William Macpherson*, The Stationery Office, www.archive.official-documents.co.uk/document/cm42/4262/4262.htm.

Mayor of London (2008) *Cultural Metropolis: the mayor's priorities for culture, 2009–2012*, Greater London Authority.

Mayor's Commission on African and Asian Heritage (2005) *Delivering Shared Heritage*, Greater London Authority.

Mbembe, A. (2002) The Power of the Archive and its Limits. In Hamilton, C. et al. (eds), *Refiguring the Archive*, Kluwer Academic.

Mirza, M. (2006) Diversity is Divisive, *Guardian*, 21 November. www.guardian.co.uk/commentisfree/2006/nov/21/diversityhasbecomedivisive.

Muir, R. (2007) *The New Identity Politics*, Institute for Public Policy Research.

Naidoo, R. (2006) *Exploring Archives: The George Padmore Institute*, MLA London.

Nestle, J. (1990) The Will To Remember: the Lesbian Herstory Archives of New York, *Feminist Review*, **34**, 86–94.

Newman, J. (2008) Project interview.

Pereira, C. (2009) Letter, *Who Do You Think You Are?*, 7 January.

Phillips, M. (2003) Obituary: Lenford (Kwesi) Garrison (1943–2003), *History Workshop*, **56**, 295–7.

Phillips, T. (2005) After 7/7: sleepwalking to segregation, http://83.137.212.42/sitearchive/cre/Default.aspx.LocID-0hgnew07s.RefLocID-0hg00900c002.Lang-EN.htm.

Schrank, A. (2006) Case-based Research. In Perecman, E. and Curran, S. R. (eds), *A Handbook for Social Science Field Research: essays and bibliographic sources on research design and methods*, Thousand Oaks & Sage.

Scott, L. (2006) John La Rose, obituary, *Guardian*, 4 March, www.guardian.co.uk/news/2006/mar/04/guardianobituaries.socialexclusion.

Sen, A. (2006) *Identity and Violence: the illusion of destiny*, Allen Lane.

Sivanandan, A. (1981 [2008]) *Catching History on the Wing: race, culture and globalisation,* Pluto Books.

Sivanandan, A. (2004) Racism in the Age of Globalisation, Lecture at 3rd Claudia Jones Memorial Lecture, National Union of Journalists Black Members Council, 24 October, www.irr.org.uk/2004/october/ha000024.html.

Sivanandan, A. (2008a) From Resistance to Rebellion: Asian and Afro-Caribbean struggles in Britain. In Sivanandan, A., *Catching History on the Wing: race, culture and globalisation,* Pluto Books.

Sivanandan, A. (2008b) *Catching History on the Wing: race, culture and globalisation,* Pluto Books.

Sivanandan, A. (2008c) Race and Resistance: the IRR story, *Race and Class,* **50** (2), 31–9.

Sivanandan, A. (2009) Catching History on the Wing: conference speech, *Race and Class,* **50** (3), 90–3.

Small, S. (1997) Contextualizing the Black Presence in British Museums: representations, resources and response. In Hooper-Greenhill, E. (ed.), *Cultural Diversity: developing museum audiences in Britain,* Leicester University Press.

Terracciano, A. (2006) Mainstreaming African, Asian and Caribbean Theatre: the experiments of the Black Theatre Forum. In Godiwala, D. (ed.), *Alternatives within the Mainstream,* Scholars Press.

Walker, S. (1997) Black Cultural Museums in Britain: what questions do they answer? In Hooper-Greenhill, E. (ed.), *Cultural Diversity: developing museum audiences in Britain,* Leicester University Press.

Wavell, C., Baxter, G., Johnson, I. M. and Williams, D. A. (2002) *Impact Evaluation of Museums, Archives and Libraries: Available Evidence Project,* Resource: The Council for Museums, Archives and Libraries.

White, S. (2008) Project Interview, 5 August.

Wild, R. and Bourne, J. (2008) Project Interview, 13 August.

Wright, P. (1985) *On Living in an Old Country: the national past in contemporary Britain,* Verso.

2

Special, local and about us:
the development of community
archives in Britain

DAVID MANDER

Introduction

Community archives in the UK encompass collecting activities that trace
their roots back to the 19th century. At the same time, these archives have also
been shaped by the ways in which the concept of community has been
interpreted and applied by local and national governments as well as by a wide
range of non-profit agencies. In some towns and counties, collecting at a local
level predated the establishment of formal collections; in others, voluntary
bodies helped form those institutions. In more remote areas, collecting began
as a result of the distance from a local government collecting body's base,
inadequacies in the policies or activities of those collecting bodies, or
suspicions that the collecting body was not a suitable repository for holding
particular kinds of source material. This article explores the growth of
community archives and community collections in the UK through a range
of voluntary bodies; the interactions among mainstream archives, libraries,
and museums; and, as a result of those interactions, the creation of a body that
seeks to act as a forum for community archives and all who are active in
working for and with them.[1]

The development of community collecting

Collecting records at a local level has a long history in England. Formal
repositories in counties[2] grew out of the need to house and preserve the court
records from 'quarter sessions', which before 1888 constituted the local

government of each county. It was not until 1926 that Bedfordshire, a county north of London, became the first record office in the country to take in records from corporate bodies and individuals to add to the historic official holdings. The creation of public libraries in the 19th century also provided stimulus for the preservation of local records, including what came to be defined as ephemera (posters, theatre programmes, sale catalogues) and photographs. Regional and local societies built up their own holdings while local voluntary activity contributed to the growth of formal record holding bodies.

In the town of Walthamstow,[3] for example, a public library service was created in the 1890s, and the second borough librarian, G. E. Roebuck, acquired records of local institutions, title deeds and manorial records, which he housed in the library. Roebuck also worked with the Walthamstow Antiquarian Society to create a local museum in a former parish workhouse, which opened in 1933 and, until the Second World War, was staffed by volunteers from the Society. Local pride fostered contributions to the development of the local history collection at the Central Library in Walthamstow and the growth of its artefacts through a picture and photograph collection and the steady acquisition of archives by Walthamstow Museum. The creation of a county record office for Essex[4] in the late 1930s led to an overlap in collecting activities, but for many years institutions lacked formal collection policies and so where depositors took their records depended to an extent on their status and relationship with potentially competing institutions. The records of landed estates tended to go to the county, those of parishes and local societies to the borough.[5]

Walthamstow can be taken as an example of voluntary and municipal bodies working closely together. In neighbouring Chingford,[6] the public library service had been less involved in collecting local history, however, the Chingford Historical Society, founded in the 1940s, took a more active role. Members acquired paintings, photographs and documents dating back to the 17th century, supplemented with reminiscences and local publications. From the 1960s, the archive and library were housed at Friday Hill House, once home to the Boothby Heathcote family, local estate owners, and latterly a community centre. The abolition of Chingford Borough Council in 1965 and the creation of the London Borough of Waltham Forest did not lead immediately to any improvement in the standards of record keeping in the three component library services – Chingford, Leyton and Walthamstow – while opposition from people in Chingford to inclusion in Waltham Forest continued by the Chingford Historical Society, which wanted to retain their own records within the former borough. It was not until 1980, with the prospect of improving standards of custody and care at the former Walthamstow Museum – by then redesignated as Vestry House Museum and serving as the record office for Waltham Forest – that the Society was persuaded to deposit their collections at the Museum. Improved cataloguing, storage and access provisions all subsequently helped to sweeten and ease the removal of the collection.[7]

The growth of county and municipal record offices did not end the collecting activity of voluntary bodies. Many local history societies maintained their own collections and saw no reason to surrender them. In some cases, distance from the county record office played an important part in the decision to keep collecting. In others, activity begun in the aftermath of social upheaval, including the closure of local industries, might stem from bodies whose primary purpose was not heritage related, including community groups. Some of this collecting was below the radar of mainstream record offices. In yet other cases, there was fear of competition based on reasonable professional desires to ensure that historic documents should be held in record offices, where standards of care were normally better. In summary, record offices generally saw themselves as the best place for those collections worthy of preservation, irrespective of the significance of the collections to the localities from which they came. In the main, communities of interest developed outside the scope of most geographically based record offices, though of interest to universities. In some cases there were additional sensitivities around the access to such collections, notably those built up by members of the gay and lesbian communities.

Concepts of community in the UK

The current concept of 'community' in Britain owes much to the development of community work in the late 1950s and early 1960s, with the community seen as the entity that policy makers and service delivery organizations needed to engage. The pivotal 1959 Younghusband Report on Social Work explored the community organization element in social work and defined it as 'primarily aimed at helping people within a local community to identify social needs, to consider the most effective ways of meeting these and to set about doing so, in so far as their available resources permit' (Smith, 1996).[8]

By the mid 1960s community work was becoming a distinct activity that was further shaped by the government community development projects in the late 1960s and early 1970s and by the Gulbenkian Foundation's report on community work and social change in 1968. Community development projects, established by the Home Office, were set up in 12 areas of social deprivation to tackle poverty and encourage self-help in deprived communities. Although many who worked with the projects rejected the analysis of the reasons for poverty, development of ideas of self-help contributed to the concept of communities playing an active role in their own growth (Smith, 1996). It was not until the 1980s that the concept of community was widened from one of geography to include the potential for common interest. According to the US Center for Disease Control (n.d.), 'A person may be a member of a community of choice, as with voluntary associations, or by virtue of their innate personal characteristics, such as age, gender, race or ethnicity . . . As a result individuals may belong to multiple communities at any one time.' In the past two decades, the focus in Britain has shifted from community self-help to community capacity building. Added to that is the idea of community cohesiveness, or the importance of communities, drawing on a shared identity, being given the tools to rebuild and regenerate.

How have the two strands of collected heritage and communities contributed to a modern definition of community archives in Britain? To that sense of local pride – whether geographic, or stemming from a business, an ethnicity or a sexual orientation – has been added the recognition of the part that the history of a community plays in fostering a vital sense of its own identity. In 2004 the Community Access to Archives Project[9] (CAAP) defined community archives as 'collections of material that encapsulate a particular community's understanding of its history and identity. This will often be personal photographs, documents, ephemera and oral history, "unofficial" records that might not normally be preserved, let alone widely available. The community itself might be geographically based, or relate to a cultural or thematic community of interest' (CAAP, 2004a).

Commanet

Community-based regeneration work brought about the development of an important initiative that has shaped the way that many local groups publicize their activities. Commanet has been a key player in raising the profile of community archives. Commanet, a not-for-profit technology support group for community archives,[10] grew out of a regeneration project in Batley, West Yorkshire, in 1994. Commanet invited local people to bring in family photographs to be copied and from these developed an educational resource for local schools. The Batley Community Archive Group, which grew from this project, started up in the following year.[11]

The act of sharing memories and using them as a bridge across the generations prompted Commanet leaders to explore how this material could be better preserved and more widely accessed. They developed Comma software, intended to be easy to use by people with relatively little technical ability. Commanet sold licences to Comma to local groups, and also offered advice on how groups can apply for funding. The software is used by local groups, which scan copies of images and documents, and it can also store audio and film clips. Each item has associated fields for metadata, and the software allows for visual pointers to be added to points on the document that link to metadata fields providing additional information. This allows individuals in photographs to be identified or for an audio clip to be added, to explain, for example, the use of a piece of industrial equipment in a photograph (CAAP, 2004b; Commanet, n.d.). The software can be used on a stand-alone basis or on the internet, thus providing emerging community archives with an online presence. Comma software has been adopted by a wide range of bodies in Britain, including over 130 local groups, two heritage societies, 12 museums, four archive services, and the government advisory group English Heritage. It was also used for the Community Memories element of the Virtual Museum of Canada and by the North Rhodesia Police Association in south central Africa.[12]

Commanet has inspired local groups to go out and copy material that might not ordinarily make its way to a mainstream record office. There are some limitations, notably the lack of a structured subject thesaurus that meets the standard of tools developed for wider application, like the UKAT thesaurus, and Commanet did not provide recommendations on standards used for the capture and storage of digital data. The website structure is also limited to displaying images, and so member bodies have no framework for publishing printed information about themselves or their activities.[13]

Typical of some of the earlier groups that have taken advantage of the Commanet software is the Hemsworth and District Community Archive (HDCA) in West Yorkshire, which has organized local scanning sessions to copy family photographs, street scenes and valuable records of coal mining equipment.[14] The HDCA also works with the Hemsworth Coalfield Partnership, which, with the assistance of a local media production company, documents its local projects. Partnership projects include the history of the Scotch Estate (named from the mass movement of workers from Scotland to the coal mines of West Yorkshire) and the conversion of a row of derelict shops from a local no-go zone to facilities that have now become the offices of the Hemsworth Initiative, a local regeneration group. The Hemsworth and District Community Archive has contributed to the regeneration of the community by collecting its documents and oral history, supporting efforts to assist local people in retaining their valued community identity and ensuring that the past would contribute to the ways in which that identity developed in future.

Community Access to Archives Project (CAAP)

In March 2004 the Museums, Libraries and Archives Council (MLA), the national (UK) development agency working for and on behalf of museums, libraries and archives and advising government on policy, released the Archives Task Force (ATF) report, which highlighted the developing UK government view of the importance of community archives. This document set out a programme for the development of community archives in Britain. A core component of the report was a plan for an Archives Gateway, 'seen as an interface between the Internet and other public networks' (CAAP, 2004a, 12). In the aftermath of the ATF report, the National Archives (TNA) put together a partnership to attempt to create the Gateway, which would provide links to existing online content as well as offering new content. Some of this was intended to come from existing mainstream providers, including local government repositories and UK home country repositories like the Public Record Office of Northern Ireland (PRONI), but the report also recognized that community-based bodies should form a key element in this new online archival world – 'archives in the community are as important to society as those in public collections' (ATF, 2004, 43).

The National Archives-led partnership, known as Linking Arms, was established in 2003 with the intention of preparing a funding bid to the Heritage Lottery Fund (HLF), a government initiative offering grant money to heritage projects. From inception, it was recognized that evidence of user need would be required, together with much more information about the developing world of community archives in Britain. Linking Arms intended to meet wider concerns over social exclusion that were reflected in the contemporary government policy on archives. The Archives Task Force report had noted that 'It was recognized that there are many sectors in the UK population who currently have little or no interaction with the Nation's archival heritage' (2004, 43). To remedy this, the Linking Arms project would need to build in programmes to increase use of archival services, with a particular focus on hard-to-reach communities.

Within the Linking Arms project, the National Archives and its partners launched the Community Access to Archives Project (CAAP). Funded by the National Archives, CAAP included the National Council on Archives, the National Archives of Scotland, the National Library of Wales, the Public Record Office of Northern Ireland, Commanet, and two local archive services, Hackney Archives Department (part of the London Borough of Hackney) and the West Yorkshire Archive Service.

CAAP's initial task was to examine the issues around community involvement in developing content projects for a projected UK Archives network and to produce a best practices model to support this involvement.

CAAP employed a small team who undertook pilot work in two areas – Hackney in London, and West Yorkshire. The West Yorkshire Joint Service had already been actively working with a variety of community groups and had a number of bids in progress to the Heritage Lottery Fund for partnered work with them. Commanet had been particularly successful in building up members in the area, including community groups from places affected by the closures of businesses and mines in the previous two decades. The West Yorkshire Joint Archive Service spanned five subregional areas (Leeds, Bradford, Calderdale, Kirklees and Wakefield) and had sufficient staffing capacity for dedicated outreach work. By contrast, Hackney Archives Department had a small staff, with limited capacity to undertake outreach work, although the service had built up a national reputation for excellence and innovation.

There were substantial contrasts between the two areas. At the time of the 2001 census, West Yorkshire had 100 times the area of Hackney, but was only ten times greater in population. Hackney had a density of 10,667 persons per square kilometre compared with 1025 persons per square kilometre in West Yorkshire. In the 20 years from 1981, Hackney's population had increased by nearly 10%, whereas West Yorkshire had remained broadly stable, with only 0.6% growth. Both areas are ethnically mixed. In 2001, 4.9% of West Yorkshire's population described themselves as Pakistani, Indian or of mixed origin. In Hackney, 26.1% were Black African, Black Caribbean or Indian (Office for National Statistics, 2001). The classification used by the National Statistics office at the time did not reveal significant populations of Turkish-Cypriot and Vietnamese people who were also Hackney residents (CAAP, 2004a, 17).

To this ethnic diversity were also added indications of deprivation and social exclusion. In Hackney, 24% of its working age population had no qualifications and almost 33% had literacy problems. Hackney had the highest rate of unemployment in London at the time, and 40% of Hackney households had an income below £15,000 per year. Some 50% rented their accommodation from the Hackney Council or a housing association – a very low rate of home ownership compared with many other areas of London.

CAAP drew on existing work in West Yorkshire and initiated mapping of communities actively engaged in archive activity in Hackney. In West Yorkshire, CAAP focused on two projects – Now Then Dewsbury and From History to Her Story.[15] These linked web projects offer a range of online source material on Dewsbury for primary and secondary school students. The projects also included partnerships working with local people (CAAP, 2004b), among whom was the Earlsheaton History Group, which produced its own book on the social and industrial area of Earlsheaton, a village in West Yorkshire.

The Dewsbury site is constructed to allow local groups to submit their own material, although the majority of the articles on the site date from the active period of the project in 2004–5. Work on the Dewsbury project drew on consultation work that the West Yorkshire Archive Service had undertaken with eight focus groups prior to a planned merger of the services onto a single site (which in the event did not come off). Feedback from the focus groups was helpful in building up evidence of local users' desires that archives perceived as belonging to their communities should stay locally based, and of non-users' perception of sources of past information (family and so on) and understandings of what archives could do for them.[16]

In Hackney, CAAP drew on the Community Information System (COMIS) database of local organizations to contact any with the potential for heritage involvement (CAAP, 2004a, 32).[17] The project also built on the active links fostered by the Hackney Museum, which had included a project with An Viet, the local Vietnamese community, and the work of the lead Hackney officer on cultural strategy, whose portfolio included a wide range of local organizations. The survey, conducted as part of the mapping of groups with an actual or potential interest in the heritage, brought to light a wide range of groups, which included residents' groups, oral history projects and ethnic minority groups.

These are some of the other CAAP-supported projects in Hackney:

- The Kingsmead Community History Project was created by the Hackney Marsh Partnership Community Development and the University of Hertfordshire's Department of Community Research around 2002. Kingsmead estate, built by the London County Council and completed in 1939, had suffered neglect under the management of Hackney Council. The creation of a community archive to record long standing residents' memories was intended to focus on the value they placed on where they lived, and to help tackle the alienation from the local authority and other parts of Hackney felt (Green, 2005) by those residents.[18]
- Hoxton Story, based at the Red Room, was another oral history project seeking to collect memories of the Shoreditch area of Hackney from people who could help document the changes the area has experienced since the Second World War. The project produced an interactive archive, a booklet and 'a limited series of intimate walkabout performances', together with a range of images and oral history testimony (The Red Room, 2004).
- The Bansonga Sport Sponsorship Association sought to put together an oral history project drawing on Congolese immigrants to Hackney (CAAP, 2004b).[19]

CAAP also set out to develop a best practice model for working with communities. In April 2004 the national Society of Archivists' Archives for Education and Learning Group held a workshop called Building Bridges: Developing Links with the Community, which set out to examine the nature of community archives and how mainstream archive organizations could work with them. Participants indicated that they needed guidance on developing and sustaining community involvement. This guidance would also form an introduction to others working in mainstream services who remained suspicious of the collecting activities of local groups, and who would need to be convinced of the value of community ownership of local heritage. The methodology drew on survey work undertaken by previous bodies, including the CASBAH Archive Survey Tool.[20] Creativity sessions in the form of workshops held in different parts of the UK brought together key individuals from the heritage sector and key community leaders to work with the developing CAAP model and test its effectiveness (CAAP, 2004a, 18).

CAAP also documented some of the diverse forms of community activity taking place across Britain. At the more traditional end these included the Mold Civic Society in Wales, which exhibited their community archive at the Festival of History in North Wales in September 2004. The archive drew on the personal family albums from one of the local landed estates in the area, and succeeding in tapping into a source that may up to then have been beyond the reach of a local mainstream archive. In Birmingham, oral histories collected by Doreen Price and held in the Birmingham City Archives were used in 2000 as the basis for a community theatre piece written by Colin Prescod. *Who Sen Me* drew on the experiences of Caribbean people migrating and settling in the Midlands in the 1950s. The play travelled around Britain and attracted audiences who would probably have not ever seen or used the source material if it had stayed in an archive. Another theatre production emerged from interviews with local people in Hackney living near a house in Sylvester Road at the time of a 15-day siege that began on Boxing Day 2002 and ended in the death of the gunman. *Come out Eli* by Alecky Blythe drew on oral testimony, including that of the principal hostage. A video installation with footage shot during the siege ran at the Arcola Theatre in Dalston in Hackney at the same time as the play in 2003 (BBC News, 2003; CAAP, 2004a, 23–4; Rod Hall Agency, n.d.).

CAAP made a successful case for the value of community archives in the UK, and in October 2004 released a final report, that included best practice guidelines together with formulas used for surveying Hackney organizations and Commanet members, advice on funding sources, and an evaluation checklist for mainstream archives working on community archive projects (CAAP, 2004c). But the Linking Arms partnership of which CAAP was a part failed to convince the Heritage Lottery Fund to support the Archives Gateway search engine. Although the initiative was seeking to meet the aspirations expressed in the Archives Task Force report, a policy document which had some government backing, the Heritage Lottery Fund did not feel that it should provide grant aid to a project which should have at least some government funding. Indeed, one of the weaknesses of the Archives Task Force was that it relied on the untested assumption that the Heritage Lottery Fund would be prepared to provide grants to infrastructure projects of this nature. Very few of the Archives Task Force recommendations have been realized five years on. Linking Arms was reshaped as a less ambitious project by the National Archives, rebranded as Archives UK or 'aUK' (not to be confused with any species of bird extant or extinct). However, after two years further deliberation, the aUK project was quietly shelved and is now believed to have passed from the endangered stage into oblivion.[21]

The Community Archives Development Group

Although CAAP finished its work in the autumn of 2004, celebrated by a launch at Hackney, the potential for community archives to help extend the reach of mainstream archive services, and for community work by those services to support the UK government agenda to tackle a range of social issues, still existed. CAAP members also wished to continue their work, and the project was reconstituted as the Community Archives Development Group (CADG) in the spring of 2005, with continued support from the National Archives. The new group chose to operate under the auspices of the UK National Council on Archives, enabling it to define and then deliver a new programme of work rather than becoming bogged down in constitutional and fundraising activities. There had been some chance that the Archives Task Force recommendation to create one or more posts for community archive development would be implemented, but this objective was abandoned by the Museums, Libraries and Archives Council (MLA). However, the MLA did make funding available to CADG, recognizing its potential value to co-ordinate community archive activity at a national level.

The Community Archives Development Group (CADG) drafted new terms of reference for its operation in January 2006, which were to 'monitor and inform developments in the field of Community Archives, act as an expert body on best practice in this area. The Group will bring together bodies and organisations concerned with Community Archives and provide a forum for the regular exchange of views and information between them' (CADG, 2007).

The aims of the new group were:

1   To work to mainstream and embed community archive work within the priorities of archive services;

2   To inform and review strategic developments in relation to the field of community archives;

3   To undertake advocacy to relevant institutions, organisations, and stakeholders on matters of current concern in the field of community archives;

4   To review and coordinate developments and activities in the field of community archives;

5   To encourage funding to promote sustainability in community archives, in conjunction with other relevant agencies;

6   To encourage the definition of standards in community archives, and to promote their application;

7   To provide advice on community archives to relevant institutions, organisations and stakeholders;

8   To encourage the development and application of evaluation models for community archive activity;

9   To oversee the activities prescribed in the work programme for the Group.

CADG, 2007

By 2010 the CADG hopes that:

- Participation in Community Archives will be open to everyone regardless of geography, background, knowledge or technical skill
- Community Archives will be acknowledged as a significant contributor to community cohesion and community based learning through inter-generational participation, cross-cultural dialogue, and the development of new skills
- Community Archives will be valued as part of the national heritage, complementing and enriching collections held in museums, archives and libraries across the UK.

CADG, 2007

Commanet was the only community-based group represented among the partners in the Community Access to Archives Project (CAAP). The Community Archives Development Group (CADG) sought to broaden its representation from community-based initiatives and community groups. However, without a formal constitution or membership, invitations to join the Steering Committee were based on personal contacts rather than on any attempt to be representative of regions or types of community archives.

CADG now worked more closely with the Museums, Libraries and

Archives Council's nine regional agency partnerships and sought to draw in more representation from community archive groups and from mainstream practitioners actively working on community archive initiatives. The group continued to have the support of the former CAAP project manager and the then policy and development officer for the National Council on Archives and was able to agree to three pieces of work, which the Museums, Libraries and Archives Council agreed to fund. These were:

- the creation and support of an online discussion forum for archives, community groups and other interested parties to share best practice, act as a 'dating agency' to bring partners together and act as a general communications network
- the creation of community archives pages for the National Council on Archives
- the creation of advocacy tools, such as professionally edited and written up case studies to support advocacy at national, regional and local levels.

The bulk of the first two parts of this programme was to be achieved through the establishment of a community archives website. The third evolved into a consultancy for the evaluation of the impact of community archives. This evaluation produced an advocacy summary, advice for community bodies in keeping records to measure their own performance, and some detailed case studies to examine the progress and range of activities of community archives, including geographically based and ethnic minority projects (Community Archives, 2007a).[22] To this programme was added the first community archives conference held in the UK.

One of the undoubted successes for CADG has been the creation of the Community Archives website.[23] Linked to the National Council on Archives pages in CADG, the website provides:

- a directory of community archives and relevant mainstream archives, including minority and ethnic projects, projects by region and home country, national and special interests covering over 340 organizations
- features such as 'how we did that', which includes descriptions of two projects, case studies from the impact assessment work, and an archive showcase with highlights from four collections
- resources such as guides to oral history, archival issues, funding sources, collection care and related issues, useful organizations, and the foremost community archive software suppliers
- information about current events, press releases, jobs and so on
- a message and subscription discussion list.

The website has been created to facilitate the inclusion of content by registered member bodies and individuals. Update work is handled by volunteers.[24] The site has offered an additional means for people to become involved in the work of CADG as updates and news features can be added remotely. Training sessions are run for new volunteers.[25]

The CADG's work on evaluating the impact of community archives proved to be challenging, both because the impact within a given community of the activities of a single group is difficult to assess in isolation from other forces and events acting on that community, and because of the lack of evidence of the reach of their activities by the majority of community groups who featured in the case studies. The work did produce some detailed case studies which ranged from a branch of a history society based in the local museum in Keswick, northern England, which was in the early stages of making its collections accessible (Community Archives, 2007b), to the Eastside Community Heritage, founded in 1993 as a community history project by Newham Museum Service (London). Eastside went on to become an independent charity, building up an oral history and copy visual collection and has worked on a wide range of community projects, often in partnership with mainstream archive and museum services in the East London area. Project work has brought different minority and faith groups together and in the process helped archive services in the area reach out to groups who do not normally use them (Community Archives, 2007c).

The benefits of community archive activity in reaching out to groups who do not use record offices was also part of the objectives of the Cambridgeshire Community Archive Network (CCAN), established in 2006 with Heritage Lottery Fund money following a pilot project in the previous year. CCAN encouraged the formation of community archive groups countywide to maintain digital collections of photographs, written word reminiscences, sound recordings and video clips. Groups operate within agreed constitutions but are encouraged to establish their own methods of working. Ownership of source material at a local level has been seen to be important, though close links are fostered with the county's archive service and with local museums. Groups use Commanet software to provide a web presence for their collections and 18 of the 40 projected groups have a website presence registered as part of the Community Archives website (2007d). Although much of the activity involves people over 45 with an interest in local history, plans for the network include a group operating with the Cambridge Ethnic Community Forum and groups set up linked to sheltered housing schemes.

The case studies also included groups who had little or no contact with mainstream archive services or museums. In 2004–2006, the Ark Youth and Community Project in Tonypandy, Rhondda, South Wales, brought together school pupils and older people in two projects: Home Front Recalled, about the life of the area in the Second World War, and Our Mining Heritage, on the mines in the area. Children captured the memories of older people and the results formed the basis of two DVD films. Although the projects used the history of the area, their primary purpose was to strengthen community bonds and break down inter-generational barriers. Collections were not established other than the two DVDs and associated resources packs and, in consequence, links to mainstream bodies were confined to some advice from the Welsh Folk Museum. Although the project comes within the operating area of the Glamorgan Record Office, which was seeking to work with local community archives at the time, staff were unaware of the work of the Ark, an indication of the knowledge gap that sometimes exists between community activity that is derived from social and regeneration-based groups and the heritage sector (Community Archives, 2007e).

Conclusion

CADG aspires to be a forum for UK community archives and, as part of its work with the public, the group launched a one-day conference in June 2007. Shared Community Memories, held at University College London, attracted representatives from community groups, mainstream bodies and academics. During the conference, the more than 140 attendees saw the launch of the impact assessment study, heard advice on preservation, use of community material and funding, and learned about the development of the Community Archives website. Three community projects demonstrated the diversity and range of the developing community scene – the Bata Reminiscence and Resource Centre, based round the Bata factory village in Essex; Community Archives Wales, which will see eight Welsh communities develop their own archives; and the Cypriot Diaspora Project based in North London.[26]

The success of the conference in bringing groups together has demonstrated the value of a forum for community archives in Britain, although the challenge is to transform CADG into a genuinely representative group. To date there has been no formal membership, and funding for projects, including the conference, has come via the National Council on Archives from the Museums, Libraries and Archives Council. There are clear difficulties for many groups in travelling to regular meetings. But while the details of establishing a genuinely member-based successor to CADG are still being worked out, a key decision has been taken to include 'heritage' in the title of a new group, and to seek to include bodies working with the built environment and transport projects such as railway and canal preservation projects. But the prognosis for the future success of this community archives project is strong. The feedback from the 2007 conference delegates clearly supported the need for a source of advice and a means of contact and communication between the growing and diverse bodies that make up the UK's community archive scene.

Notes

1 Most of this article draws on examples from England; however, the wider bodies that have developed, notably the Community Archives Development Group, cover the whole of the UK which also includes Scotland, Wales and Northern Ireland.

2 Counties are territorial divisions of England, which were created for reasons of political, administrative and geographical demarcation. There are currently 82 metropolitan and non-metropolitan counties (http://en.wikipedia.org/).

3 From 1894 to 1965 Walthamstow was successively an urban district council and a borough within the county of Essex, and had its own library service. From 1965 it was merged with Chingford and Leyton to form Waltham Forest, one of the 32 boroughs within Greater London.

4 Walthamstow was successively a parish, urban district council and borough in the county of Essex until 1965, when it became part of the London Borough of Waltham Forest in the north-east part of Greater London.

5 In the only recorded instance of a dispute over the transfer of a Walthamstow manorial register by another record office to a suitable place of deposit, the matter was resolved by a delay of some 25 years, when the document was transferred by mutual agreement to the archives at Waltham Forest.

6 From 1894 to 1965 Chingford was successively an urban district and a borough in the county of Essex. It became part of the London Borough of Waltham Forest in 1965.

7 The author was successively senior local studies assistant and borough archivist at Waltham Forest from 1977 to 1983.

8 I am indebted to Janet Keighley for this summary of the development of the concept of community.

9 For the development of the Community Access to Archives Project (CAAP) see below.

10 'Commanet: The Community Archives Network' at www.commanet.org/default.aspx.

11 'Batley Community Archive' at www.communityarchives.org.uk/page_id__140_path__0p2p12p31p.aspx.

12 Commanet went into liquidation in June 2008. However, the software developed by Commanet is still supported in the UK, and continues in use by a wide range of groups. The Commanet website was still live when this article was in composition.

13 Ibid and from personal observations at Commanet demonstrations. While this

article was being written Commanet went into receivership, though arrangements
are in hand to ensure the continued operation of the Commanet website.

14   Web page from the Hemsworth Coalfield Partnership site gives current information
on the Group: www.one2one-development.com/hemsworthpartnership/
page.asp?idno=70.

15   See www.nowthen.org/articles/singlearticle.php and www.historytoherstory.org.uk/.

16   WYAS. Consultation undertaken towards the development of the WYAS. Chapter
5, Consultation findings - focus groups with users and non-users.

17   The survey found some 30 groups out of 520 that were from the Black and ethnic
minority communities which might have an interest in history, heritage, skills
development or possibly an online presence.

18   Roger Green, the Director of the Centre for Community Research, worked with
the residents. His book *Voices from the Mead: people's stories of the Kingsmead Estate* was
published by Arima Publishing in 2005. Source:
http://perseus.herts.ac.uk/uhinfo/staff/?uuid=D9F074A7-987E-C971-
7EF4234E4224398E.

19   The BSSA received grant aid from the London ESF Social Grants programme and
LB Hackney in 2003-4. It appeared to be still active in 2007 but has not produced
anything which is available online. This paragraph also draws on the CAAP case
studies.

20   Developed to survey archive collections for sources on the history of Caribbean and
Black and Asian people in UK archives.

21   The author was a member of Linking Arms and aUK in its early stages -
information from personal observation and unpublished documents.

22   The impact assessment work was completed in March 2007 and launched at the
CADG conference at University College London on 27 June 2007.

23   See www.communityarchives.org.uk/.

24   Initially there were training programmes to bring in new volunteers. At the time of
writing the volunteer role is under review and CADG may move to using some of
the resources it receives from the NCA to pay for the website to be professionally
maintained.

25   *Community Archives Development Group: key development opportunities for CADG*,
updated to May 2008.

26   CADG Conference programme, 'Shared Community Memories', June 2007.

References

ATF (2004) *Listening to the Past, Speaking to the Future. Report of the Archives Task Force*,
Museums, Libraries and Archives Council,
www.mla.gov.uk/what/publications/2004.

BBC News (2003) In Pictures: Hackney Siege, 10 January,

http://news.bbc.co.uk/1/hi/england/2645007.stm.

Calouste Gulbenkian Foundation (1968) *Community Work and Social Change: a report on training*, Longman.

Commanet (n.d.), www.commanet.org.

Community Access to Archives Project (2004a) Final Report, www.nationalarchives.gov.uk/documents/finalreport.pdf.

Community Access to Archives Project (2004b) Case Studies, www.nationalarchives.gov.uk/documents/casestudies.pdf.

Community Access to Archives Project (2004c) Outreach Pack.

Community Archives (2007a) http://communityarchives.org.uk/.

Community Archives (2007b) Keswick Historical Society Archives Group: case-study showing the impact of community archives, http://communityarchives.org.uk/documents/Community_Archives_Case_Study_Keswick_HA_final_rev_07_51.pdf.

Community Archives (2007c) Eastside Community Heritage: case-study showing the impact of community archives, http://communityarchives.org.uk/documents/Community_Archives_Case_Study_Eastside_CH_final_May_07_rev.pdf.

Community Archives (2007d) Community Archives in Cambridgeshire: case-study showing the impact of community archives, http://communityarchives.org.uk/documents/Community_Archives_Case_Study_Cambridgeshire.pdf.

Community Archives (2007e) Home Front Recalled: bridging the generation gap in the Rhondda Valleys; and Our Mining Heritage, coal mining in the Rhondda and the South Wales Valleys, www.communityarchives.org.uk/documents/Community_Archives_Case_Study_The_Ark_Youth_Community_Project.pdf.

Community Archives Development Group (2007) *Key Development Opportunities for CADG*, unpublished.

From History to Her Story, www.historytoherstory.org.uk/.

Green, R. (2005) *Voices From the Mead: people's stories of the Kingsmead Estate*, Arima Publishing.

Museums, Libraries and Archives Council, Archives Task Force (2004) Listening to the Past, Speaking to the Future, www.arts-research-digest.com/archive/digests/1587.

Now Then Dewsbury, www.nowthen.org/.

Office for National Statistics (2001), www.statistics.gov.uk/census2001/profiles/00AM-A.asp.

The Red Room, www.theredroom.org.uk/hoxton.htm#.

Rod Hall Agency (n.d.), www.rodhallagency.com/?art_id=000532.

Smith, M. K. (1996, 2006) 'Community work', *The Encyclopaedia of Informal Education*, www.infed.org/community/b-comwrk.htm.

US Center for Disease Control (n.d.) Community Engagement: definitions and
organizing concepts from the literature,
www.cdc.gov/phppo/pce/part1.htm.

West Yorkshire Archive Service (WYAS) (2003) Report by ABL Consulting.

Part 2

Communities and non-traditional record keeping

3

The Single Noongar Claim: native title, archival records and aboriginal community in Western Australia[1]

GLEN KELLY

[Editor's note: In August 2008, the Fourth Annual Conference on the History of Records and Archives (ICHORA IV) was held in Perth, Australia. The theme of the conference was 'Minority Reports: indigenous and community voices in archives'. The following keynote address by Glen Kelly is reproduced, with some minor editing, in its entirety.]

Introduction

First of all, let me acknowledge the Traditional Owners of this place, the Whadjuk Noongars. This isn't something that I say flippantly; my family are Traditional Owners in the lower south west of the state. I am a Wardandi Noongar, so I make that acknowledgement as an outsider, to state that I recognize the primacy of the Whadjuk Noongars in this country and to pay my respect to these people.

Let me also acknowledge the organizers of this conference and thank them for asking me to present this keynote address. I must say that the history of archives and records is an area that is a little out of my expertise; however, in developing this address, I have been able to reflect on a number of things that are important to my business and it has given me some fresh insight into a number of areas that are central to my role in a native title representative body and the creation of evidence to support native title claims.

By way of introduction, my name is Glen Kelly. I am a Wardandi Noongar, obviously with European heritage as well, and am the Chief Executive Officer of the South West Aboriginal Land and Sea Council (SWALSC).

SWALSC is a community organization with a membership of some 2500 Noongar people,[2] and we are very much an organ of the Noongar community. SWALSC is also the Native Title Representative Body (NTRB) for the south west of Western Australia, that is, we have been certified by the Commonwealth Government to deliver services as defined in the Native Title Act (1993). As a result, SWALSC has statutory functions which are, broadly speaking, the representation of native title claims.

This of course shapes the types of things that I am going to speak on today, and the general context will be from the direction of a native title representative body and native title claims. Presenting from this backdrop, however, there are many things of relevance to mainstream practice and to the themes of this conference.

The areas I will touch on today are distinct yet related, and I hope to tell a story that links together the European record and the Noongar knowledge set, cultural memory or indigenous archive, whatever you wish to term it. The topics I will speak on are:

- the short background of native title claims and their content
- the development of the anthropological records interpreting people and culture, which transferred to archives and became, in the eyes of many, 'truth'
- the types of records that have been kept by the state in particular about Aboriginal people, and the purpose of these records
- the ways that these things have fed into the native title claims that we represent and the role of records
- indigenous archives and their treatment in the native title arena and how in this arena they relate to the non-indigenous record.

Native title claims – a backdrop

The reason that native title is relevant here is that a native title claim is essentially an exercise in gathering information and then using that information to prove a level of traditional connection that is 'acceptable' to the courts.[3] In its essence, a native title claim is like any other legal claim be it insurance, workers' compensation, a civil writ, and so on. It is a claim to certain rights defined through traditional law and custom and interpreted through the Native Title Act and the common law over a people's traditional land. In addition, native title claims are lodged in the Federal Court and processed through that court, except in cases where there are higher appeals, and these go to the High Court of Australia, which is, as the name suggests, Australia's highest court.

As in any other writ or claim, there is a burden of proof. In the case of native land claims, the burden of proof falls onto the claimants to prove that they have in fact withstood the harsh effects of colonialism and have maintained a body of traditional law and custom which can be proven to be derived from the law and custom of their ancestors as at sovereignty. That may sound a bit less complicated than it is, because proving it is no mean feat.

So how do you do it? Well, you develop a body of proof that is derived from both the non-indigenous record and the indigenous record, and, hopefully, the two match up to the satisfaction of the court. First of all, you need to prove a normative system, that is that a structured society existed at sovereignty. To do this, your team trawls through all the historical records it can in order to develop evidence about whether a normative system exists and then to describe it.

You then trawl through all the records that follow so as to establish continuing physical connection to lands and a continuity of society, and then you gather evidence from the indigenous record in order to establish the continuing existence of the normative system and ongoing connection. So in the case of native title cases, you actually rely on both the indigenous and non-indigenous record. Sometimes they work well together, sometimes they don't, and it's this interplay which makes the native title context relevant for today. In all of this, the burden of proof is skewed well towards the written record and it treats the indigenous record as in some way less reliable, less authentic and in many ways, less truthful.

The Single Noongar Claim

The main vehicle that SWALSC has used to pursue native title in the south west of Western Australia is the Single Noongar Claim, and, without going into all the technical details, I need to describe this claim to you due to its significance to us. You see a claim is not just about land rights, it's also firmly entrenched in the socio-economic realm. Using mechanisms like native title claims, people are able to carve themselves out a space in today's world, but you need to prove your case first.

The Single Noongar Claim covers a large territory. Its western and southern borders are the coastline and its eastern border runs approximately diagonally from north of Jurien Bay (some 250 km north of Perth) to east of Hopetoun (some 750 km south east of Perth). This covers a very large area of several thousand square kilometres. By way of comparison, the Single Noongar Claim is bigger than the Australian State of Victoria (Figure 3.1).

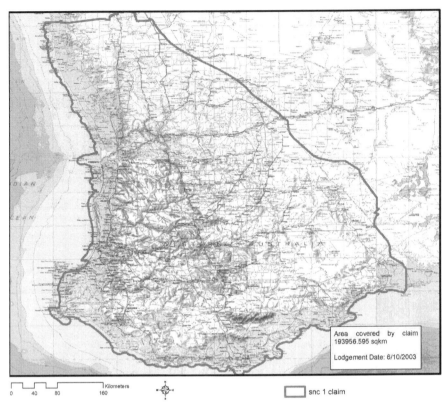

Figure 3.1 The Single Noongar Claim

The Single Noongar Claim is a societal claim. It asserts the existence of a Noongar society in this area of land that is distinct from its neighbours and is governed by a uniform set of laws and customs. It doesn't assert that the people are uniform, as there are widely different environments in this area of land, and indeed Noongar people have always organized into subgroups, clans, families, moieties and other things. The claim is described by a set of apical ancestors. Basically this means that there is a list of Noongar people and couples who were around at sovereignty or shortly after,[4] and the members of the claim group are descendants of these people. The number of claim group members is about 35,000 people, that is, all Noongars currently alive.

The State Government was not willing to negotiate in relation to the Single Noongar Claim, particularly the Perth metropolitan portion. As a result, the metropolitan portion was cut out and listed for hearings. Our argument was that as the metropolitan area is a small portion of the larger societal claim, if native title was to be recognized in the metropolitan area it would be as a portion of the larger Noongar society. Further, in order to prove this society, evidence needed to be taken from around Noongar country, not just the metropolitan area. So that's what happened.

In September 2006 the trial judge handed down a judgement which recognized the existence of a Noongar society at sovereignty and the existence of a Noongar society today, which adhered to laws and customs derived from those at the time of sovereignty. Further, as a result of this, the judge recognized that, except for where it was already extinguished (an extensive area), native title existed in the Perth metropolitan area.[5]

To say this caused a strong reaction would be a bit of an understatement. We had politicians ranting in Parliament, the local newspapers going off, even the Federal Attorney General at the time was peddling lies about what a native title determination meant, and saying publicly that access to beaches, rivers and parks was in danger. Of course, and by law, it never was. The judgement sent shockwaves across Australia. In the first instance, it was a shock that native title had been recognized in a metropolitan area, but it was also a shock that Noongar people had been recognized; well, a shock to everyone but the Noongar people of course. The reason for this was that until that point, people had been living under the misconception that Noongar culture, and therefore society, was gone, finished, dead, extinct. Justice Wilcox, on the other hand, saw first hand that it wasn't, but it's worthwhile noting that he himself was surprised by the result, and he said as much when he handed down the judgement.

Of course, the Single Noongar Claim was appealed in a very aggressive manner. Normally in an appeal you say that the judge applied the law wrongly to the facts that were found. In this case, the appeal contained that, but it also asserted that the facts themselves were wrong. From this, the state and the Commonwealth 'threw the kitchen sink' at the appeal. In the end, during April 2008, the appeal court ruled that it upheld the state's appeal about the application of the facts, but that the facts regarding a Noongar society stood. It then referred us back to the docket judge to begin again.

So, as one Noongar man remarked, half time, scores are even. We have gained great mileage out of the Single Noongar Claim. We have advanced ourselves politically in a short time in a greatly accelerated fashion. There is now a greater amount of calm in relation to the Single Noongar Claim, and the state has recently indicated it is now actually ready to negotiate a settlement. This is a huge advance for us as Noongar people but also for society at large, as it has brought society along as well. Of course, none of this would happen without proof, and this proof is gained from access to both the white and the black record in the manner I spoke about a short time ago. Let's start examining the record.

The historical record – anthropology

There are many types of non-indigenous records that are taken and kept that have relevance here. One of the critical types in a native title context is what may be loosely termed the anthropological record. I use the term 'loosely' as anthropology became a discipline well after the settlement of the Swan River Colony in 1829, so there are really two stages to this. The first is the observations about Noongars in early colonial times and the second and later stage is the emergence of the professional studier of people, the anthropologist.

In the early stage, what we have is a set of records that are in many cases observations of earlier settlers, explorers, farmers, police, military and civil officials and even newspapers. In many cases these are direct observations, sometimes in journals, sometimes in military or police reports and sometimes in deliberate first-hand observations that were written specifically to be first-hand observations. The common theme about these is they don't really apply interpretation, they are just straight recording designed to be seen as true records of events.[6]

Of course they do have thoughts attached to them which interpret events, but in the main they are a pretty dry or 'objective' catalogue, at least as objective as the lens of colonialism allowed. They catalogued events, conversations, language, place names, creation stories, dress, markings, hunting strategy, moieties, clans, marriage, ritual, rites, ecological knowledge and so on, to which the writers in many cases don't really seek to apply strong values or interpretation. The other key feature of this type of record – and this is important in our case – was that many of these early record takers never really collaborated, and across the south west, which is a very large area, it emerged that there were strong commonalities between what was written about Noongars by independent people in very distant locations.[7]

This type of information litters our archives and official records. It's not organized in a way that is designed to be easily interrogated through evidence gathering in a native title case, it was never designed for this. It is, however, in its totality, a rich source of information about Noongar people at sovereignty, which can be interpreted by today's professionals. In fact the depth of the record in Noongar country is so deep and widespread with so many commonalities that you are able to build up ideas of a normative system of society. As previously discussed, this is a fundamental and key point to proving a native title case – remembering that what you are trying to do is to prove that people today have ostensibly maintained the same normative society as the one that existed at sovereignty.

The fact that proving a society in a native title case relies not on talking to today's Noongar people, but solely through interrogating and interpreting the white record is the first skewing of the burden of proof towards the written record and away from the Noongar record. Woe betide you if your land got settled by a bunch of illiterates or worse, people who were only intent on clearing you from your land and therefore deliberately failed to record things, lest their atrocities be known. Because if that were the case, then there is no foundational evidence to prove a normative society, and so how can you prove that today's people have ostensibly maintained the laws and customs of this society at sovereignty? The answer is, you can't and your claim fails. No matter how good the oral record from the indigenous people, no matter how convincing the evidence from the claimants themselves, without this very early white record, it is assumed that claimants' information is basically unreliable and your claim is fairly sure of failing. And this is not uncommon.

Fortunately, however, in Noongar country there is a vast amount of early record keeping and this has worked in the favour of Noongar people. The second 'phase' of this anthropological record was the development of the anthropologists themselves. Initially amateur, they gradually gained commission from colonial governments in the late 1800s and early 1900s to gather information on 'the natives', in many cases for posterity. Some of these people were trained, some were untrained, but the basic difference of this movement was that they started to apply a level of interpretation.

One of the most famous of these people in the south west of Western Australia was Daisy Bates. She was one of the untrained but her work is of great importance. She was a peculiar person, and it's worth dwelling on this for a moment as we consider the reliability of records, whose are trustworthy and what knowledge they give rise to. Daisy Bates said that she hated three things: 'Germans, trades unionists and half castes' (Bates, 1985, 22). So while by her own admission, she hated a significant proportion of the Noongar population, she recorded a lot of information from and about Noongar people, even though her mission was, as she said, to help a 'dying race, whose final pillow she had a duty to smooth' (Bates, 1966, xi; Bates, 1985, 17). Perhaps she was trying to establish a field of 'palliative' anthropology. You see Daisy Bates shared an idea with many people of the time, one derived from social Darwinism, which believed that Aboriginal people were a doomed race. As a result of this, they thought they'd better get a bit of information down for the benefit of future generations, although presumably not for the benefit of future Noongar generations.

To further illustrate the person, Daisy Bates was married for a time to a man by the name of Breaker Morant, called 'Breaker' because of his skills in breaking in horses to the harness. Breaker Morant is the centre of a famous Australian story. After his divorce from Daisy, he went to the Boer War where he was made a scapegoat and executed by firing squad for following bad orders – at least I think that's how the story went, it's been a long time since I watched the movie that was made which was based on the events.

Daisy also raised the ire of her colleagues, although some of this was probably intellectual snobbery due to the fact she was pretty much self-trained. Prominent anthropologist Alfred Radcliffe-Brown noted that 'Bates' mind was somewhat similar to the contents of a well-stored sewing basket after half a dozen kittens had been playing there undisturbed for a few days' (Bates, 1985, 7–8). She was also considered to be peculiar by Noongars. Part of the oral history that I have heard about Daisy Bates is that when she would visit reserves to speak to people, even though it might be 40 degrees, she would always wear jet black, full Victorian-style dresses. Noongars thought this was pretty strange. After all, it was very hot – shorts and sandals would have done.

I once told this story about her dress to an anthropologist friend of mine who confirmed it and told me that the reason she always went overboard with the clothes was that she was trying to set an example. For all her 'quirks', however, Daisy Bates did have real friends among the Noongar people and she also wrote a lot of material. In the early 1900s, she interviewed some of the last Noongar people who had 'first contact' with Europeans but disregarded any Noongar person with any European heritage as being inauthentic or of no consequence (Bates, 1985, 52–4).

To a great extent, it was the perspective of Daisy Bates and those who shared her social Darwinist lens that gave rise to the myth that Noongar people, society and culture were dead and gone. Never mind that there was cultural passage occurring with the half-castes she so despised, these were ignored and, as a result, completely missed. To all intents and purposes, then, it probably seemed to Daisy Bates that the prophesies of social Darwinism had pretty much come to pass. These myths became accepted as truth in anthropological circles and seem also to have become the basis on which later work was done. As a result, some of her ideas tainted the future record, long after her materials were part of the archive. Unfortunately the effect of this was that work in later decades served only to perpetuate the white mythology created at the beginning of the 20th century.

An excellent example of this 'white mythology' was work done by noted anthropologists Ronald and Catherine Berndt in the 1960s and 1970s (Berndt, 1979, 81). They regarded Aboriginal people in 'settled areas' as not 'authentic' Aboriginal people and did not even deign to do fieldwork with a people whom they assumed had lost their culture. Berndt, without engaging in any fieldwork in the south west, concluded that by the 1930s the Aboriginal people of the south west 'possess little or nothing of their traditional heritage' and that most of them were 'of considerably mixed Aboriginal affinity' (Berndt, 1979, 81).

By this time, of course, for reasons that I will explain soon, no Noongar in their right mind was going to talk to any anthropologist anyway, so their conclusion confirming Bates' ideas was really a self-fulfilling prophecy. But this conclusion was baseless. Still, it reinforced the growing record that Noongar culture was gone. In fact, this work by the Berndts, which today forms part of the anthropological record, was used by the state at the Single Noongar Claim trial to seek to display a lack of continuity and a breakdown of Noongar culture. The point here isn't to attack the Berndts, but rather to demonstrate how earlier prejudices by a European recorder and interpreter entered the record and created myth that was uncritically accepted as truth even by those who had rejected the ideas of social Darwinism. It goes further though because, as noted previously when discussing reaction to the Single Noongar Claim, the original perspective about the end of Noongars and its uncritical reinforcement effectively became social convention or part of the common sense of broader Western Australian and even Australian society.

The white record in relation to Aboriginal people is full of these myths, which have somehow converted to truth. Why then, when this happens, is the indigenous record seen as unreliable or untruthful? There is no question that the direct record of people like Daisy Bates is invaluable, but their interpretations are extraordinarily destructive, and somehow, in the white record, these incredibly destructive 'truths' take root and, for some reason, seem unassailable. This is a tragic outcome, as their acceptance by broader society has given rise to generations of incredibly pervasive racism, which has affected and continues to affect all parts of Noongar life.

Historical record – 'native welfare'

One of the attitudes that these social Darwinist myths supported was assimilation and what can be broadly called 'the native welfare system'. I'd now like to turn my attention to the record left by the people behind these systems. The native welfare system wasn't really about the welfare of the natives, it was designed to facilitate the process of first segregation then assimilation. Not content with the idea that Noongars and indeed Aboriginal people were a doomed race, serious efforts were actually undertaken to facilitate and control this outcome. The system of native welfare which was to dominate Aboriginal people and Noongar people especially was created in 1886 with the Aborigines Protection Act. This Act sought to provide for the 'better protection and management' of Aborigines. This was the start of a dazzling and destructive series of legislative acts under various names, which continued to blight Aboriginal people until the early 1970s.

The 1905 Aborigines Act instigated the position of 'Protector of Aborigines' (Aborigines Act 1905). It created a system whereby the protector, through the police, could place people in reservations, in which Noongars had to be between 6pm and 6am – to be caught in a town, for example, during this time meant jail. The Act also required the protector to grant permits for Noongar people to travel, get jobs and marry, and for many other aspects of daily life. Many of these permits were refused (Haebich, 1988, 2000).

Worst of all, the Act made the protector the legal guardian 'of every Aboriginal and half-caste child' under 16 years. This gave him the legal right in white law to decide on the disposition of Aboriginal children. In support of the assimilation policies the Act was based on, the protector could, and did, through the legal sanction of the Aborigines Act, order the removal of children from their parents and their placement in Christian missions for re-education – read assimilation. Older Noongar people who were considered too dark for absorption into the white community were left at Moore River Native Settlement where they could live out their days (Haebich and Delroy, 1999).

This entire 'welfare' system (which underwent significant changes in legislation and name in 1936 and 1954) with its obsessive recording of the intimate details of every Aboriginal person gave rise to incredible records and archives.[8] Obviously, in order for the protector to administer the system, he needed to have a detailed knowledge of where people were, what they were doing, how they were acting, where they were working, who they were with and a whole variety of other things.

This has left us with a host of individual native welfare files – now held at the State Records Office of Western Australia – files which are the most pervasive record imaginable. They are also incredibly offensive and full of official lies about the condition of people and the parenting of adults in order to justify the genocidal practices they were designed to support. They are also extremely detailed in relation to times, places, movements, work and a whole variety of other materials.

The native welfare system also gave rise to another set of records, 'the caste card'. These cards were used to track the caste or blood quantum of people through the generations with the aim of being able to give the protector the ability to calculate whether a particular person would be classed as a native or not. This was then used to justify the further segregation of children from each other. For example, where it was calculated (through mathematical calculations on the actual card) that a child was a quadroon, an octoroon or something less in blood quantum, they were separated and sent to particular missions where they could be raised as white children before being released into general society. You can see then that these cards, these records and the way they were able to be used held power. Thankfully this ceased when the native welfare system was abandoned in the early 1970s.

In mentioning the studies performed by Ronald and Catherine Berndt in the 1960s and 1970s, you can now get an idea of why no Noongar was going to say anything to any anthropologist, and why it was a fair assumption on the part of Noongar people that these researchers were there to somehow further disadvantage them, even if they weren't. In fact, the effect that the native welfare system had was that Noongars closed ranks. You can't expect that when you put people on reserves, in a concentrated space, that cultural information wasn't being passed on; you can't expect that with a lot of people working in agriculture, often with their children even only periodically, that cultural information wasn't being passed on, because it was. But it was done in hushed tones and in secret, because to be public had some very serious consequences. But the record, either native welfare or anthropological, during this time missed this. It was only able to scratch the surface of Noongar society as no access to outsiders was granted. Of course, this furthered the idea in the white record, an idea that was further entrenched as truth, that the Noongar culture was over. Still, while it's hideous and terrifying to think about the native welfare system and to know that it operated in recent history, what it left was an amazing record. There are now thousands of records and literally tons of paper that are now part of archive systems spanning the best part of 70 years and that contain an extraordinarily detailed record of Noongars and their families.

And incredibly, despite this record being intended as a tool to cement segregation and later assimilation to see the end of a society, it was in this respect a complete and utter failure. Ironically enough, we see this in these very records. As previously discussed, a key point for a native title case is that of connection, which is not only about cultural connection but physical connection, and it must be proven that people have maintained an unbroken connection to the country they are claiming traditional rights to. The contention of the state and the Commonwealth was that there couldn't be a recognition of native title due to the effects of moving people off country as well as the removal of children, all of which amounted to a breakdown of connection. However, the native welfare records actually helped us to establish that although people did move around, they also figured out how to exploit the system by moving around in their own traditional lands. This point was completely missed by the state and everyone else who studied Noongar people for the best part of 100 years until the Single Noongar Claim litigation.

Now when we try to establish physical connection to country, we can actually map through birth, death and marriage registers and through the native welfare files and cards, the fact that through the generations, Noongar people pretty much stayed on their own country and connection was not broken. This is the most delicious irony I have had the pleasure to come across. The people who developed the system to assimilate Noongars, that is see the destruction of Noongar society, actually helped us to prove its existence. Gladly, their life's work was rendered a failure and their disgraceful and disgusting but detailed and voluminous records played a key role in our claims for native title in the south west.

The Aboriginal Archive

Of course, in the end, it comes down to the evidence that Noongar people themselves give. You can have the best legal strategy in the world as well as the best archival record, but if you don't have evidence, your claim is not going to succeed. This evidence is based on our researchers, with the context defined by our lawyers, going out to speak with Noongar people on matters of law and custom. The raw materials are then transferred to sworn witness statements which can be submitted to a court.

The Single Noongar Claim faced some obvious prejudices through the mythology that had been built up and reinforced in the white record. Indeed the paucity of good materials during the middle parts of the 20th century was used as evidence that Noongar society was extinct, even though there were some strong reasons for never speaking to a 'whitefella' about your Noongar business during this time. This led to a perception that maybe, just maybe, the evidence coming from these Noongars today is kind of made up, invented to suit the circumstance, unreliable, untruthful.

And we see this sort of perception well beyond Noongar country, and doubts over the veracity of oral records coming from Aboriginal people is a constant theme in Australia. The talk is always about how they are exaggerated or pushed by a political agenda or some other impetus. But if we pause to think about the personalities and the prejudices of the people who laid out the white record as well as the manner in which officials misrepresented things in the official record that we deal with, this is a bit hard to take.

Let me put it this way, if Noongar people have a cultural memory of Rottnest Island being connected to the mainland and other questionable things, all of which were scoffed at by Europeans when they became aware of these bits of information, I'm sure we can remember things that happened over the few generations since sovereignty. You see, many of the Noongar people who gave evidence are grandchildren of the apical ancestors listed on the claims. Others are great-grandchildren and some further. Underneath it all, however, is the fact that the type of information that is gathered in a native title case from witnesses isn't necessarily factual information such as events, times or dates, but cultural information and understandings. So even if detail on days, times and the like becomes hazy through the oral record, the principles of Noongar law and custom don't. And this shone through in the evidence.

There's also another interesting phenomenon in relation to the indigenous oral record. It seems that if it is spoken first hand, there may be some doubts, but if mediated by a non-indigenous professional, although doubts remain, it gains more credence. To my mind, this is further evidence of the type of institutionalized racism that Aboriginal people in Australia experience daily.

Still, the evidence gathered in the Single Noongar Claim from Noongar people was and is excellent. It had the effect of undermining the interpretations made through the white record and it will give rise to a new discourse in relation to Noongar history and culture that debunks many of the suppositions and so called 'truths' that have been accepted through the use of the white record. It will also have the effect of correcting the previously written record and, while not rendering it obsolete or of no use, will allow a more enlightened interpretation of it. This new discourse has already commenced and we ourselves plan to publish what we consider a more accurate version of Noongar history which includes consideration of the fact that no one wanted to speak to any anthropologist or official on the topic of Noongar business for a very long time.

Concluding remarks

I hope that today I have been able, using a native title claim as the backdrop, to offer some insights first into the manner in which all sorts of record have been important to us and, second, into how the records have interacted with each other. It's not often that you work in a field that requires so many different types of information, and the challenge of making them work together, considering the reasons these records came into existence in the first place, is not an inconsiderable one.

In the end, though, our ability to bring these things together to develop a body of evidence has had a great effect. Not only will it result in a correction in the interpretation of these records themselves, but it has and will have a great and positive effect on the lives of Noongar people, now and into the future. Because based on even what we have now, people are starting to take Noongars seriously. We are starting to see movement in all sorts of areas that we never saw before and, who knows, we may even settle the Single Noongar Claim out of court based on the materials that we have been able to gather to date. All in all, times have changed, and I certainly hope that there is in the future a more harmonious and constructive interaction between the white and black records sparked by things such as the Single Noongar Claim and the sometimes surprising things that come out of them.

Notes

1　The author acknowledges Chris Owen, Yvette Bradley and Denise Cook for their research assistance.

2　For more information about the Noongar people, see the website of the South West Aboriginal Land and Sea Council at www.noongar.org.au/.

3　For Justice Wilcox's 2006 judgement see www.austlii.edu.au/au/cases/cth/FCA/2006/1243.html.For the appeal outcome see www.austlii.edu.au/au/cases/cth/FCAFC/2008/63.html.

4　For the purposes of this particular case, the date of acquisition of sovereignty is identified as 1829. See www.minterellison.com/public/connect/Internet/Home/Legal+Insights/Newsletters/ Previous+Newsletters/A-C-Noongar+case+first+to+uphold+native+title.

5　See the judgement at Federal Court of Australia, *Bennell* v. *Western Australia* [2006] *FCA* 1243 (19 September 2006), www.austlii.edu.au/au/cases/cth/FCA/2006/1243.html.

6　See, for example, G. F. Moore, *A Descriptive Vocabulary of the Language in Common Use Amongst the Aborigines of Western Australia, with Copious Meanings, Embodying Much Interesting Information Regarding the Habits, Manners and Customs of the Natives and the Natural History of the Country*, London, 1842.

7　Historical sources show how Aboriginal people of the south west had been identified as 'Noongar' (or variations 'Nyungar', 'Nyungal' or 'Yungar') since at least the 1840s and Aborigines in places as far apart as York, Perth and Albany were 'Yung-ar' and spoke the same language. Moore's 1842 descriptive vocabulary (part 1) lists the word 'Yungar'(s) with the meaning 'People. The name by which they designate themselves' (Moore, 1848, 84).

8　For example, the Native Administration Act (1936) and the Native Welfare Act (1954) made wide ranging legislative changes to the powers of government over Aboriginal people and asserted the government's ability to remove children from their families and make them wards of the state.

References

Aborigines Act 1905, 5 Edw. V11.14.

Aborigines Protection Act 1886, 50 Vict. 25.

Bates, D. (1966) *The Passing of the Aborigines: a lifetime spent among the natives of Australia*, Heinemann.

Bates, D. (1985) *The Native Tribes of Western Australia*, edited by I. White, National Library of Australia.

Bates, D. (1992) *Aboriginal Perth and Bibbulmun Biographies and Legends*, edited by P. J. Bridge, Hesperian Press.

Berndt, R. M. (1979) Aborigines of the South-West. In Berndt, R. M. and Berndt, C. H. (eds), *Aborigines of the West*, University of Western Australia Press.

Green, N. (1979) *Nyungar - The People: Aboriginal custom in the southwest of Australia*, Creative Research.

Haebich, A. (1988) *For Their Own Good: Aborigines and government in the South West of Western Australia 1900-1940*, University of Western Australia Press for the Charles and Joy Staples South West Region Publications Fund Committee.

Haebich, A. (2000) *Broken Circles: fragmenting indigenous families 1800-2000*, Fremantle Arts Centre Press.

Haebich, A. and Delroy, A. (1999) *The Stolen Generations: separation of Aboriginal children from their families in Western Australia*, Western Australian Museum.

Hassell, E. (1975) *My Dusky Friends*, East Fremantle.

Moore, G. F. (1842 [1978]) *A Descriptive Vocabulary of the Language in Common Use Amongst the Aborigines of Western Australia, with Copious Meanings, Embodying Much Interesting Information Regarding the Habits, Manners and Customs of the Natives and the Natural History of the Country*, W. S. Orr & Co. [University of Western Australia Press].

Moore, G. F. (1884 [1978]) *Diary of Ten Years Eventful Life of an Early Settler in Western Australia*, M. Walbrook [University of Western Australia Press].

Mulvaney, J. and Green, N. (eds) (1992) *Commandant of Solitude: the journals of Captain Collett Barker 1828-1831*, University of Melbourne Press.

Salter, E. (1971) *Daisy Bates: 'the great white queen of the never never'*, Angus and Robertson.

Shann, E. O. G. *Cattle Chosen*, University of Western Australia Press, originally published in 1926.

4

Oral tradition in living cultures: the role of archives in the preservation of memory

PATRICIA GALLOWAY

Introduction

Vanishingly few purely oral cultures – those that do not even communicate with a literate culture – still exist in the world. There are numerous indigenous cultures with many nonliterate members; there are also myriad modern literate subcultures that preferentially preserve all or some tradition in oral form. Both, however, are embedded to greater or lesser extent in a web of global literate cultures of varying local intensities. Some historians have argued that tradition preserved orally is not valid evidence, while others recognize it as a category of 'memory' that has its own rules of resonance. Modernist western archivists, themselves reflexively literate, sit uneasily in between: charged with supporting the preservation of records of the past, they have until recently adhered to a practice almost exclusively focused on written textual objects. Now they are being confronted with memory modalities that challenge the model of sequential written text as sufficient documentation for all human cultural phenomena.

Production of information, oral and written: the 'orality and literacy' episteme

Although few communities in the early 21st century completely lack some kind of literacy, it is also true that few are completely documented by the written word, or will ever be so. Thus nearly all communities' communication and recording of memory take place in a mixed environment. The discussion of orality and literacy as modalities for recording and preserving the past has most frequently been focused, somewhat abstractly, on cultures and communities seen as characterized by 'pure orality' – that is, communities where no written language is produced at all – or by 'literacy' – taken as communities where everyone is literate. Further, this discourse has been connected historically with an orientalist discourse that placed 'oral' and 'literate' in a family of binary oppositions including ancient–modern, primitive–civilized and inferior–superior, together with an argument that holds that literacy 'transforms consciousness' (for the better, of course) (Ong, 1991). Yet the adequacy of this whole approach to ranking the value of written and oral documentation, with its implication that the written word is more accurate or true than the orally transmitted word, has been set aside as historians and anthropologists have turned away from a positivist view of history and culture and have recognized that all literate cultures still retain many oral practices (Olson and Torrance, 1991). From the archival point of view, this gives a new and significant place to oral texts,[1] from whatever source.

Recognition of the value of orally transmitted texts was already important to anthropologists, for whom the collection of oral tradition and folklore from cultures that were still transmitting the majority of their cultural knowledge orally was foundational to their discipline. An interest in oral history as such came with a broader concern by social historians with the everyday lives of ordinary people for understanding the past, as evidenced by the oral history movement beginning in the 1960s.[2] Both disciplines have been influenced by the work of Maurice Halbwachs (1992) and his notion of collective memory and by Pierre Nora's ideas about 'places of memory' (1989, 7–24), even though both disciplines have also questioned these two approaches. Most important, perhaps, mainstream anthropology and history have been challenged recently by the documented communities themselves, which have begun to voice their own opinions about how to collect, use and value their orally transmitted texts (Wilson, 1998).

Memory and orality: why, how and who?

Oral texts are dependent on memory, but retention in memory and oral transmission are strongly influenced by the context of remembering: why, how, by whom, and for whom (Shopes, n.d.). This will of course come as no surprise to archivists, for whom context is a primary value, and oral historians have also come to conduct their work more critically as the issues of evidence in oral testimonies have been addressed.[3]

Why?

The motivations for preserving memories instead of written texts at all can be many, but where an embedding culture is literate, one must first ask why, if it is possible to externalize a text, it would be retained only in oral form or even primarily in oral form. In fact, although people who are not literate do not seem to have the choice of converting oral text to writing, it is worth considering that they may also not have the need or motivation to seek to have it so converted, even where the opportunity presents itself through solicitations from potential interviewers. Secrecy or security may demand that the memory not be externalized except in being passed on orally to an apprentice or shared with a peer, thereby effectively restricting access; or the oral text may seem not to be a text at all but rather a performative tool, as in the case of magical or healing formulae. People who are literate may have similar reasons not to record oral texts, where they represent persecuted speech or are only used to accomplish short-term goals.

How?

Yet these carriers of memory do remember. One may observe that the material that is remembered has the quality of being memorable; almost a century of study has shown at least some things about what that means, although human memory is still not by any means well understood.[4] But psychologists interested in naturalistic observation of human memory and qualitative interviewers agree with archivists that context is paramount as a factor in the production of oral texts, since the mere presence of an interlocutor (including an imaginary one) introduces a co-creator into the event of production. As far as memory itself is concerned, at the present juncture we are in the middle of serious changes in conceptions of human memory. Active research on memory in naturalistic contexts as well as simulation experiments by cognitive scientists are beginning to reveal the complexities of actual memory use; it is now accepted that, like the epic recitations of Yugoslav singers studied by Albert Lord in the 1950s, most things produced 'from memory' are actually reconstructed out of pieces supplied by memory and by the situation in which the memory is produced (Lord, 1960; Niethammer, 2007). It has been understood for a long time that information couched in narrative form is preferentially memorable.

Who?

As to who remembers, there may be many motivations. My examples here will look at two very different groups: medical students who choose to adopt opportunistically a method of memorization of acronymic mnemonic phrases or sentences as a shortcut strategy for acquiring rote command of a body of knowledge; and Choctaw elders who are traditional experts, recognized by their community as especially skilful and authoritative in the relation of traditional narrative and as especially careful of the responsibility of doing so.

Preservation of tradition in a mixed environment: two case studies

I am interested here in the construction and reproduction of orally preserved tradition in the presence of a surrounding literate culture. As examples, I will look at the preservation and transmission of an oral medical student culture of mnemonics as narrative vignettes in the context of the standard texts and record-keeping practices inculcated and formally rehearsed in medical schools; and at traditional memory preservation in the context of modern record keeping and archiving currently practised by the Mississippi Band of Choctaw Indians (MBCI).[5] Both of these cases are at the cusp of epistemic shifts in their respective knowledge environments. The nomenclature supported by anatomical mnemonics is in the process of a slow trans-formation to a more descriptive and therefore more obvious terminology, while increasing specialization makes gross anatomy more of a rite of passage than a vital acquisition for a large number of medical practitioners. The living tradition of Choctaw oral narratives that preserve traditional belief, history and practices is now at risk as Choctaw culture accommodates to modern American culture, while the stories and their language preserve a symbolic significance as a symbol of tribal sovereignty and uniqueness. I think that these two cases can shed light on the appraisal, acquisition and preservation questions raised for archivists by orally transmitted cultural materials, especially because both cases exhibit documentary values that make them worth preservation to their respective communities. Juxtaposed, they allow us to consider additional factors, especially concerning the transmission and reception of memory: Is memory always transmitted? Is it promoted or suppressed? How does memory work relate to an embedding literate culture? Can memory be said to be preserved apart from oral transmission?

Medical student mnemonics

One interesting category of oral memory embedded in a profoundly literate context is the persistent use of mnemonics in literate learning or practice situations; a familiar example, cited in nearly all discussions of pedagogical mnemonics, is the use by medical students of mnemonic phrases or sentences to remember anatomical structures. Linguist Alan Dundes has pointed out that such mnemonics are fundamentally related to literacy, implied by their use to remember a list of specific words by means of their initial letters, and by the fact that the arrangement of the elements in a mnemonic phrase or sentence reinforces memory by means of grammatical structure.[6] Francis Bellezza (1981) categorizes them as single-use (that is, only applied to a single specific memory task) peg-type (that is, using a structure to cue memory that is extrinsic to the subject matter) mnemonics, particularly appropriate for learning materials that need to be retained permanently in semantic memory.[7]

Context

Although most educators no longer advocate rote learning, the study of human gross anatomy is still a process of acquisition of a complex and extensive terminology, in a dead language, for the description of physical structures that are at best partly indeterminate, in order to inculcate a specific way of identifying and communicating observed phenomena. The embedding literate subculture, then, is the discipline of human anatomy, which has a history going back to western antiquity but whose 'gross' portion (visible to the human eye) has been superseded as an active research area. Yet anatomy is a basic science of venerable importance to the study of medicine, since practising physicians require a knowledge of anatomical structures and their locations in order to examine, diagnose and treat patients in a clinical setting, particularly if they intend to be surgeons; in some settings, notably the emergency room, it is still critical that anatomical knowledge be instantaneously available. It is a literate tradition because from the beginning observed structures have been named in order to make them objects of study, and over two millennia several canonical types of teaching textbooks have emerged and are still used in the study of gross anatomy. These include the *anatomy text*, which discursively describes gross structures and correlates them with function and other issues, like abnormalities and disease; the *anatomical atlas*, which today consists of densely labelled illustrations with minimal description; and the *dissector*, which contains another kind of description of structures, designed to provide the student with procedures for dissecting and exposing them for examination in a preserved dead body. There is also a considerable scientific literature on gross anatomy, although most of it is now old and most medical students have little or no occasion to be exposed to it. The anatomy course commonly consists of lectures from faculty including some demonstrations of dissection technique, dissection of a dead human body over an extended period of months, and testing via both written tests and laboratory practical examinations.

The striking fact that favours the oral preservation of medical-school mnemonics and its continual reproduction comes from its character as mildly persecuted speech: these oral phrases and sentences are primarily used for passing exams, and therefore are at least partly seen by the anatomy faculty as cheating (although sometimes faculty themselves will pass on some particularly pithy or hallowed mnemonic phrase).[8] The student is supposed to be learning anatomy through a primary identity between terminology and structures, mediated by visual recognition. The use of mnemonics has been condemned repeatedly by both anatomy faculty and students looking to reform the teaching of anatomy, which has been seen as taking thought out of the process of learning about the body (McDonald, 1941, 327–9).[9] Yet the fact remains that the primary method of testing for anatomical knowledge is the laboratory practical exam, in which the student is confronted with a roomful of 'stations' comprised of a cadaver with one or more structures tagged with numbers, each of which the student is required to identify in a restricted period of time, usually 90 seconds. Students follow a path around the room with a test paper, pencil and probe in hand. In order to make a correct identification, it is not good enough that students have a clear visual recognition of the structure in question and that that visual identification be connected with physiological, developmental and clinical information; they must also produce the precise latinate term for the structure. To accomplish this task, students believe that memory aids are necessary, and whatever memory aids students have, they must come into the laboratory in their heads.[10]

Examples

A large part of the interest of anatomy mnemonics is historical. The contemporary American use of medical mnemonics in this way may be traceable to gross anatomy as taught by Franklin Paine Mall, the enormously influential anatomy professor at the Johns Hopkins medical school at the turn of the 20th century. In fact, the evidence of the oldest current mnemonics themselves points to this time period. The older of these texts appear to have been fairly inoffensive, but over time the mnemonics have become sophomorically obscene, reflecting both the dominant male population of medical schools and the problematic relationship between students and their cadavers. They also contain many references to cultural fads and the cultural contexts of their users, as well as references to outdated anatomical nomen-clature.[11] Of course the actual words pointed to by the usually acronymic mnemonics do indeed reflect a constructed literate terminology that acts as a scientific abstraction, comprising elements of classification by location, function and appearance. These issues can be briefly exemplified by citing a pair of the best known mnemonics:

On Old Olympus' Towering Tops A Finn And German Viewed Some Hops
(mnemonic for the 12 cranial nerves: Olfactory, Optic, Oculomotor, Trochlear, Trigeminal, Abducens, Facial, Auditory, Glossopharyngeal, Vagus, Spinal Accessory, Hypoglossal). Can be dated by the assumption that the user of the mnemonic will have had some exposure to a classical education.

Robert Taylor Drinks Cold Beer
(mnemonic for the five divisions of the brachial plexus: Roots, Trunks, Divisions, Cords, Branches). Can be roughly dated by the era of popularity of Robert Taylor's movies, 1930s–1950s.

Transmission

How do students manage to produce and reproduce the mnemonics? Unsurprisingly, they may first hear them orally, from fellow students or, less likely, from faculty members – or indeed some clever student may look for recognition by inventing a new one, whether as a variant of something already used or as something completely new. The same mnemonics will tend to be localized, as lab partners or study groups within a class study together and rehearse through mutual quizzing both the mnemonics themselves and the identification of the structures they represent. Common practice will be likely to be found among lab partners, particularly since dissection practice primarily develops in the context of the student team-cadaver group. But the mnemonics are basically seen as a common possession of students in general, since they like to consider them a form of resistance against the nearly unbounded task of assimilating anatomical nomenclature.[12] Like the linguistic play of schoolchildren, they are communicated from one class of students to another but are dropped from active use by individuals in fairly short order, which means that they must remain in constant use to survive. Whether they are indeed effective for the purpose of memorizing subject matter is another question that has not really been studied. Several of the most important of them can frequently be recalled at least in part by physicians many years after their training, but are not usually complete or precise enough to be used for their original purpose; the physicians in question have long since integrated such anatomical knowledge as they need for their specialization into their practice as contextualized knowledge and have abandoned much of the rest.

Preservation

Anatomy mnemonics are unlikely to be preserved intact by the people who use them. The fact that they are not official discourse and their reproduction is or has been primarily oral makes preservation by archives difficult. Although several printed collections of mnemonics have been published in the past,[13] and there are currently multiple medical mnemonic websites available on the internet (which may change the dynamic of transmission),[14] the mnemonics actually used by students have in the past generally only been found scattered in students' diaries or class notes.[15] Further, local traditions of mnemonics, where a single student has produced something memorable for its humour or obscenity or local reference, are very difficult to document without a specific and ongoing effort. Hence, although mnemonics and their use in the study of anatomy have been cited in medical memoirs for at least 100 years, they remain poorly documented because they are hard to collect, relatively invisible to outsiders, and are officially disapproved of in their context. Their value lies in their documentation of changing historical contexts, local uptake of changing standard nomenclature, and the pressure of intensive learning on medical students.

Mississippi Band of Choctaw Indians traditional knowledge

An apparently very different case is represented by the oral transmission of traditional knowledge among the Choctaw Indians of Mississippi, whose elders continue to preserve large parts of the tribe's intangible cultural heritage through the repetition of oral traditions.[16] Here I will concentrate on serious narratives, narratives which interestingly have their own mnemonic force in that they provide schemas for right behaviour.[17] The reproduction of these narratives still takes place primarily in natural settings, sometimes learned simply through sustained repetition, sometimes through intentional tutelage. Although this process has been familiar to anthropologists documenting nonliterate cultures, the Mississippi Choctaws as a modern tribe now find themselves deeply embedded in literate American culture, a fact that has its own impact on the continued reproduction of oral tradition.

Context

The Mississippi Band of Choctaw Indians (MBCI) is a federally recognized Indian tribe now located in east-central Mississippi, centred on a reservation community near Philadelphia, Mississippi. In 1830 a large number of the original Choctaw tribe were forced to move to Oklahoma in order to preserve their tribal governance, while the rest remained behind in

Mississippi and became legally Mississippi citizens. Forced to divide up their land, swindled out of it, and therefore inclined to withdraw from much contact with incoming white settlers, the Mississippi Choctaws began to come back together when a beginning was made in the 1920s to buy back land to make up a centralized reservation proximate to the major concentrations of Choctaws; in 1945 the tribe received federal recognition as a sovereign Indian tribe under the name of the MBCI.

The people of the MBCI were very isolated for many years because of poverty, racial discrimination and a way of life that concentrated on subsistence farming. As a fortuitous result, and in contrast to the Oklahoma Choctaws, they retained their language to a remarkable degree, such that even today several dialects that reflect a multicultural origin in the 16th century can be distinguished in Mississippi Choctaw speech from the different regional communities. Because the Choctaws retained their language, significant amounts of language-based tradition were also retained and passed on by elders to younger people as a matter of course. Mississippi Choctaw legends and traditions have been collected as written texts by linguists, ethnographers and folklorists and often translated into English, but much of the living tradition has remained unrecorded except in memory.

In the 1990s the MBCI used the legal advantage of their tribal sovereignty to begin to create a tourist resort in east-central Mississippi, which today consists of two major casinos, two world-class golf courses, a water park and other attractions. Building on existing cultural programmes, including a cultural affairs programme supporting the reproduction of cultural practices since the 1980s, a museum started in 1981, an archives dating from 1995, and a language programme also dating from the 1990s, the MBCI is in the process of creating a cultural centre to house these activities. But just as the prosperity brought to the region by the resort development has transformed the lives of many Choctaws, so has it also accelerated Choctaw assimilation into the English-speaking southern culture of the region. Monolingual Choctaw-speaking elders are literally a dying population.

Modern record keeping by the MBCI in its governmental and business dealings has been done primarily in English, since the tribe has kept many of these records in response to the requirement for formal interactions with external non-Indian governmental entities.[18] In contrast, a significant part of Choctaw oral tradition is dependent on living Choctaw elders' knowledge and especially on Choctaw language, which itself serves as a guarantee of authority. Although still spoken regularly by thousands of speakers, Choctaw language *literacy* has not been widespread. In the 1980s efforts began to be made to encourage Choctaw language use in reservation schools with the development of a bilingual programme. In aid of that programme, tape recordings were made and teaching materials were developed. Over time, the language programme has attained a separate identity and developed into a significant element of Choctaw early education, now including the development of a modern dictionary to support full Choctaw language literacy for older students. Oral tradition of history, belief, medicine and surfaced tacit knowledge of practices has also been recorded on audiotape and more recently on videotape in support of the cultural affairs programme.

Examples

Folklorist Tom Mould, who undertook to collect what he called 'Choctaw tales' for first a thesis and then a dissertation study of Choctaw oral tradition in 1996 and 1997, is the most recent outside collector of Mississippi Choctaw oral tradition. As a folklorist he was especially attentive to the context of transmission, and on that basis he placed orally performed stories in two categories: '*shukha anumpa*', or informal storytelling for entertainment, and 'elders' stories', or the more serious transmission of tradition through stories and other oral forms (Mould, 2003, 2004).[19]

The narratives that are of the greatest interest to the tribe for preservation fall into the latter category. They concern traditional history, legend and belief, including genealogy; accounts of traditional practices, like crafts, sport or ceremony; and traditional healing. This last topic, interesting though it might be to outsiders, is unlikely to be collected into an archive at all, however; some say that there are no more traditional healers who might transmit this knowledge, but if there were it would be unlikely that the practitioner would be willing to agree to anything other than human transmission, as the possession of this knowledge has over historical time come to be considered dangerous by many (Mould, 2003, 119–23). Other such elders' stories, however, are available to MBCI members as performances on varied occasions. Explanatory commentary on traditional practices is conveyed when the skills are shared, while the more reflective narratives about the past and the elements of Choctaw identity can be heard within families and other social circles as well as on occasions that have been formally organized by the cultural and language programmes so that children can be exposed to their traditions. Because the narratives of interest are long and can be accessed through Mould's book and several other sources (Swanton, 1931), I will limit myself to describing two of them briefly:

> Migration Legend (Swanton, 1931, 10–33; Mould, 2004, 71–2)
> This legend tells how the Choctaw migrated from the west together with the Chickasaw, led by two eponymous brothers and a tall pole,

which was set in the earth every night and which by morning leaned in the direction of the next day's march. When the party arrived at the Nanih Waiya mound in east central Mississippi, the pole remained upright. The Choctaws took this as a sign that this was the place for them to settle, but the Chickasaws continued their march further and the two groups split.

Origin of Corn (Swanton, 1931, 208–10; Mould, 2004, 77)
Two hunters preparing a meal after their day's rather unproductive hunt heard a voice and discovered a beautiful woman standing on the Nanih Waiya mound who asked for food. They gave her all their meal and in return she told them to return to the spot after a period of time. When they returned, the men found a new plant, corn.

Transmission

The transmission of oral traditions among the MBCI brings up many troublesome issues connected with the growing fragility of the link with the past maintained in the oral medium.[20] There is not apparently a jealously guarded ownership of the narratives told, but there is nevertheless a frequently reported practice of source citation by the current tradition-bearer, indicating the person from whom he or she learned it. The production of the traditional 'elders' stories' takes place today in varied settings, which may be casual or more formal, but it is nearly always carried out by elders: the transmission is cross-generational and must exploit a limited window of opportunity, frequently directed at children rather than at their parents (who presumably had already heard them in their turn), although interviewers have heard stories from younger adults when elders were not available to tell them, thus implying an etiquette of honouring elders' preferential authority by younger adults who still see themselves as learners. Where everyday life severs elders from the lives of children and youth, transmission is likely to fail, hence there has been a sustained effort by the MBCI to get Choctaw language (and indeed Choctaw elders) into the classroom. The language is also still central to the genuine transmission of the traditions (among Mississippi Choctaws transmission of tradition has not acceptably crossed over into English as it has with many other Native American groups), and where fewer children and youth can speak fluently or where they are too preoccupied by other distractions, another threat presents itself. Finally, different dialects may be at issue, since the actual spoken language is not a single standardized entity and understanding and especially transcription may be difficult even for a Choctaw speaker.

For transmission to continue as in the past, some adults who are not yet elders may have to undertake to continue to learn the traditional narratives. Current evidence seems to suggest that this is taking place to some extent, where the narratives are being preserved in families. The current generation of 'rising elders' and those who follow them are and will be literate, whereas many of the current elders tend to be 'lay literates' who seldom communicate in writing (Illich, 1991, 28),[21] and it is hard to forecast the effect that this change may have on the traditions.

Preservation

Previous to the collection of oral tradition by the MBCI itself, ethnographers, linguists, folklorists and historians had actively collected specific information for their own use and sometimes had worked at length to collect extended narratives. Although there are some traces of Choctaw traditions to be found in colonial-period documents, very little reflection of the actual language or extended narratives from Choctaw speakers exists from the 18th century, and not until the mid 19th century do we begin to see serious efforts of this kind being made by external scholars. Some of this material has been at least partly published, but much of the work of these scholars remains in manuscript in scattered archives.[22]

Although there has been a good deal of effort expended on these projects, the preservation of traditional narrative that they have achieved has been shaped by the purposes of the individual researchers. Swanton's work assembled an enormous amount of material, including the earliest published narratives collected in the 18th and 19th centuries as well as material from Cushman, Halbert and other early 20th-century observers, but the texts were not published in full and remain with Swanton's papers in the National Anthropological Archives. The linguists as a group have been responsible for the gathering of much spoken material, but because they have been interested mostly in grammar and language history, this material has not been published in a coherent narrative form and is also mostly unavailable except for that prepared by Kwachka for the tribal language programme.

Implications of a community's 'mixed-media textuality' in archival practice

Existing formal records management and archival practices in both the medical school and MBCI environments either fail to capture the oral sources at all (in the case of the medical school example) or fully (in the MBCI case) but preserve the written without much problem when written materials are sought out. Yet it is clear in both cases that the oral cultural materials have a robust history that is important to the identities and even to the well-being of those who participate in their creation and reproduction, and on them may hinge not only the documentation but perhaps the survival of the culture or subculture itself. Hence it is important to consider how robust are the actual reproduction environments of the oral traditions and the appropriateness of archives' acting to preserve them and thereby to keep the traditions alive in memory.

The emergence of indigenous protocols for archives and libraries around the world suggests that archival participation in the preservation of orally transmitted materials will be complicated unless such archival participation, if judged to be warranted, is undertaken by insider archival institutions.[23] Oral transmission, though apparently public in that it is transmitted to an interlocutor, is frequently not meant to cross cultural boundaries, as in both of the cases discussed here. The evidence of online medical mnemonic websites apparently contradicts this assertion; yet most of these sites are operated by students or former students, solicit donations of mnemonics from students to help other students, and do not represent educators as stakeholders.

Documentation strategy (documentation movement?)

The task of archiving both medical mnemonics and Choctaw oral tradition calls for a strategy of documentation to accommodate the oral memory practice in both cases: to document student activities as a minor part of the pedagogical process in the former case, and to document fundamentally important orally supported traditional knowledge in the latter. I am referring here both to a strategy of documentation as discussed by Gerald Ham and Hans Booms and the notion of a shared 'documentation strategy' that would organize groups of archives interested in particular topics to collect strategically in order to cover them co-operatively (Ham, 1975; Booms, 1987; Hackman and Warnow-Blewett, 1987). This archival approach seeks to document an overall phenomenon in enough depth to provide both content and context for its subsequent study through archival collections. Archives that stand in an insider relationship to the orally transmitted materials we have been discussing can thus follow a documentation plan in order to pursue the building of effective collections. I can suggest several options for carrying out such a plan, moving from the conventional to strategies more suited to oral narrative.

Freeze-dried tradition (multiple systematic captures)

The archives can initiate its own oral history/tradition gathering programme, with the purpose of recording repeatedly oral materials from willing and respected informants in order to assemble a longitudinal documentation of a changing tradition. The recordings would be carefully preserved, probably in several ways (analogue, digital, transcribed), and the original informants would be followed until they passed their legacy on to others, who would be followed in their turn.

Archivist-as-apprentice (archives as performance)

The archivist or an appropriate archival employee can become a tradition-bearer by apprenticing to someone who does possess the materials, learning them orally together with their conventions of performance, and performing them regularly for educational and research purposes. This would be a tricky option, since the archives would either have to adhere to the assumptions of the 'freeze-dried' position that the oral narrative had to be learned by rote and not allowed to change (which would entail devising some method to check that the performance had not changed); or it would have to accept that each oral performance is unique and that the oral narrative will simply change over time, whoever preserves it.

Postcustodialism (keeping oral performances in circulation)

In view of the realities of transmission and the reservations that bearers of oral tradition often have about sharing what they know, and especially in view of the felt need in situations like the Choctaw case to keep spoken tradition alive, it is worth discussing how an archives might carry out a 'postcustodial' strategy with respect to oral tradition. A concept that emerged with the development of digital record keeping, postcustodialism refers to the practice of an archives' advising and/or supervising records creators in carrying out the preservation of their records themselves. An archives that wished to assist in this way in the preservation of oral traditions would assist the 'natural' oral reproductive process as necessary by supporting awareness of oral narratives and their importance (to help encourage their 'natural' reproduction by recruiting potential tradition-bearers) and attempting to formulate best practices for their oral transmission and preservation according to advice from current tradition-bearers. Having documented the content of the narratives, should the danger of loss become acute such an archives could function as a repository of last resort, undertaking emergency capture of materials as detailed above pending the appearance of an appropriate person willing to take up the task of preserving the narrative in oral form.

Specific recommendations: anatomy mnemonics, MBCI traditions

Collecting anatomy mnemonics, especially given their tendency to local modifications, is clearly a task that the archives of medical schools might undertake – documentation strategy in the latter sense of collaboration between institutions. This would mean adopting practices as suggested by Helen Willa Samuels (1998) for the collection of university student materials, although her recommendations, made on behalf of a university doing its own archiving, applied to more acceptably public student activities, and in the case of anatomy mnemonics, disapproved as they are, this would require either gaining students' trust (and educators' tolerance) or assisting students to carry out postcustodial preservation. Medical archives might also consider collecting mnemonics that have been made public through paper or online publication, although both environments would perhaps have to be con- sidered secondary sources, disconnected from actual practice. It is unlikely that anatomical mnemonics are in danger of disappearing entirely as long as anatomy continues to be taught as it now is, but medical school archives might monitor various student-learning practices in any case; it may prove to be true that changes in student mnemonic practices prove to be important clues to pedagogical effectiveness.

The collection of oral tradition as in the case of the MBCI, however, is likely to be a localized task undertaken by the MBCI archives and its cultural programmes in partnership. It would be rare for any other archives to possess the linguistic skills needed, to begin with; and issues like trust and confidentiality intrinsic to the most treasured of these materials mean that control of them should rest with the community for whom they are of primary importance. To start with, the MBCI as a whole and Choctaw students in particular can benefit if the MBCI archives undertakes to procure copies of traditional oral materials that have been collected in the past by outsiders. These might include recordings and field notes from the Smithsonian as well as from scholars who have worked on Choctaw language and/or tradition, and would provide comparative material for the oral tradition that is being collected now and may be collected into the future. That is not to say that the archives itself needs to mount an oral collecting programme in the MBCI case. In the context of the several cultural programmes of the tribe, each with its own specialization in terms of traditional knowledge (and including individuals committed to becoming tradition-bearers themselves), the archives can continue to be the repository of collected oral materials as it has been in the past. But it can also collaborate with those programmes by playing a postcustodial role in encouraging preservation and serving as the ultimate repository for any culturally approved fixed captures of traditional performance or at a minimum for security copies of such captures.

Theorizing archives of orally transmitted materials in a discourse of collective memory

Wulf Kansteiner cites Jan Assman's distinction between 'communicative memory', that which is used in everyday, instrumental communications, and 'cultural memory', that which is rehearsed, chosen and preserved in order to 'stabilize and convey that society's self-image' (Assman, 1995, 132). Seen in such terms, archives have conventionally served as repositories of cultural memories, chosen and preserved to stabilize a society (the similarity is striking between this view and the archival appraisal method advocated in the 1980s by Hans Booms and later by Terry Cook (2007, 169–81) in the name of 'total archives').

This role can be further specified in terms suggested by Pierre Nora, who has argued that premodern societies were characterized by the originary person-to-person transmission of oral tradition; modern societies in nation-states resorted to archives containing specifically chosen traditions (which he referred to as first-order simulations); while postmodern societies depend on ubiquitous consumption-driven media to create second-order simulations of the past (Nora, 1989; Cox, 2004). Clearly, however, both examples discussed in this chapter immediately contest Nora's categories simply because together they represent cases where oral (premodern) traditions persist in complex combinations with a literate environment (modern) where media penetration (postmodern) is having noticeable effects on the transmission process. In the case of both the mnemonics used in the learning process in the modern setting of medical education and the narrative performed by Choctaw elders in the course of premodern, natural transmission of tradition, when oral materials are preserved by the archives they can of course be used as a resource for learning to perform them orally. In Nora's terms, these will become modern, first-order simulations if repeated verbatim (for the purpose of direct pedagogy, whether of anatomy, Choctaw culture, or Choctaw language), simply because a fixed simulacrum of human memory held in the archives is the source, rather than a living person. When such materials taken from archives are repurposed, for example via media exploitation (in medical dramas on television, or in televised performance of Choctaw traditional dance), they would according to Nora become postmodern, second-order simulations.

But what does this really mean? Might it be changed when control of archived oral materials is in the hands of the community that created them? The interesting thing about the postmodern cultural arena, as our two examples show, is that it does not wholly displace premodern and modern practices, just as modern culture has not wiped out premodern practices. People don't cease to be capable of the construction of oral narrative when they become literate, and some have even pointed to the increased importance of sound and visual media as a sort of return of repressed orality with modalities that 'oral cultures' are especially capable of exploiting (Turner, 1991; Portelli, 2006).[24] Hence Nora's concern about the loss of premodern Gemeinschaft-style solidarity may be misplaced: communities may be able to make use of modern and postmodern media and knowledge institutions to achieve such purposes. When a community preserves its own cultural repertoire, it may have to adopt different practices depending on what is being preserved; preservation may have to be construed in several ways. Where official records of university class schedules and curricula or a tribal government's governing and business dealings are being preserved, the (distinctly modern) standard archival practices aimed at documenting the performance of the institution in its duties would be appropriately applied; in such situations, the archives may necessarily aid the institution in 'seeing like a state' (Scott, 1998). Where the cultural aspects of the life of an institution are concerned, however, the archives may consider the ideas behind the 'intangible cultural heritage' definition and choose to adopt premodern and postmodern practices suggested above: archivist-as-apprentice to bring authentic oral preservation of cultural materials into the archives itself, and postcustodial preservation of the capacity for oral performance such that the object of preservation remains in active circulation. Such practices have long been undertaken by museums to assist with the perpetuation of traditional material culture, and there is no reason why word-borne intangible culture should not prosper with similar support.

Notes

1   Of course it is a contradiction to refer to 'oral texts', but I could not find a more accurate and similarly uncumbersome locution to refer to the chunks of meaningful sound I am talking about here.

2   Social historians already had before them as an example the oral life stories collected across the US by the Federal Writers Project of the Works Progress Administration in the 1930s. The stories were certainly uneven in value but also preserved

astonishing amounts of rich documentation of cultural memory (Frisch, 1991).

3　See Lutz Niethammer (2007) for specific interview techniques designed to provide background information richer than the usual demographics together with exposure of informants' narrative styles and memory practices, developed in the course of the life-history interviews for the Deutsches Gedächtnis project.

4　For observations on the poor state of understanding of memory in natural settings, see Ulric Neisser (1982, 3-19).

5　These two examples reflect research I carried out and experience I acquired for two projects: my 2004 dissertation in anthropology and extended work with the MBCI as a historian beginning in the 1980s extending to collaborative work on a museum exhibit in the 1990s and advisory work on reorganization of the tribal archives in 2008.

6　Dundes (1961) was interested in their role in supporting human memory in general; he discusses examples from the navy, electrical engineering, geology, astronomy, physics, music and English grammar as well as medicine.

7　Bellezza specifically cites anatomical mnemonics as exemplifying this type.

8　In a letter to the editor of the *Canadian Medical Association Journal*, L. H. Johns (1976, 207), in musing about his retention of anatomical knowledge, wrote: 'But of course, a few bits still stick - a couple of mnemonics, for example. I can still remember the reported outraged cry of Wharton's duct on finding itself double-crossed and also the outrageous conduct of Timothy towards all nervous housemaids.' Johns went on to relate an occasion on which his anatomy professor was alleged to have prompted a nervous student: 'Come, come! - Timothy, Mr Smith, Timothy!' The relevant mnemonic, which refers to structures at the ankle, is 'Timothy Doth Vex All Very Nervous Housemaids. Bad Lad.'

9　McDonald deplores the 'traditional' learning of anatomical facts through mnemonics. Interestingly, Bellezza (1981, 253) contrasts learning via mnemonic devices with that by assimilation, where 'information is presented whose underlying conceptual structure reflects the structure of some memory schema possessed by the user' such that the new information is assimilated into the existing schema. This latter procedure is just what the faculty outline when they urge students to read and study the material before dissection, attend carefully to dissection, and explain dissections to each other, but few students have adequate time to achieve this ideal and most see mnemonics as a shortcut.

10　During the process of dissection, the canonical books are poised near the scene of action on special stands attached to the dissecting table, although student teams will often dedicate one 'sacrificial' anatomical atlas to actually being draped over the body so as to hold the relevant illustration near the actual dissection process. The goal becomes to make the dissection look like the illustration. An additional memory aid is the process of 'reading': one lab partner is allocated the task of reading the dissection process step by step from the dissector text as the dissection takes place, and the dissection narrative and process also enter into the memory-creation process. During the test, of course, atlases, dissectors and the dulcet tones of one's lab partner are not present.

11 This makes it possible to date them roughly, recalling the appearance of historical events in nursery rhymes and tales (Stevens, 1968).

12 Many of these characteristics of anatomical mnemonic usage are also present in the oral lore of children, as presented in the classic work by Iona and Peter Opie (2001).

13 A particularly often-cited work is Alistair Smith, *Irving's Anatomy Mnemonics* (1969), which is especially informative about the activities of Timothy mentioned above (see McLachlan, 2000, 866). I was also able to find a privately printed booklet available for purchase on the internet: *Mastering Gross Anatomy Using Mnemonics, Acronyms, and Other Techniques* (Hines-Libak, 1991). A more precise work, *Mnemonics and Tactics in Surgery and Medicine* (Shipman, 1984), offers 450 mnemonics that the author devised or collected. Finally, a recent book, *Surviving Gross Anatomy* (Haggerty, 2007) (available only via online order, some profits benefiting a New Orleans health clinic and Doctors Without Borders), includes a large fund of mnemonics as part of a strategic method of outsmarting common testing protocols.

14 A Google search for the terms *anatomy* and *mnemonics* will yield many pages of citations. Whether such sources are becoming archives remains to be seen, but none would meet any reasonable definition of archives.

15 Mnemonics are rare in these sources, and the sources themselves are rare because they have been seen by the record creator and archivist alike as too instrumental and unimportant to keep. An example of the kind of exception that may be made when the author is significant for other reasons is the medical school papers of playwright Tom Stoppard, included in his collection at the Harry Ransom Humanities Research Center at the University of Texas (Stoppard refers to his periodic deposition of materials there as 'cleaning out the trash').

16 For the expression 'intangible cultural heritage', see the definition adopted by UNESCO in 2003: 'Intangible Cultural Heritage means the practices, representations, expressions, knowledge, skills – as well as the instruments, objects, artefacts and cultural spaces associated therewith – that communities, groups and, in some cases, individuals recognize as part of their cultural heritage. This intangible cultural heritage, transmitted from generation to generation, is constantly recreated by communities and groups in response to their environment, their interaction with nature and their history, and provides them with a sense of identity and continuity, thus promoting respect for cultural diversity and human creativity. For the purposes of this Convention, consideration will be given solely to such intangible cultural heritage as is compatible with existing international human rights instruments, as well as with the requirements of mutual respect among communities, groups and individuals, and of sustainable development.' This definition clearly does not expect that intangible cultural heritage will remain unchanged over time.

17 Basso's (1996) book on the Western Apaches' traditional stories reviews the use of
    geographically situated narratives as frames for the communication of behaviour
    norms. Mould (2003, 2004) similarly points to Choctaw use of traditional narrative
    of several kinds as important to the definition of Choctaw identity.

18 And as is the case with business and government records everywhere, these records
    are increasingly kept in digital form.

19 Both books discuss this classification of Choctaw stories from the Choctaw point of
    view.

20 Linguist Pat Kwachka, who has long been involved with Mississippi Choctaw
    language programmes, remarked in 1999 that when she began to work with them
    in 1976, the need was for English-language improvement in the schools, but that
    within 20 years there had been a more than 50% decline in Choctaw fluency
    among children, to 40%, and a need for Choctaw-language teaching in schools was
    pressing (Gugliotta, 1999).

21 'Lay literacy', as described by Ivan Illich, refers to a person who is not, or is only
    barely, literate but who shares the assumptions of 'clerical' literacy about the
    possibilities for preserving memory as text.

22 The external scholars mentioned include - ethnographers: John Swanton, David
    Bushnell, John Peterson, Clara Sue Kidwell; linguists: Cyrus Byington, Dale Niklas,
    Emanuel Drechsel, Greg Keyes, George Broadwell, Pat Kwachka; folklorist: Tom
    Mould; miscellaneous: H. B. Cushman, Henry Halbert, Works Progress
    Administration interviewers. Some of these materials are in the MBCI archives,
    including interview materials from Peterson and Mould, as well as interviews on
    material culture carried out in the 1970s, a group of 'legends, myths, and stories'
    gathered by the language programme, and interviews carried out for an oral history
    programme in 2001.

23 See Aboriginal and Torres Strait Islander Library and Information Resource
    Network (1995) and First Archivists Circle (2006).

24 It is worth noting that the MBCI has had its own video unit and community
    television station since the 1980s, which now functions under the aegis of the tribal
    museum.

References

Aboriginal and Torres Strait Islander Library and Information Resource Network (1995)
    Aboriginal and Torres Strait Islander protocols for libraries, archives and information services,
    www.alia.org.au/policies/atsi.protocols.html.

Assman, J. (1995) Collective Memory and Cultural Identity, *New German Critique*, **65**,
    132, quoted in Kansteiner, W. (2002) Finding Meaning in Memory: a
    methodological critique of collective memory studies, *History and Theory*, May, 179-
    97.

Basso, K. H. (1996) *Wisdom Sits in Places: landscape and language among the Western Apache*, University of New Mexico Press.

Bellezza, F. S. (1981) Mnemonic Devices: classification, characteristics, and criteria, *Review of Educational Research*, **51** (2), 247-73.

Booms, H. (1987) Society and the Formation of a Documentary Heritage: issues in the appraisal of archival sources, *Archivaria*, **24**, Summer, 69-107.

Cook, T. (2007) Remembering the Future: appraisal of records and the role of archives in constructing social memory. In Blouin, F. X. and Rosenberg, W. G. (eds), *Archives, Documentation and Institutions of Social Memory: essays from the Sawyer seminar*, University of Michigan Press, 169-81.

Cox, R. (2004) *No Innocent Deposits: forming archives by rethinking appraisal*, Scarecrow Press, 231-58.

Dundes, A. (1961) Mnemonic Devices, *Midwest Folklore*, **11** (3), 139-47.

First Archivists Circle (2006) *Protocols for Native American Archival Materials*, www2.nau.edu/libnap-p/protocols.html.

Frisch, M. (1991) *A Shared Authority: essays on the craft and meaning of oral and public history*, SUNY Press.

Galloway, P. (2004) *Mortal Knowledge: anatomizing the person*, PhD dissertation, Department of Anthropology, University of North Carolina.

Gugliotta, G. (1999) A Tribe Races to Teach its Mother Tongue, *Washington Post*, 19 August.

Hackman, L. J. and Warnow-Blewett, J. (1987) The Documentation Strategy Process: a model and a case study, *American Archivist*, **50**, Winter, 12-47.

Haggerty, A. (2007) *Surviving Gross Anatomy*, self-published.

Halbwachs, M. (1992) *On Collective Memory*, edited by L. Coser, University of Chicago Press.

Ham, G. (1975) The Archival Edge, *American Archivist*, **38**, January, 5-13.

Hines-Libak, P. (1991) *Mastering Gross Anatomy Using Mnemonics, Acronyms, and Other Techniques*, Annie Enterprises.

Illich, I. (1991) A Plea for Research on Lay Literacy. In Olson, D. R. and Torrance, N. (eds), *Literacy and Orality*, Cambridge University Press, 28-46.

Johns, L. H. (1976) Letter to the editor, *Canadian Medical Association Journal*, 115, 207.

Lord, A. B. (1960) *The Singer of Tales*, Harvard University Press.

McDonald, D. (1941) The Future of Medical Education: a medical student's view, *British Medical Journal*, 327-9.

McLachlan, J. C. (2000) Queer People Enjoying Anatomy, *The Lancet*, 356, 866.

Mould, T. (2003) *Choctaw Prophecy: a legacy of the future*, University of Alabama Press.

Mould, T. (2004) *Choctaw Tales*, University Press of Mississippi.

Neisser, U. (1982) Memory: what are the important questions? In Neisser U. (ed.), *Memory Observed: remembering in natural contexts*, W. H. Freeman, 3-19.

Niethammer, L. (2007) Contrastar métodos de recogida e interpretación de datos,

Historia, Antropología y Fuentes Orales, **38**, 123-8.

Nora, P. (1989) Between Memory and History: les lieux de mémoire, *Representations*, **6**, Spring, 7-24.

Olson, D. R. and Torrance, N. (eds) (1991) *Literacy and Orality*, Cambridge University Press.

Ong, W. (1991) *Orality and Literacy: the technologizing of the word*, Routledge.

Opie, I. and Opie, P. (2001) *The Lore and Language of Schoolchildren*, rev. edn, New York Review of Books.

Portelli, A. (2006) Lookin' for a Home: independent oral history archives in Italy. In Blouin, F. and Rosenberg, W. (eds), *Archives, Documentation, and Institutions of Social Memory: essays from the Sawyer seminar*, University of Michigan Press, 219-24.

Samuels, H. W. (1998) *Varsity Letters: documenting modern colleges and universities*, Scarecrow Press.

Scott, J. (1998) *Seeing Like a State: how certain schemes to improve the human condition have failed*, Yale University Press.

Shipman, J. J. (1984) *Mnemonics and Tactics in Surgery and Medicine*, 2nd edn, Lloyd Luke Medical Books.

Shopes, L. (n.d.) Making Sense of Oral History, http://historymatters.gmu.edu/mse/oral/oral.pdf.

Smith, A. G. (1969) *Irving's Anatomy Mnemonics*, 4th edn, Churchill Livingstone.

Stevens, A. M. (1968) *The Nursery Rhyme: remnant of popular protest*, Coronado Press.

Swanton, J. R. (1931) *Source Material for the Social and Ceremonial Life of the Choctaw Indians*, Smithsonian Institution, Bureau of American Ethnology Bulletin 103, US Government Printing Office.

Turner, T. (1991) Representing, Resisting, Rethinking: transformations of Kayapo culture and anthropological consciousness. In Stocking Jr, G. W. (ed.), *Colonial Situations: essays on the contextualization of ethnographic knowledge*, University of Wisconsin Press, 285-313.

Wilson, A. C. (1998) Grandmother to Granddaughter: generations of oral history in a Dakota family. In Mihesuah, D. (ed.), *Natives and Academics: researching and writing about American Indians*, University of Nebraska Press, 27-36.

5

We are our memories: community and records in Fiji

SETAREKI TALE AND OPETA ALEFAIO

Fiji is a Pacific nation of 330 islands (a quarter of which are inhabited) lying at the heart of the 'South Pacific'[1] midway between the equator and the South Pole. It has a population approaching 900,000 people, and archaeological evidence has established that the group of islands was probably first settled around three and a half thousand years ago (Yaqona, 2004, 10–11). As with most other former colonies, change has been a constant theme for our nation. The idea of nationhood is itself relatively new, unlike countries such as China, Japan, France or Egypt, which have a long and colourful record of nationhood.

We in Fiji, on the other hand, were originally a collection of variously structured kin groups headed by chiefs who contested for predominance within their immediate areas. The more successful chiefs sought to extend their power and influence as far as possible.

After a number of failed attempts at centralized government, and under the growing threat of increasingly disruptive elements within the settler community, the leading chiefs of the time decided to cede Fiji to Britain and on 10 October 1874 Fiji became a crown colony of Britain (Lal, 1992, 10–11). A mere 96 years later, on 10 October 1970, after considerable growing pains and earnest dialogue among Fiji's communities and the British, Fiji became an independent nation.

For the last 150 years, the people of Fiji have had to deal with great waves of change, and challenge. This becomes especially clear when dealing with issues such as culture, identity and what seems to be competing perceptions of knowledge. Against this backdrop archives and records managers are struggling to implement relevant, effective record-keeping systems in a society that is losing parts of its traditional heritage, and is not yet convinced of the need to manage records over time. What then are the challenges to retaining our memory? What role do archives play? And where do we go from here?

Oral tradition is the synthesis and transmission of knowledge and histories in a community from one generation to the next. The approach is not about 'data' or 'facts' that are captured in the 'formal record-keeping environment', but rather it is a knowing which comes from doing and sharing. In Fiji, a person's ancestry for example is not learned by consulting documents, it is learned through song and dance. Knowledge of the sea and marine life is not acquired by studying biology texts, it is acquired by interaction with the sea and marine life and by using carefully constructed narratives to expand and reinforce the insights gained from those experiences. Knowledge and information is not an abstraction, it is with us, it is within us. This means that we *are* our memories, we *are* our knowledge.

The question then becomes how does this relate to the 'formal' record keeping of the modern age, and what are the stakes for the community? The answer is complex, and to unravel it we must start at the beginning, then explain the different challenges that confront us and suggest possible solutions for the future.

Not just fairy tales

Oral tradition has played a leading role in the history of the Pacific, and is as relevant today as it has ever been: 'Our archives does not have written documents and books. Our culture and historical records are contained in oral histories and legends, which are stored in the collective memories of the people of Melekeok and which have been passed from generations to generations over the centuries' (Ngirmang, 2001). Unfortunately these legends and parables have been belittled by those with neither the patience nor the desire to understand. Our traditions and lore have on more than a few occasions been dismissed as quaint little fables or as romanticized self conceptualizations. In reality, they contain technological and scientific knowledge on navigation and seafaring, fisheries, agriculture, medicinal preparations and so on. This information is also recorded through handicraft (such as weaving, woodcraft and pottery), poems, songs and dance (Briggs, 1977, 1–5).

This knowledge is dynamic and collaborative, evolving through phases of transmission between generations. It is passed on within the village, tribe, clan, family or whichever unit this knowledge resides in. It is understood to be communally owned, a combination of experiences and ideas, not the sole possession of an individual. The inherent value of a particular item or artistic expression is the pride of the unit or community in which it resides (Peteru, 1999, 9–10). However, the relative isolation that permitted this oral tradition to thrive came to an end in the 1850s with the official establishment of American then British Consuls. Things were about to change on a scale our forebears could never have imagined.

A new wind

The establishment of consular offices brought the introduction of many new ideas, and 'formal' record keeping was one of these. The formation of a centralized government administration in 1871 with the setting up of the Cakobau Government (Brown, 1973, 299) further inspired record keeping and provided some continuity in how records overall were being generated. What has been observed from records is how meticulous the colonizers and early administrators were with record keeping. Records of these administrations, which included those of the Cakobau Government and the subsequent government up to the Colonial Government which governed Fiji from 1875 to 1970, survived difficult conditions and their importance is being increasingly recognized by the public of Fiji. These records were systematic and detailed, and today their completeness makes them some of the most useful and sought after resources for research.

The emphasis placed on record keeping by administrators was significant and an indication of this was the secondment to Fiji in 1930 of a records clerk[2] with experience in the management of official records. The effectiveness of his work was felt immediately with the reviewing of the records registration system of the Colonial Government, and a new system was adopted from 1931. The system is still widely used today.

However, things seemed to have slackened off after Fiji's independence in 1970.[3] It appeared that from a certain point record keeping was relegated to the back seat. This is understandable to a degree as this is the period when all sectors were competing for attention and resources from government leaders.

Looming collective memory loss

This contact with the outside world and the introduction of modern records, centralized government and rapidly evolving technologies brought many changes and challenges. One of these is the steady erosion of oral traditions. While oral tradition is still a strong factor in today's Pacific, different 'items' and knowledge are slowly but surely being lost. For example, a village in Fiji almost lost its signature *meke* (dance) because knowledge of the song had died with the elders. This was a catastrophic situation because that *meke* was a large part of the village's identity. Fortunately an old recording of the song for the *meke* was found in the archives of the former government radio station, and the *meke* was salvaged.

Another example with a less certain ending is that of the once skilful canoe builders of the Fiji islands who made great double-hulled canoes capable of carrying many men along with food and water on long voyages. One such canoe was the *Rusi I Vanua*. She was 118 feet long, her deck was 50 feet long and 24 feet wide and her mast 68 feet high and the two yards were 90 feet long. With only the most rudimentary tools she took seven years to build, and fully laden with 200 men and food and water for a long journey and under wind power alone was able to reach speeds of 15 knots (Derrick, 1946, 19). Sadly the art of canoe building has long lain dormant, and in the modern age of cheaper transportation it remains to be seen whether the traditional methods of oral tradition can ensure its survival into the future, see Figures 5.1 and 5.2.

While it is clear that oral tradition is being eroded the 'memory' of Island communities is being compromised in a much less obvious way. While oral tradition is slowly conceding ground, the mismanagement or under-management of 'formal records' is also a threat to 'memory'. Awareness of records and their role in society is very low in Fiji society. For some time now records have been treated as the by-product of daily business, and their management is generally addressed in a piecemeal way. This has resulted in mini information empires established around certain individuals who tend to guard jealously their turf. This tendency to resist addressing records in a systematic manner makes capturing records of permanent value problematic, with negative implications for the collective memory of the community.

In the past few years information and communications technologies (ICTs) have invaded both government and the private sector reaching out into almost all sectors of the community. Government agencies and users now recognize the potential of ICT and the opportunity it provides for development where both great distances – which characterize the Pacific Islands – and traditional methods have tended to hamper progress. But ICT evolves at an exponential rate, and the issues that come with managing ICT systems and the records they create seem to grow in the same way. This has made a significantly difficult situation considerably more complicated. In a manner of speaking, it has taken our canoes from the precarious but familiar ocean, and warped them out into the unfamiliar and unforgiving territory of cyberspace.

At the same time, it must also be made clear that many record keepers in the island states have very little or no support and do not have the capacity and skills to carry out the basic record-keeping tasks required of them effectively. The challenges they face are many. These include the tyranny of distance, condemning records officers to operate with meagre resources and without the

Figure 5.1 A pair of craftsmen take a break from Drua building (courtesy of the Fiji Museum)

Figure 5.2 A fleet of Drua double-hulled canoes approaching Levuka in 1855 (courtesy of the Fiji Museum)

benefit of interaction and advice from experienced colleagues. In addition the field of records management is generally unrecognized as a profession, and record-keeping positions and responsibilities are usually allocated near the bottom of organizational structures. This leaves record keepers without the resources or clout to make management decisions and contribute on policy matters. The rapid evolution of technology is only exacerbating the situation.

In to the future?

What then are the prospects for oral tradition and archives in Fiji? The question is a tricky one, for it represents two very different assumptions. The first is that knowledge is locally owned and resides within communities of living people who are its manifestation and who shape it. The other, that knowledge is the collation of records from disparate locations into a central repository for research and enlightenment.

The reality is that with the increase in modernization, archives and other collecting institutions must improve their capacity to engage and participate with local communities to record their memories before they are lost to time. The issue of ownership must never be in question. Archives can only act as trustees of the knowledge which is owned by those who allowed it to be recorded and their descendants.

On the issue of records and their management, governments and civil society in the global community are increasingly recognizing the importance of information for good governance. Quality information enables government to function properly and to make sound decisions. Authentic and accessible records are authoritative sources of information that support government activities and provide evidence of its transactions. They support fundamental values such as the protection of rights and entitlements, openness in governance, and public participation in the process of governance.

In light of global developments a good strategy would be to emphasize the business benefits of good record keeping. Taking this approach, as opposed to the 'big stick' approach, leads to an organization-wide culture reflecting an overall willingness to practise good record keeping, and records units are seen as providers of solutions to the information challenges faced each day (Sweeney, 2006, 24).

The first step therefore would be to make a concerted effort to raise the profile of record keeping across government. Without proper recognition our memory is again in jeopardy. It is noted that many problems that affect record keeping in Fiji and the Pacific such as limited resources, lack of training, tendency of staff to leave after training, and so on, are related to the lack of recognition of the profession. Vigorous awareness and marketing programmes properly planned for specific target audiences are avenues that can be used to address these issues, and to propel the profession forward.

Conclusion

Though very different, it is clear that oral tradition and records and archives are both large portions of the memory of communities, in UNESCO terms the 'Memory of World', and both must be allowed to play their part. In the face of all constraints and difficulties we believe solutions to the problems in Fiji and perhaps all small island states of the Pacific do not lie in drastically overhauling the system and acquiring new technology and equipment. Technology will require specific skills, additional resources, costs for maintenance and so on, for which we do not have the means.

What is needed is an increased societal awareness of the role of records. This will help generate a groundswell of support for records and protecting the community's memory. In turn, this momentum will allow us to deal with records in a more systematic manner, and will naturally spawn innovative means of dealing with challenges as they appear. The first lesson from such a journey is to realize that evolutionary change is better than revolutionary change where evolutionary change equates to a gradual adaptation to the environment or specific requirements (Sweeney, 2006, 24).

Notes

1   A group of Pacific island nations whose boundary runs from the Solomon Islands in the west, Tahiti to the east, the Marshall Islands to the north and the Kingdom of Tonga to the south.

2   John Murray Jardine assumed duties as a records clerk in the Colonial Government on 21 March 1930.

3   Fiji gained independence from Great Britain on 10 October 1970.

References

Briggs, B. (1977) What is Oral Tradition? In Vatu, S. (ed.), *Talking About Oral Tradition*, University Printing Unit, Extension Services, University of the South Pacific.

Brown, S. (1973) *Men from Under the Sky: the arrival of westerners in Fiji*, Charles E. Turtle Company.

Derrick, R. A. (1946) *A History of Fiji*, vol. 1, Printing Department Suva, Fiji.

Lal, B. V. (1992) *Broken Waves: a history of the Fiji Islands in the twentieth century*, University of Hawaii Press.

Ngirmang, R. R. B. (2001) Welcome address, *Pacific Archives: connecting, capturing, preserving*, PARBICA 9th Conference, Palau, 1 August.

Peteru, C. (1999) Protection of Indigenous Knowledge, paper presented at the WWF and Department of Environment (Fiji) Preservation of Local and Indigenous Knowledge Workshop, Suva 16–17 November.

Sweeney, P. (2006) Corporate Compliant Without Burdening the User: change management lessons from the ergon energy, *InfoRMAA Quarterly*, **22**, November.

Yaqona, L. (2004) Radiocarbon Results Indicate Oldest Lapita Site yet to be Found in Fiji, *USP Beat*, **4** (10).

Part 3

Records loss, destruction and recovery

6

Archiving the queer and queering the archives: a case study of the Canadian Lesbian and Gay Archives (CLGA)

MARCEL BARRIAULT

As a young teenager I looked desperately for things to read that might excite me or assure me I wasn't the only one, that might confirm an identity I was unhappily piecing together.

Edmund White, Out of the Closet, on the Bookshelf (Kester, 1997, 121)

Introduction[1]

In 1987 Canadian sociologist Gary Kinsman published a landmark study titled *The Regulation of Desire – Sexuality in Canada*.[2] It is widely considered to be the first critical examination of the history of homosexuality in Canada, or, in Kinsman's own words, an 'excursion towards a queer history of Canada' (1987, 65). In outlining his research methodology, Kinsman acknowledges a problem with sources and interpretation:

> Because of the socially organized 'private' or 'personal' character of intimate sexual relations there has been little public record of same-gender sex aside from the 'deviant' or 'criminal' behaviour found in police records, government reports, newspaper articles, medical and psychiatric discourse, and sex advice literature. Since same-gender eroticism was stigmatized, historically valuable diaries and letters have not been preserved. The voices of those people engaged in same-gender sex have thereby been silenced.   Kinsman, 1987, 66

Kinsman concludes that, given the absence of personal records, researchers interested in queer[3] studies in Canada have often had to rely on the evidential value of public records, which necessarily document only the official version of this issue. Researchers have thus had to read the records 'against the grain' in order to grasp some sense of the everyday lives of queer Canadians in the past. The focus that public archives had placed on records that describe individual homosexual acts as criminal offences necessarily excluded from the archival fold any records that spoke of a community of people marginalized by the sexual policies of the state. What Kinsman strongly implies is that traditional archival institutions in Canada have not been accountable to queer people and to researchers interested in the historical construction of sexuality.[4]

Same-gender sexual activity in Canada, as in most Western democracies, had almost always been prosecuted by the state, condemned by the Church and pathologized by science. The situation remained more or less the same until the 1960s, when the emerging civil rights movement began to foster a growing social awareness of homosexuals as a disenfranchised and marginalized group of people. It is now generally recognized that the legal case of Everett George Klippert was the touchstone for the queer rights movement in Canada.

In 1965 the Royal Canadian Mounted Police (RCMP) questioned Klippert, a 39-year old mechanic from Pine Point, North West Territories, in connection with an arson investigation. It soon became clear to investigators that Klippert was in no way involved with the crime; however, during the course of the interrogation, he volunteered information related to his having had sexual relations in the past with four separate consenting male adults. Klippert was subsequently charged with four counts of gross indecency, and on 24 August 1965 he was sentenced to three years in prison. Following an evaluation by two court-appointed psychiatrists, Klippert was deemed to be 'incurably homosexual', and was subsequently declared a dangerous sexual offender under Section 661 of the *Criminal Code of Canada*. As a result, Klippert was sentenced to 'preventive detention', which really amounted to life imprisonment. An appeal to the Court of Appeal for the North West Territories was dismissed, as was an appeal to the Supreme Court of Canada in 1967 (Klippert v. The Queen).

The Klippert trial received extensive national media coverage and contributed to a discursive shift away from private morality to the broader issue of civil rights.[5] The case also pressed the federal government to bring much needed amendments to the *Criminal Code of Canada*. On 14 May 1969, a full month before the Stonewall Riots in New York City, the Liberal government of the Right Honourable Pierre Elliott Trudeau passed Bill C-150, an omnibus bill which brought a large number of amendments to the *Criminal Code*, including a provision to decriminalize homosexuality in Canada. This eventually paved the way for Everett George Klippert's pardon and release from prison in July 1971.

Reflecting on the proposed legislation in 1967, when he was Minister of Justice in the Cabinet of Prime Minister Lester B. Pearson, the charismatic Trudeau famously quipped, 'there's no place for the State in the bedrooms of the nation' (Columbo, 1987, 311). At a time when the official legal discourse had defined homosexuality as a criminal offence, when the official medical discourse had diagnosed it as a pathological perversion, and when the official religious discourse had branded it as an abomination to God, Trudeau's bold political statement placed homosexuality squarely in the public space, thus inviting public debate on an issue that had seemed irrevocably decided. The decriminalization of homosexuality in Canada allowed queer Canadians themselves to speak publicly about their own sexuality, in their own voices, without fear of incarceration or other forms of legal reprisal.

The Body Politic

It is chiefly within this socio-political context that the influential publication, *The Body Politic*, first emerged in 1971. Not only would it become the leading Canadian queer news magazine until it ceased publication in 1987, but it would also lead directly, in 1973, to the founding of what would eventually become the Canadian Lesbian and Gay Archives (CLGA). In September 1971, Jearld Moldenhauer, a gay activist based in Toronto, proposed the founding of a newspaper that could be the mouthpiece for the Canadian gay liberation movement. He and a few other activists formed a small collective that oversaw the production of this new publication, and, in November, the inaugural issue of *The Body Politic* appeared in print. The newspaper did much to help create a stronger sense of community identity for individuals who saw themselves as engaged in a common struggle for equal rights. It did this in several ways, but chiefly by reporting on current social and political events that were happening in various cities across the country, in a feature on its 'community page'. What quickly became apparent was that the newspaper was becoming the voice of a very diverse and multifaceted community that encompassed individuals from all walks of life, races, age groups and socio-economic backgrounds. The diversity of the newspaper's readership was stunning, and readers demonstrated a wide range of experiences. For example, the life experience of a transitioning male to female (MTF) transsexual who identified as a lesbian was very different from that of a Native Canadian who identified as two-spirited. Clearly, it was fallacious to believe that the 'gay community' was homogeneous in its composition and in its aspirations, even if members often shared similar experiences with homophobia and heterosexism. Divisive and polarizing issues such as the availability of pornography and same-sex marriage have since completely dispelled the myth of any unified political 'gay agenda'.[6]

The Canadian Gay Archives

By 1973 the editorial collective of *The Body Politic* had amassed a collection of documents that were no longer required for the newspaper, and Jearld Moldenhauer and another collective member, Ron Dayman, began to recognize the archival and historical value of these non-operational files. It was Dayman who primarily began to collect these materials and to store them in the basement of his home in Toronto. These materials would form the core of the collection, but Dayman would soon begin to contact various gay groups from across the country to add more materials to his archives.

In the autumn of 1973 Dayman proudly announced the creation of the Canadian Gay Liberation Movement (GLM) Archives, which was in effect an extension of the work of *The Body Politic*. In essence, this early relationship proved to be symbiotic: *The Body Politic* generated archival materials for the newly-minted GLM Archives, and, in turn, the archives made use of advertisement space in the newspaper to communicate with a readership that might include potential donors. An early advertisement laments the fact that gay history had nearly been obliterated by 'straight historians and other "guardians of morality"' and states: 'One way to encourage accurate historical research is to gather, and make available, resource material relevant to all aspects of gay history. To this end, *The Body Politic* has founded the Canadian GLM Archives' (*The Body Politic*, 1973). The advertisement then goes on to invite interested readers to add to the growing collection, by donating documents relating to any homophile groups active in Canada in the 1950s and 1960s, any personal memoirs and correspondence, and early editions of works by pioneering gay rights advocates, Edward Carpenter (1844–1929) and Magnus Hirschfeld (1868–1935).

In 1974 the GLM Archives was relocated from its basement home to a new repository in an office building it shared with *The Body Politic* and the Toronto-based rights group, Gay Alliance Towards Equality (GATE). The move was practical in that it brought the archives closer to its parent body and allowed for readier public consultation of archival materials. By early spring 1975 Edward Jackson, another member of the newspaper collective, had inherited the care of the archives. In an effort to move the collection beyond the realm of political activism, the GLM Archives was renamed the Canadian Gay Archives (CGA). Under Jackson's direction, an archives collective was formed to guide the activities of the archives. A formal statement of purpose, which was drawn up that year by the collective, made explicit the need for a gay archives in Canada. It states: 'A conspiracy of silence has robbed gay men and lesbians of their history. A sense of continuity which derives from the knowledge of a heritage is essential for the building of self-confidence in a community. It is a necessary tool in the struggle for social change' (Fraser and Averill, 1983, 60). To 'aid in the recovery and preservation of [this] history', the archives collective gave the CGA two basic aims: the first, to acquire, arrange and preserve queer records in all media, with a particular emphasis on Canadian documents; and the second, to make this material accessible to researchers, and to enable them to locate additional relevant sources outside its holdings (Fraser and Averill, 1983, 60). This document served as the professional framework of the CGA, and it was instrumental in guiding the activities of the archives.

One of the earliest and most critical decisions of the archives collective was to decline an offer by the Archives of Ontario in 1975 to acquire some of the holdings of the CGA. From a purely theoretical perspective, this decision was pivotal in defining what the fledgling archives should be. By looking at past practices, one could easily point to the systematic exclusion of queer records from public archives as an example of Michel Foucault's idea of power relations at play, with evidence that the state was deliberately dominating the discourse on homosexuality. In this light, the choice to withhold these records from public archives would become a politically empowering act, allowing members of the queer community itself to decide what the ultimate fate of its records would be. By distancing itself from public archives, the CGA would be able to challenge, to deconstruct and to redefine what an archival institution should be. It would be able to adopt a total archives approach, which would eventually enable it to deal with a wide range of queer records in all media (textual documents, photographs, documentary art, cartographic and architectural plans, moving images, audio recordings and digital records). Furthermore, its continued awareness of some specialized queer publications and artefacts that were seldom being collected by libraries and museums would lead it to become an integrated knowledge-based institution, whose core mandate would be to function as archives, library *and* museum. Free from the rigid constraints of what constitutes a traditional archival institution, the CGA would be able to acquire records that are fundamental to the queer community and that have traditionally been discarded as ephemera by most other archival repositories. These would come to include such key holdings as queer erotica and pornography, buttons (like the 'Lick Dick in '72' button to protest Richard Nixon's presidential campaign), banners from AIDS marches, trophies and uniforms for all-queer sports teams, board games like 'Gay Monopoly' and even a lamp from the St Charles Tavern, once a prominent gay bar in Toronto.

By the spring of 1977 the CGA had produced the first issue of its official newsletter, *Gay Archivist* (later *Lesbian and Gay Archivist*). This was an important achievement for the CGA because the publication became a vehicle for the archives to report on its ongoing activities and to give it greater visibility within the queer community. At roughly the same time, the archives collective welcomed James Fraser, the first professional archivist at the CGA. Fraser brought much-needed archival standards to the existing collection, while continuing to acquire, arrange, describe and make available new acquisitions to the collection. This work continued unabated until the police raid later that year.

Police search the archives

In its December 1977 issue, *The Body Politic* had run an investigative article on hebephilia, titled 'Men Loving Boys Loving Men'. The publication of this story immediately led to a police raid of the newspaper's offices and the seizure of materials. Since *The Body Politic* shared office space with the CGA, the police incursion extended to the archival space as well and archival materials were also confiscated. In total, 12 large shipping boxes of records were taken. The newspaper was subsequently charged with 'use of the mails for the purpose of transmitting or delivering anything that is obscene, indecent, immoral or scurrilous', under Section 164 of the *Criminal Code of Canada* (*The Body Politic*, 1978). Over the course of the next six years, *The Body Politic* would appear in court three times, the first two trials resulting in two acquittals and two subsequent appeals from the Crown. In 1983 the court ruled decisively in favour of the newspaper and the Toronto police force was ordered to return all confiscated materials to their rightful owners. The police finally returned documents to *The Body Politic* and to the CGA in 1985, a full eight years after the raid.

The CGA is recognized as an archival institution

The archives collective was justifiably worried that the police search of the CGA had set a dangerous precedent. Not only had the raid occurred at closing time on the Friday evening before the New Year's long weekend, leaving the archives with no recourse for several days, but the raid itself had resulted in the forced removal of documents from an archival institution. What made the matter worse still was the fact that the police had searched through materials entirely unrelated to the charges they were investigating, and they had seized copies of publications like *The Joy of Gay Sex* and *The Joy of Lesbian Sex* (*The Body Politic*, 1978). The preservation of the integrity of the archives became an even greater concern at this time, as was the need to assure prospective donors that donated materials to the archives would not be confiscated by the state, and that their own privacy rights would be respected.

Prior to the police raid, the CGA had already been looking into the issue of being incorporated as an independent, non-profit organization, as a means of obtaining charitable status. This would enable it to issue tax receipts for financial donations, which would then provide the CGA with another source of funding. After the raid, it was generally believed that incorporating as a separate body would also help prevent further police incursions into the archives should there ever be more charges laid against *The Body Politic* (Kester, 1997, 109). The incorporation of the CGA finally occurred on 31 March 1980, but an application for registration as a charitable organization was initially denied by Revenue Canada. The federal agency argued that the work of the CGA was not 'directed to the benefit of all members of the community', and that it had been 'formed by a group of individuals primarily for the promotion, advocacy or performance of a particular purpose peculiar to them' (*Gay Archivist*, 1981). Perhaps more surprisingly, Revenue Canada also claimed that the CGA did not qualify as an archives because it did not acquire government records. The agency's response was firm, and it did not even make mention of any appeal process. The CGA did in fact appeal the decision, also sending supporting documentation to show that the vast majority of archives in Canada did not acquire government records, and Revenue Canada eventually overturned its decision, granting the archives charitable status in November 1981 (Kester, 1997, 109).

The CGA had finally become a firmly established archival institution, even though its funding remained precarious for many years. It was beginning to be recognized both nationally and internationally for its holdings, which were growing exponentially every year and which documented all aspects of the queer community in Canada. In addition to its impressive work related to core archival functions, in December 1979 the CGA launched its Archives Publication Series. This initiative was designed to assist researchers in locating queer source material in Canada and abroad, and a number of prominent scholars contributed to its success. Over the years, many leading works were published in the series, such as *Homosexuality in Canada: a bibliography* (1979) by Alex Spence, which was updated in 1984 by William Crawford; *Medical, Social and Political Aspects of the Acquired Immune Deficiency Syndrome (AIDS) Crisis in Canada: a bibliography* (1985) by Donald W. McLeod and Alan V. Miller; and *Our Own Voices: a directory of lesbian and gay periodicals, 1890–1990, including the complete holdings of the Canadian Gay Archives* (1991) also by Alan V. Miller. In response to numerous requests received by the CGA for information on the creation and the operation of a queer archival institution, it also published

Organizing an Archives: the Canadian Gay Archives experience (1983) by James A. Fraser and Harold A. Averill. This manual offered practical advice to people interested in founding an archival centre dedicated to queer records and was largely based on the pioneering experience of the CGA in this area.

That the CGA was increasingly active in queer scholarship was also attested by the fact that it became involved in academic conferences in the 1980s. The first of these, 'Whitman in Ontario', which was co-sponsored by the CGA, was held in October 1980 to mark the 100th anniversary of the visit to Canada of American poet Walt Whitman (1819–92). Other conferences included 'Wilde '82', one of the earliest international gay and lesbian conferences in the world, which was held to mark the centenary of the North American tour by Irish writer Oscar Wilde (1854–1900), and 'Smashing Borders, Opening Spaces', the 7th International Gay Association Conference, in 1985. These conferences brought greater visibility to the CGA in the queer community and they helped consolidate its identity as a leader in the emerging field of queer studies. In turn, this visibility brought more and more members of the community into the archives, either as researchers, as donors or as volunteers.

The Canadian Lesbian and Gay Archives

In 1992, at the annual general meeting of the CGA, members voted in favour of administrative changes which would help reorganize the archival institution. The archives collective, which had served its purpose for over 15 years, was officially dissolved, and the CGA established an elected Board of Directors. In keeping with this spirit of renewal, the following year the CGA adopted what was felt to be a more inclusive name, the Canadian Lesbian and Gay Archives (CLGA).

Very early on, the Archives had realized that, unlike many people who identify primarily with a given community (ethnic, multicultural or religious), members of the queer community do not generally inherit from their parents a sense of queer identity or history. Often this education must come from outside the family unit, and the CLGA began to play an important role in making this history known to the general public. The Archives Publication Series and the conferences were clearly ways to do this in a more academic setting, but the CLGA also undertook a number of outreach initiatives that brought the archives to a wider audience. Among the countless examples over the years were an evening with Vito Russo and a screening of film excerpts that had informed his work, *The Celluloid Closet*, in 1988; the 'Pass It On!' exhibition of lesbian and gay histories in 1995; an evening of readings and conversation with friends of Andy Warhol in 1998;

and the 'Exposing Ourselves' exhibition on Toronto's queer past in 2002. These initiatives served at least three main purposes: first, to bring greater social awareness of queer history; second, to raise the community profile of the CLGA and to highlight the importance of its work; and finally, to function as outreach and fundraising events for the institution.

Thanks in large part to the greater visibility of the CLGA through its own outreach activities, many businesses that cater primarily to the queer community began to organize their own fundraising events in support of the CLGA. These activities, of a mostly social character, have supplemented the public and private donations that have allowed the CLGA to continue operating over the years. Among the more creative events planned were fashion and drag shows hosted in Toronto's Gay Village, like 'Leather and Feathers' night; the Pride and Remembrance run, a benefit for both the AIDS memorial and the CLGA; a bingo night at the Club Baths in Toronto; various dances like the Big City Hoedown; numerous book launches and film premieres; and, more recently, an annual fowl supper, which in 2007 was promoted as 'Oklahomo'.

In 1998 the CLGA celebrated its 25th anniversary by launching the National Lesbian and Gay Portrait Collection. Initially encompassing 25 portraits of outstanding queer Canadians who 'have contributed to the growth of an out and proud community' (Tompkins, 1998), the Collection has grown as more honoured individuals have been inducted into the gallery. It now includes portraits of such internationally recognized queer Canadians as Nicole Brossard, Tomson Highway, k. d. lang, Ann-Marie MacDonald, Carole Pope, Jane Rule, Shyam Selvadurai and Michel Tremblay. The enduring impact of the CLGA on the queer community was recognized on the occasion of its silver anniversary with its designation as the honoured group for Pride Day. CLGA president Edward Tompkins and vice president Robin Brownlie joined Svend Robinson of the New Democratic Party (NDP), Canada's first openly gay federal politician, in a convertible at the head of the Pride Parade that year. Also during Pride Week, the Metropolitan Community Church (MCC) of Toronto presented a special award to the CLGA for 'service and commitment to the community' (CLGA, n.d.). Since then, promotional materials for the Pride Parade in Toronto include information on the CLGA, and they clearly identify the archives on their parade route as a vital part of the community it serves with pride.

The visibility of the CLGA, which was already quite prominent by 1998, grew to unprecedented levels after the launch of its website. The site has since become an invaluable resource. It currently hosts more than 500 pages of online content that describe the mandate of the CLGA and the history of the institution, along with detailed information on its holdings. Moreover, it includes a link to the National Lesbian and Gay Portrait Collection, which has been digitized and is now available online, as well as a link to the complete run of *Lesbian and Gay Archivist*. The website even features a link to the Lesbian Gay Bisexual Transgendered (LGBT) Community Calendar, which posts information on upcoming events in the queer community (Canadian Lesbian and Gay Archives).

Today the CLGA is one of the largest repositories of queer archival holdings in the world, second only to the ONE National Gay and Lesbian Archives in Los Angeles. As it now moves its extensive holdings to new, larger quarters in downtown Toronto, which will serve as a permanent off-site storage space, the CLGA continues to live up to its slogan to 'Keep Our Stories Alive'. One of the most innovative ways it has found to do this was to launch its first national essay contest in the summer of 2008. The contest invited interested applicants to submit a first-person narrative on the topic, 'Once I Was A Child', and, in addition to the promise of cash prizes, all entries were considered for publication in the first volume of *Keeping Our Stories Alive: a journal of the Canadian Lesbian and Gay Archives*. What on the surface appeared to be an ordinary essay-writing contest was in fact a creative way to encourage queer people to write autobiographical sketches as a means of capturing narratives that may otherwise not be preserved. This could actually prove to be one of the least invasive ways of acquiring oral history.

Conclusion

In light of this brief study, there can be little doubt that the CLGA has been instrumental in restoring and preserving the collective memory of the Canadian queer community. Acutely aware, as Gary Kinsman had been, of the past silencing of queer voices in the archives, the CLGA has worked diligently to preserve the documentary heritage of a marginalized group whose missing records had caused a very genuine crisis of memory and identity. These records are not merely the by-products of past LGBT activities: in and of themselves, they point to the richness and the diversity of the Canadian queer experience. And ultimately they continue to sustain and to redefine the queer community in Canada.

Notes

1   This text is a revised and expanded version of a paper I presented at the Association of Canadian Archivists (ACA) Conference in Montréal on 29 May 2004, titled 'Out of the Closet, Into the Archives: the struggle to preserve the records of gay, lesbian, bisexual and transgendered people in Canada'. I would like to express my heartfelt

thanks to several people whose assistance has proven to be invaluable. First and foremost, I would like to thank the personnel and volunteers at the Canadian Lesbian and Gay Archives (CLGA): Robert Windrum, general manager; Harold Averill, Clifford Collier, Don McLeod and Alan Miller. I would also like to thank a number of friends and colleagues whose inspired comments and annotations have been very much appreciated: Greg Bak, Michael Dufresne, Katherine Lagrandeur, Martin Lanthier, Nick Nguyen, Kara Quann and Johanna Smith, all from Library and Archives Canada; my former partner Marc-André LeBlanc; Amber Lloydlangston, assistant historian at the Canadian War Museum; my friend Darren MacKinnon; and Laura Madokoro, doctoral student at the University of British Columbia. And finally, I would like to dedicate this essay to the memory of James Fraser (1946-85), the first professional archivist at the Canadian Gay Archives (CGA), forerunner of the CLGA.

2   A revised and updated edition appeared a decade later. See Kinsman (1996).

3   I use the inclusive word *queer* to designate gay men, lesbians, bisexuals, transgendered, transsexual, intersexed, two-spirited and questioning individuals, whose sexual orientation has traditionally been perceived as contrary to heteronormative standards.

4   The absence from public archives of personal records documenting the lives of queer people is not unique to Canada and is arguably universal. Compare for instance the following comment from American playwright and actor, Harvey Fierstein: 'History offers few records of homosexuals as a people . . . . Where are our records? Our lives seem to be evidenced only in the fecal materials of lawsuits, police files and pornography. For most of history, our everyday lives were cloaked in shame and secrecy' (Fierstein, 2008, xi).

5   Consider for instance the comment of Bud Orange, Liberal member of Parliament for the North West Territories, immediately after the Supreme Court ruling: 'I think that when two male adults wish to engage in an act which to me is a most repulsive act, but it's something that they themselves want to consent to, I think it's their private business, and provided they don't interfere with anybody else in society, I think it's their right as citizens in this country to be able to do so' (CBC Digital Archives, n.d.).

6   The issue of pornography has provoked a fierce debate in the queer community, with its proponents arguing that it is a celebration of sexual freedom, and its opponents declaring that it promotes sexual inequality. For a more detailed discussion, see Morrison (2004). Likewise, same-sex marriage has polarized the queer community, with advocates stating that this is a question of equal rights, and opposers maintaining that it is contrary to the spirit of gay liberation from social norms. See Sullivan (2004). For a general overview of tensions in the queer community, see Sullivan (2003b).

References

Canadian Lesbian and Gay Archives, www.clga.ca/.

Canadian Lesbian and Gay Archives (n.d.) Vertical file on the CLGA.

CBC Digital Archives (n.d.), http://archives.cbc.ca/on_this_day/11/07/.

Columbo, J. R. (ed. and comp.) (1987) *New Canadian Quotations*, Hurtig.

Fierstein, H. (2008) Foreword to *Out Plays - Landmark Gay and Lesbian Plays of the Twentieth Century*, by B. Hodges, Alyson.

Fraser, J. A. and Averill, H. A. (1983) *Organizing an Archives: the Canadian Gay Archives experience*, Canadian Gay Archives.

Gay Archivist (1981) Charitable Status Denied: appeal planned, September, 1.

Kester, N. G. (ed.) (1997) *Liberating Minds - the stories and professional lives of gay, lesbian, and bisexual librarians and their advocates*, McFarland.

Kinsman, G. (1987) *The Regulation of Desire - sexuality in Canada*, Black Rose.

Kinsman, G. (1996) *The Regulation of Desire - homo and hetero sexualities*, Black Rose.

Klippert v. The Queen [1967] *S.C.R.* 822, 7 November.

Morrison, T. G. (ed.) (2004) *Eclectic Views on Gay Male Pornography: pornucopia*, Haworth.

Sullivan, A. (ed.) (2004) *Same-Sex Marriage Pro & Con: a reader*, Vintage.

Sullivan, N. (2003a) *A Critical Introduction to Queer Theory*, NYU Press.

Sullivan, N. (2003b) Community and its Discontents. In Sullivan, N., *A Critical Introduction to Queer Theory*, NYU Press.

Tompkins, E. (1998) Celebrating Our 25th Anniversary. In *Lesbian and Gay Archivist*, June, 1.

The Body Politic (1973) Gay Archives, *The Body Politic*, (10) Autumn, 2.

The Body Politic (1978) TBP Raided & Charged, *The Body Politic*, (41) February, 8.

7

A living archive, shared by communities of records[1]

ERIC KETELAAR

Introduction

In 1993 the United Nations Security Council (UNSC) established the International Criminal Tribunal for the Prosecution of Persons Responsible for Serious Violations of International Humanitarian Law Committed in the Territory of the Former Yugoslavia since 1991 (ICTY) 'for the sole purpose of prosecuting persons responsible for serious violations of international humanitarian law committed in the territory of the former Yugoslavia' (UNSC, 1993; Bassiouni and Manikas, 1996; Scharf, 1997; Bass, 2000). The central purpose of the ICTY, as of any criminal court, is the deterrence of, and retribution for, serious wrongdoing (Osiel, 1997). But from the start, expectations of what the Tribunal could achieve went beyond the primary judicial goal of establishing the truth about and giving an historical record of what happened, contributing to healing individuals' and communities' traumas, and to reconciliation (Power, 2002). Connected with the diverse expectations of the outcomes of the Tribunal's work are expectations of the role the Tribunal's archives can play. Expectations are mounting as the ICTY's work is near completion and decisions about the legacy of the Tribunal are imminent.

In this essay, I explore the potential of the ICTY archives in establishing truth, engaging with history and practising memory – all of which may help communities in former Yugoslavia and elsewhere not only come to grips with their own past but also acknowledge a past shared with neighbouring ethnic and political communities.[2] I will argue that these expectations can only be met by a living archive as a place of contestation, allowing for what Hayden White has called different kinds of discourse about 'what happened and what is to be done' – the archive not merely as a storage technique but primarily as a force for delegitimation of mythified and traditionalized memories (White, 2000, 55).

> 'Sarajevo joins race for ICTY archive' (*Dnevni avaz*, 2007)
> 'Discussion on the fate of ICTY archive' (*Nezavisne novine*, 2007)
> 'Fighting for the Hague documents' (*Nedeljni Telegraf*, 2008)
> 'BiH, Serbia, Croatia all lobby to take over ICTY archives' (*Vecernji list*, 2008)

With headlines like these, the media in Bosnia and Herzegovina, Republika Srpska, Serbia and Croatia brought the archives of the ICTY into the limelight. The headlines also attest to contesting views on the fate of the archives, which vary by region in the former Yugoslavia.[3] And even within one region there are competing views. The mayor of Sarajevo reportedly claimed that the ICTY archives contain 'the only established version of the truth, unlike the three versions that currently exist' in Bosnia and Herzegovina (Miller, 2006; Škuletić, 2008).

In the 15 years since its establishment, the Tribunal has indicted 161 persons. Proceedings against 116 have been concluded. Proceedings are ongoing with regard to 45 accused, and two (Mladić and Hadžić are still at large.[4] In 2003 the Security Council called on the ICTY to take all possible measures to complete the work. It is now estimated that all trials and appeals will be concluded in 2012. A key component of the ICTY completion strategy concerns the appropriate disposition of its archives.

In 2005 I submitted to the registrar of the ICTY a report called *The Legacy of the United Nations International Criminal Tribunal for the former Yugoslavia (ICTY)*, based on research carried out between September 2004 and July 2005 (Ketelaar, 2005a).[5] Concurrently, the US Institute of Peace and the National Peace Foundation sponsored Trudy Huskamp Peterson to undertake a comparative review of the temporary international tribunals and the records they create (Peterson, 2006; see also Peterson, 2005). While my report focuses on the measures to be taken with regard to the ICTY records in the framework of the Tribunal's completion strategy, Peterson's report offers a conceptual framework for creating a central international judicial archives under UN auspices and for standards to select, preserve and manage the records of temporary international criminal courts.

I reconnected with the ICTY archives when I was appointed as a member of the Advisory Committee on the Archives of the UN Tribunals for the former Yugoslavia and Rwanda (ACA), established by the registrars of the two tribunals in October 2007.[6] The ACA was mandated to provide an independent comparative analysis of the potential locations for the archives of each of the tribunals and to examine related issues concerning those archives. The ACA submitted its report to the registrars in September 2008.[7]

ICTY archives

The ICTY archives comprise video and audio recordings, 2200 gigabytes of electronic material, artefacts and 1449 metres of paper records.[8] Nearly 82% of the paper records exist in both paper and digital format. The bulk (70%) are the substantive records of the Office of the Prosecutor (OTP). These include records and material obtained in the course of investigations, such as witnesses' statements and other evidence. All over the former Yugoslavia, the OTP seized documents by the truckload, and from various sources tons of documents, photographs, intercepts of telecommunications, and videos were received (Hagan, 2003). They are from public and private provenances and include records of military and civil government agencies in and outside the former Yugoslavia, personal correspondence, audiovisual items, diaries and other similar material. In most cases, the originals have been returned to the owner or provider, leaving a copy in the archives of the Tribunal.

A second category are the judicial records comprising all court files and records obtained or generated by the Tribunal in support of and during the indictment phase, the pretrial, trial and appeal procedures, as well as procedures relating to the transfer of cases. These include English and French transcripts and the audiovisual recordings of the proceedings, evidence tendered in court, motions, decisions and all other documents and relevant correspondence created by the judges and the parties.

Other types of records that relate to the judicial process, but are not part of the official case files, are records of meetings; general correspondence files; records concerning the privileges and immunities of the Tribunal; agreements with the host country, with other states, and with intergovernmental organizations; correspondence with individual states in order to help enforce sentences and the relocation of witnesses; press files; publications by the Tribunal; and, lastly, the Tribunal's website (www.icty.org), which is, among other things, an archive from which the public can download the public version of transcripts, and more. In 2008 the website recorded more than one million page hits each month for the English site and close to one million each month for the Bosnian/Croatian/Serbian site.

The administrative records include records concerning human resources, procurement, finance and other administrative support functions. Judges, the prosecutor, the registrar and members of staff will have kept working papers. To the extent that they relate to the conduct of the Tribunal's activities, they have value as part of the ICTY's legacy (Sax, 1999). This applies equally to the records created and received by the defence counsel and not submitted to the Tribunal.

The ICTY's Judicial Database (JDB) provides electronic access to court records in most of the Tribunal's cases (Pimentel, 2004; Peterson, 2006). The JDB includes court filings, judgments, decisions, exhibits (but not 3D arte-facts), transcripts and statistical information needed for registered users (usually from the OTP and the defence counsel) to conduct legal research. The database has to be separately accessed for public records, and confidential material may only be accessed with the appropriate security access. The JDB is a legal research tool and not designed to function as a database of archival records.

As early as 1994, the judges instructed the registrar to make and preserve 'a full and accurate record of all proceedings, including audio recordings, transcripts and, when deemed necessary by the Trial Chamber, video recordings' (Mason, 2000; Haufek, 2006; Peterson, 2006; United Nations, 2006, rule 81). All courtroom sessions have been recorded on video (with audio track) and audio. The complete video contains all confidential material (for example testimonies by witnesses whose identity has to be kept secret), while a redacted version contains only public material. The audiovisual record of the proceedings is more comprehensive than the official transcripts. The transcripts exist in two versions, English and French, while the audiovisual record contains Bosnian, Croatian and Serbian as spoken by defendants and witnesses. Moreover, in the transcripts 'the entire visual content of the footage of atrocities committed throughout the region is in most instances reduced to two words: [videotape played]' (Lennon, 2005).

Legally, the records created and received by the Tribunal are the property of the UN. However, they do not belong to the Tribunal; they constitute a legacy, a 'joint heritage', shared by a number of 'communities of records' (Ketelaar, 2005b, 44–61). These communities consist of different stakeholders (to be identified in the following section), each with a *right to know* from the ICTY archives.

Stakeholders

The stakeholders with a concern in the ICTY archives occupy different spatial and temporal positions, depending on the degree of their involvement in the core business of the Tribunal. The interests of stakeholders change over time. Some will not have an immediate interest; others' interests may gradually increase or decrease.

The first category of stakeholders comprises those who now or in the near future have an interest in the primary legal business of the ICTY: to bring to justice persons responsible for serious violations of international humanitarian law committed in the territory of the former Yugoslavia since 1991. This goal will not be reached on completion of the Tribunal's mandate in 2012. Part of the completion strategy is to transfer to competent national jurisdictions (inside and outside the former Yugoslavia) those cases involving the accused of intermediate and lower rank (Raab, 2005). For domestic courts, prosecutors and defence counsel, the ICTY records will continue to be *active* records.[9]

So far 15 states have agreed to enforce the Tribunal's sentences. The judicial authorities in these countries need to have access to the medical files and other records concerning convicts, which were created by the ICTY. The Tribunal retains certain supervisory responsibilities (Tolbert, 2004; Peterson, 2006), which (on completion of the Tribunal's mandate) have to be transferred to a successor agency. That successor agency will need access to the relevant records. Other stakeholders with an interest in ICTY's archives because they were involved in the core legal business of the Tribunal, are the UN, former ICTY staff and defence counsel, governments in the region, indicted and convicted persons, and witnesses.

Slightly more distant from the core legal business of the Tribunal, but nevertheless with an interest in the primary values of the Tribunal's records, are victims and their relatives, many of whom live outside the former Yugoslavia (Huttunen, 2005); victims' groups and other non-governmental organizations; the media; the International Criminal Tribunal for Rwanda; the International Criminal Court; and other criminal justice organizations (Adami and Hunt, 2005; Peterson, 2006). Scholarly researchers (in law, history, political science, and so on) intersect this first category of stakeholders as well as the second, which comprises all those who were not directly involved in the trials before the Tribunal but whose interest in the Tribunal's archives will develop over time.[10] The ICTY archives have a significant secondary value for several reasons, analogous to the arguments recently proposed by Bruce Montgomery with regard to the archives of human rights organizations:

- The archival record is important for historical accountability, and will be 'used by researchers, prosecutors, and victims alike with the aim of analyzing and making known the dimensions of particular human rights violations'.
- The archival evidence 'is important for the memory of the thousands of victims and survivors of human rights abuses, their relatives, and others

who must individually confront the truth of what transpired. Retaining
the memory of victims and survivors is also important to preserve at
least some semblance of identity for those who suffered extreme
depredations . . .'
• Archival records of human rights abuses will likely assume new and
critical importance as this evidence becomes pivotal in the adjudication
of cases. Post-authoritarian governments can only be helped if they
confront the crimes of the past and end impunity with the aim of
building new democratic societies based on the rule of law
(Montgomery, 2004, 23).

Truths, histories and memories
Truths

> Tribunal's archive of truth.   Lazović, 2008

In February 2007 the Humanitarian Law Centre in Belgrade, along with its
partners the Research and Documentation Centre in Sarajevo and
Documenta: Centre for Dealing with the Past in Zagreb, jointly organized a
forum called Establishing the Truth about War Crimes and Conflicts. The
conference agreed that the ICTY archives will play a very significant role in
truth-telling and truth-seeking. During the conference, however,
representatives of victims' organizations expressed their disapproval of its title
'claiming that victims are the only rightful owners of the truth' (Documenta,
2007). What did they mean by 'the truth'?

Four notions of truth were used by the South African Truth and
Reconciliation Commission: factual or forensic truth; personal or narrative
truth; social or 'dialogue' truth; and healing and restorative truth (Truth and
Reconciliation Commission, 1998; Chapman and Ball, 2001). Richard
Wilson (2001) proposes to categorize these into two truth paradigms: forensic
truth and narrative truth. The former is 'the familiar legal or scientific notion
of bringing to light factual, corroborated evidence, of obtaining accurate
information through reliable (impartial, objective) procedures' (Truth and
Reconciliation Commission, 1998, 111). As an ICTY president wrote,
establishing the truth in the courtroom of the ICTY means that the atrocities
in former Yugoslavia will become 'facts established by law' (Jorda, 2004,
577). However, defendants, witnesses, prosecutors and judges tell, hear and
record something that *counts as true* in a particular case, a particular trial,
within the legal context (Edkins, 2003; Montgomery, 2004). The legal
forum is not interested in anything but the forensic truth. It cannot 'move

beyond categorising through abstractions that are necessarily reductions in the scope of possible categorisations of persons and events' (Christodoulidis, 2000).

This 'legal myopia' continues to cause misunderstanding and frustration to victims who want to tell *their* truth, but for whom only a legal forum is accessible. They are 'tools in the prosecutors' case, confined in their testimony to only those fragments of their experience that meet the legal standard of relevant evidence' (Minow, 2000, 238; see also Dembour and Haslam, 2004; Booth, 2006; Hafner and King, 2007, 104). One can only guess what many of the thousands of witnesses before the ICTY may have endured (Klarin, 2004; Stover, 2004, 2005; Leydesdorff, 2008). One of the Tribunal's fundamental contributions to international humanitarian law is its jurisprudence on sexual slavery and rape (Wald, 2002, 2004; Niemann, 2004). However, as a former senior trial attorney regretfully remarked, 'the priority in the case seemed to be on legal theory rather than on the more immediate purpose of illustrating and showing how, and explaining why, sexual assault is used as a weapon of terror' (Schrag, 2004, 431). On the other hand, for many witnesses giving testimony gave 'a little bit of dignity' (Sachs, 2006, 12; see also Goldstone, 2000, 65–6). Also, several of ICTY's judgements contain a narrative explaining the origins and contexts of the conflict, thereby providing a broader picture of which the particular case forms only a part (Robertson, 2006). Still, the rules of the legal procedure generally prevent the ICTY (or any court) from providing an all-encompassing narrative framework, involving bystanders within and outside the region, and 'the complex interactions among ideologies, leaders, mass frustrations, historic and invented lines of hatred, and acts of brutality' (Minow, 2000, 238; see also Minow, 1998, 40; Balint, 2001, 136).

Narrative truth includes the categories of personal, social, and healing (or restorative) truth, emphasizing narrative, subjective dimensions of truth. Narrative truth does not strive at factual truth, but attempts to explain why, according to the narrator, things happened and to give meaning to these events, both to the individual narrator and to society (Wieviorka, 2006a). Currently, civil society groups in the former Yugoslavia and international actors are focusing on forensic truth, while there are few attempts to heal and reach reconciliation through story telling or involving communities on the local level (Zupan, 2006). While forensic truth can be shared, narrative truth will always be contested. As Michael Ignatieff argued in his renowned piece 'Articles of Faith',

> [T]ruth is related to identity. What you believe to be true depends, in some measure, on who you believe yourself to be. And who you believe yourself to be

is mostly defined in terms of who you are not. To be a Serb is first and foremost not to be a Croat or a Muslim. Even people who fought to maintain a moral space between their personal and their national identities are now unable to conceive that one day Zagreb, Belgrade and Sarajevo might share a common version of the history of the conflict.

Ignatieff, 1996, 114

It is clear that the truth that victims claim as being their monopoly (Jelin, 1994) – as is the truth claimed by aggressors and bystanders – will be at odds with the forensic truth contained in the ICTY archives. Moreover, 'the idea of accessible court records that speak for themselves . . . is problematic' (Minow, 1998, p.125). Indeed, records do not speak for themselves; their 'tacit narratives' echo the user's interests, hopes and fears (Ketelaar, 2001). It is the autonomous responsibility of the user to determine what information he or she gets out of the archives (Menne-Haritz, 2001; Macpherson, 2002). This empowers the user to re-create in his or her own way what is found in the records that were created by the Tribunal in its way. That is why archives are never closed and never complete: every individual and every generation are allowed their own interpretation of the archive, to reinvent and to reconstruct its view on and narrative of the past.[11] That is to say (in Hanna Arendt's words), it has 'the right to write its own history. We admit no more than that it has the right to rearrange the facts in accordance with its own perspective; we don't admit the right to touch the factual matter itself' (Arendt, 1977, 238–9).[12] That factual matter is – if one has to choose between the four truths – ultimately *the* truth. The selectivity and the constructedness of the criminal trial may have frustrated survivors and their families, either present in the courtroom, or left behind where the atrocities were still fresh in the memories of the land and the people. However, once the selectivity and constructedness are frozen in the Tribunal's records, they are no longer an obstacle for telling your story, your truth, and storing your myth in what Hayden White calls the 'communal traditionalised memory' (White, 2000, 53).

A number of sociopsychological studies affirm that it takes a long time (20 to 30 years) before individuals and communities are ready to revisit and to reconstruct their past. Apparently, and for different reasons, they need some distance in time (Pennebaker, Paez and Rimé, 1997). As Jeffrey Olick contends, the only collectivity 'that can be healed and can learn the lessons of history and make something of them, is the next generation' (2007, 148). We should therefore not be surprised when society's immediate use of the Tribunal's archives turns out to be rather limited. Over time, both the current generation and their children will (re)discover the possibilities of the archives as sources of history.

Histories

> The archive material of the Tribunal is of crucial importance, our history will be
> written based on it.   *Vecernji list*, 2008

It is not only the victims and their families who have to come to grips with
the past; their communities and society at large have to acknowledge it as
well. What Elizabeth Jelin maintains for post-totalitarian Argentina is true for
the former Yugoslavia too: 'Only when the incorporation of historical events
becomes an active and dynamic process can it feed into the construction of a
democratic culture and collective identity' (Jelin, 1994, 53). What function in
this process would the ICTY archives have as a historical record?

The expectation that the ICTY would establish a historical record can be
traced back (Allcock, n.d.) to the words of Robert Jackson, the chief
prosecutor at the Nuremberg trial, who said that the prosecution had
documented from German sources the aggressions, persecutions and
atrocities 'with such authenticity and in such detail that there can be no
responsible denial of these crimes in the future and no tradition of martyrdom
of the Nazi leaders can arise among informed people' (Harmon and Gaynor,
2004, 404). Jackson's words were echoed by the ICTY's first president,
Antonio Cassese, who observed that the Tribunal 'has established a record of
events that will go down in history and may not be impugned in future'
(Cassese, 2004, 597).[13] The ICTY cites in its Krstić judgement the words of
Nuremberg prosecutor Telford Taylor who said that it is 'important that
these incredible events be established by clear and public proof, so that no one
can ever doubt that they were fact and not fable' (ICTY, 2001, para. 95).[14]
The objective is not so much creating a record contributing to
historiography, but to prevent denial. As Ruti Teitel wrote, 'The ICTY's
responsibility should be to forge and disseminate a record that limits the
possibility of historical denial' (2005; see also Orentlicher, 2008). However,
she also argues that a court that tries to go beyond individual accountability
to assess the historical reality at large risks 'sacrificing individual rights to the
societal interest in establishing a historical record' (Teitel, 2000, 76; see also
Zacklin, 2004).

Indeed, the findings of any trial can be nothing more than a contribution to
creating a larger historical record because the focus is on specific crimes and
perpetrators, not on wider historical events (Schiff, 2002). A trial has to be
selective, focusing on the indicted individual or individuals, on their
accountability for crimes committed by them or because of them. As the
Israeli court in the Eichmann case stated very clearly:

> The desire was felt – readily understandable in itself – to give, within the limits of this trial, a comprehensive and exhaustive historical account of the events of the catastrophe . . . [But] the Court . . . must not allow itself to be enticed to stray into provinces which are outside its sphere. The judicial process has ways of its own . . . whatever the subject-matter of the trial . . . The Court does not possess the facilities required for investigating general questions of the kind referred to above.
>
> Osiel, 1997, 80–1; see also Bayard, 2000[15]

Can one expect from the ICTY that, within the limits of the judicial process, it investigates the historical, political, sociological and economic causes that led to the conflict in former Yugoslavia (Basic, 2007)? The Tribunal in its first judgement (in the Tadić case) devoted some 48 pages (out of 285) 'to say something in a preliminary way about the relevant historical, geographic, administrative and military setting about which evidence was received' (ICTY, 1997, para. 53).[16] In a later judgement (in the Krstić case), the judges were more negative about their role as history writers:

> The Trial Chamber leaves it to historians and social psychologists to plumb the depths of this episode of the Balkan conflict and to probe for deep-seated causes. The task at hand is a more modest one: to find, from the evidence presented during the trial, what happened during that period of about nine days and, ultimately, whether the defendant in this case, General Krstić, was criminally responsible, under the tenets of international law, for his participation in them. The Trial Chamber cannot permit itself the indulgence of expressing how it feels about what happened in Srebrenica, or even how individuals as well as national and international groups not the subject of this case contributed to the tragedy. This defendant, like all others, deserves individualized consideration and can be convicted only if the evidence presented in court shows, beyond a reasonable doubt, that he is guilty.   ICTY, 2001, para. 2

Nevertheless, the ICTY has been praised because it was able to put its judgements in a broader historical context. Richard Wilson commends the ICTY judgements in the Tadić and Krstić cases for their extensive historical interpretation of the causes of the conflict, adding that their 'approach to historical interpretation forces a reconsideration of the long-standing view that the pursuit of justice and the writing of history are inherently irreconcilable' (Wilson, 2005, 922; see also Schiff, 2002). However, in his final conclusion Wilson seems to leave the actual history writing, as the ICTY itself elucidated in the Krstić case, to people outside the Tribunal who may use the ICTY records. The ICTY's judgements, Wilson writes, 'could become an indispensable part of the process of writing a common, credible history of political violence in the 1990s' (Wilson, 2005, 942). Prosecutor Carla Del Ponte said, 'Governments, NGOs and historians should use the millions of pages presented in court to recount history as it really happened' (ICTY, 2007). Robert Donia (who appeared before the Tribunal as an expert witness several times) testifies that the ICTY has 'produced histories that are not only credible and readable, but *indispensable* to understand the origins and course of the 1990s conflicts in the former Yugoslavia', and that it provided 'a detailed, thoroughly investigated and comprehensive account of what happened at critical times in the battle for Bosnia from 1992 to 1995' (Donia, 2004). Nevertheless, according to Donia, the judges' 'historical essentialism' took only those elements into account that they felt were essential to comprehend the atrocities, and that they heard about from witnesses in each case.

The Tribunal's time is in conflict with the time of history; the former emphasizes presence (justice here and now), the latter focuses on absence (justice in the past) (Bevernage, 2008).[17] The law aspires to a degree of finality now and for the future. Therefore, a trial seeks closure through a full and final sentence. On the other hand, there 'is no such expectation of relative fixity in the realm of historical understanding, or of the collective memory to which such understanding contributes' (Osiel, 1997, 217; see also Minow, 1998). Subsequent events, new interpretations, new sources – they will inevitably change the view, and reopen the case. The court's verdict is final, but its reading of the historical event is not. Court records have, therefore, not more value than other records (Ketelaar, 2001). Law's closure has to be rejected in favour of history's recurrence. History is never finished or final because with the passage of time historical interpretation undergoes change (Teitel, 2000). History is provisional and thereby allows a contrapuntal narrative doing justice to adversarial and contested stories (Maier, 2000). Instead of asking for *the* truth or *the* history, one should show and teach that there are many truths and histories.

Memories

> The ICTY has already become an institution of great importance for social memory in the region.
>
> Donia, 2006, 400

The psychologist Nico Frijda suggests that appropriating the past is an element in the construction of an individual's identity. It does so in a double way, by 'shaping or affirming the identity of one's group, and by accepting or redefining membership within that group' (Frijda, 1997, 109). This argument is shared by James Booth who puts forward that gathering in the past, appropriating it, 'gives us identity and a moral narrative of pride, shame, and indebtedness, that ties us across time to *our* past and the burdens this past imposes simply by virtue of being ours' (Booth, 1999, 254; Booth, 2006). The common, often mythical, past, sustained through time into the present, is what gives continuity, cohesion and coherence to a community (Morley and Robins, 1995; Stråth, 2000). Any community is therefore a community of memory, especially a community living after mass atrocities, where the past continues to torment because it is not past. They 'are not living in a serial order of time, but in a simultaneous one, in which the past and present are a continuous, agglutinated mass of fantasies, distortions, myths and lies' (Ignatieff, 1996, 119). For victims and survivors of mass atrocities, the past stays on, as Frijda asserts, as 'unfinished business': they and their families keep on searching for meaning to understand how the humiliations, the cruelties, the systematic destruction were ever possible (Frijda, 1997). They may label their search for meaning, searching for *the* truth or *the* history, but it is in fact no more and no less than a meaning-making process to confirm and reconfirm identity (Fuhrer, 2004), constructing and reconstructing their community's memories and narrative truths, engaging the community in rituals of commemoration. The ICTY cannot – or can only minimally – live up to the expectations of a 'secular ritual of commemoration' (Akhavan, 1998, 784).[18] Such a ritual with its beneficial effects on individuals and communities has to be set up elsewhere, with the help of people and institutions engaged in memory-practice (Osiel, 1997). Among these institutions are, of course, memorial museums, including sites, that are established in 'the global rush to commemorate atrocities', as the title of Paul Williams' recent book on memorial museums includes. Williams acknowledges that we only have a fuzzy awareness whether and how 'concrete spaces like memorials and museums are effective social spaces for aiding reconciliation' (2007, 170). But they provide space for rituals of commemoration, as for example the Srebrenica memorial and cemetery in Potočari (Bosnia), where annually on 11 July commemoration ceremonies are held (Williams, 2007, 17–18).

Archives could also become such spaces of memory-practice, where people can try to put their trauma in context by accessing the documents, not primarily seeking *the* truth or searching *the* history, but transforming their experiences into meaning. Accessing the archives of the ICTY, and weaving them into private and public memories, may constitute a healing ritual. Archives as a space of shared custody and trust. Archives as places where records are preserved through time, long enough perhaps to destroy the agony and heal the communities (Ketelaar, 2008).

A living archive

Even after completion of the primary mission of the ICTY the archive will continue to be a living archive, used by prosecutors and judges within and outside the former Yugoslavia, defence counsel, and other stakeholders. At the same time – and stretching far beyond the time the documents have to serve judicial purposes – the archive will be a living archive for the causes of truths, histories and memories. The archive will be a living archive because it will continue to be challenged, contested and expanded. I will deal with these successively.

Challenging the archive

According to one of the UN Human Rights Commission's principles, people are entitled to challenge the validity of the information in archives concerning them by exercising their right of reply (Ketelaar, 2006a). The challenged document should include a cross-reference to the document challenging its validity and both must be made available together whenever the former is requested. A comparable right of correction, enshrined in the data protection legislation of all European Union states, should be given to people involved in trials before the ICTY, especially because in some cases discrepancies between the witness' evidence and the official record of it have been found (Human Rights Watch, 2004).

Contesting the archive

Any archive is a place of contestation (Harris, 2000, 80; Harris, 2007). Like memorial museums, archives are spaces where battles about the politics of memory are fought. Like memory, an archive is not just an agency of storage, but a process, a mediated social and cultural practice (Ketelaar, 2006b). A living archive allows for what Hayden White calls

> three different kinds of discourse about 'what happened' and 'what is to be done'. First, the disaster can be assimilated to communal memory by its mythification. Secondly, it can be assimilated to communal memory by the conventions of classification, cataloguing, and storage techniques of the rationalising sciences. And thirdly, the disaster can be assimilated to communal memory in such a way as to force a revision and delegitimation of traditionalised memory itself.
> White, 2000, 55[19]

Different as these kinds of discourse may be about what happened and what is to be done, they have to be related. Myth and rationality are not entirely independent of collective memory; they are mutually constitutive (Olick, 2007). The third component – revision and delegitimation – entails hospitality to contestation and renegotiation. As Michael Moss writes: the archive is 'a place of "dreams" of re-enactment for both the user and the archivist (curator), who together always are engaged either passively or actively in the process of refiguration that is never ending' (Moss, 2008, 83). I believe that the archive is not merely (as White suggests) a rational storage technique but primarily a space to escape from a monolithic truth, history and memory, by allowing questioning myth and rationality – including the myth and rationality contained in the archive.

This is even more relevant in the former Yugoslavia, where the past is no common past. After the Second World War there was 'never a discourse on how a multiethnic society whose population consisted of extremely divergent individual and collective memories could manage this complex legacy sufficiently to come to terms with its complex past' (Hoepken, 1999, 204). And when the Yugoslav state disintegrated, the historical memory disintegrated too. The post-Yugoslav republics created 'a new fragmented memory along not only ideological, but ethnic, borderlines' (Hoepken, 1999, 226). Different ethnic groups each claim their own memory of suffering, to be framed in a space only trusted by and accessible to members of their own group. This 'ethnization of memory' (Corkalo et al., 2004, 157) may lead to 'ghettoization of history' (Williams, 2007, 168). The archives of the ICTY, however, cannot be split up according to the ethnic provenance of perpetrators, victims and witnesses. It is a joint albeit a contentious heritage that should be accessible from any of the places in former Yugoslavia (and from anywhere in the world) where people live who want to use the archives. The contentiousness of the archive might even prove beneficial because it can show 'how people can live with continuing disagreements about what exactly happened in the past and why, and still respect each other as fellow citizens' (Gutmann and Thompson, 2000, 35). Reconciliation, as Christodoulidis (2000) argues, has to take risks, and one of them is that memories and identities are not arbitrated, that constituencies for communities are not fixed. I believe that the risk of contentiousness of the archives should be taken, too.

Expanding the archive

The living archive should be expanded, in the first place by linking the content to the holdings of the broad range of governmental and non-governmental agencies within and outside the former Yugoslavia that continue to collect material about the conflict (Djordjevic, 2002). Second, the archive should be expanded by gradually releasing the numerous classified documents, classified because of protection of witnesses, privacy and state secrets. Most of the transcripts contain redacted passages, sometimes amounting to more than 50% as in the case of Miletic et al., where 7994 pages of the more than 16,000 pages of transcript contain redacted passages. And third, by allowing people to enrich the ICTY record with their comments and stories. Witnesses, victims, as well as convicted and indicted people (and bystanders) should be allowed to tell their stories. Stories are not only vehicles for understanding, they are also a means of remembrance (Atwood and Magowan, 2001). Writing down and submitting their stories – co-creating and constituting the archive – allows people to articulate their own war histories and, in psychoanalytic terms, gives them an opportunity to express and thus begin to incorporate them into the present (Twomey, 2003; Pillemer, 2004; Adler et al., 2009). I propose permeating the boundaries between what Hayden White calls the communal traditionalized memory and the communal rationalized memory; the first consisting of stories of the past, the second of 'accounts of a community's past, contained in its archives and catalogued and processed in the form of written or visualized "histories," so that it can be "accessed" on demand' (White, 2000, 53).

Of course archival institutions, as the rationalized receivers of story, should, in Verne Harris's words, 'Be ever vigilant. Cherish what story gives us, but always probe its telling, explore other tellings and other stories. Know that as compelling as it might seem, as seamless and satisfying and healing, it remains story not truth. We should never allow story to be more than a platform to our own search for meaning' (2007, 415).

Archival institutions around the world are moving into new ways of capturing, storing and using public and private documents, stories, images and sound. Digital systems of distributed custody of the holdings of both public institutions and private individuals and communities are already in place. Web 2.0 applications stimulate social navigation, and uploading 'evidence of me' (McKemmish, 1996) to an archival institution's server thus creating and maintaining a living archive out of private and public documents (Ketelaar, 2003, 2008; Šajkaš, 2007). The ICTY archive presents 'an unprecedented challenge to use new technology and innovative finding aids to assure access and usability to future generations' (Donia, 2006, 400; Donia and Becirevic, 2008).

Conclusion

The ICTY archives, as any other archives, allow for contestation. But paradoxically that quality may help members of a community not only to come to grips with their own past but also to acknowledge that the past they share with neighbouring ethnic and political communities is not a monolithic truth, history or memory, but allows, even requires, questioning and contestation. For this, the archive provides a space. As South African judge Albie Sachs stated, archivists are caring for archives 'not as we used to think, to guard certainty: they are doing it to protect uncertainty because who knows how the future might use those documents' (2006, 14). Each community is a community of records, marking the limits to other groups and their members. The risk of 'ethnization' (or exclusiveness) of memories may be abated by giving each community in the former Yugoslavia not just a share in a joint heritage, but by making each community a co-custodian of the living ICTY archive, constantly challenged and challenging.

Notes

1   A slightly different version constituted my paper 'Truths, Memories, and Histories in the Archives of the ICTR and the ICTY', presented at the conference '60 Years Genocide Convention' organized by the Amsterdam Center for Holocaust and Genocide Studies, the Amsterdam Center for International Law and the Peace Palace Library, The Hague, 8 December 2008.

2   I refrain from dealing with 'memoricide': eradicating communities' identities by destroying their archives. See Kolanovic, 1996; Kovacevic, 1996; Riedlmayer, 2007.

3   The territory of the former Yugoslavia comprises the states of Bosnia and Herzegovina (consisting of two entities: the Federation of Bosnia and Herzegovina and Republika Srpska), Croatia, Kosovo, Republic of Macedonia, Montenegro, Serbia and Slovenia.

4   See www.icty.org.

5   I was assisted by postgraduate students enrolled in the Master of Archival Science programme of the University of Amsterdam: Ernestine Baake, Esther Balkestein, Jelle Bosma, Marie-Christine Engels, Kees Fluyt, Wim Mastenbroek and Natasja Pels. I presented some of the results of this research to the Second International Conference on the History of Records and Archives (ICHORA2) in Amsterdam, 1–3 September 2005.

6   The other members of ACA were Justice Richard Goldstone, former Chief Prosecutor of the ICTY and the ICTR (chair), Saliou Mbaye, former national archivist of Senegal, Judge Mohamed Othman, a member of the Tanzanian High Court, former Prosecutor at the East Timor UN Administration and former Chief of Prosecutions at the ICTR, and Cecile Aptel, former staff member of both the ICTY and ICTR. I have benefited greatly from the insights and fellowship of the ACA. I also want to record my gratitude to Hans Holthuis, registrar of the ICTY, and his staff for their invaluable assistance and support to my research.

7 Unlike my 2005 study and the ACA report the present paper does not deal with the current management and the future location of the ICTY archives.
The views expressed in this paper are those of the author in his personal capacity and do not necessarily represent the views of the UN.

8 The term archives applies, according to the UN administrative instruction ST/AI/326 of 28 December 1984, 'to those records to be permanently preserved for their administrative, legal, historical or informational value'. Records are, following the definition in that instruction, 'all documentary materials, regardless of physical type, received or originated' by the Tribunal. I have updated some figures (Peterson, 2006) on the basis of information provided by ICTY staff, as of November 2007/August 2008.

9 According to Rule 11bis (D) of the ICTY Rules of Procedure and Evidence, when a case is referred to another court, 'the Prosecutor shall provide to the authorities of the State concerned all of the information relating to the case which the Prosecutor considers appropriate and, in particular, the material supporting the indictment' (United Nations, 2006).

10 The archives of the International Military Tribunal and the US Nuremberg Military Tribunals are, some 60 years since their creation, used very rarely by lawyers and professional historians, but mostly by private individuals interested in a relative who testified or served in some capacity with the court, or people who are a relative of a victim of Nazi aggression and so on (T. K. Nenninger (US National Archives and Records Administration), personal communication to E. Balkestein, University of Amsterdam, 15 March, 2005).

11 This reasoning resembles James Booth's (2006, 182) argument that we have some measure of choice in determining how our understanding of the past will be shaped.

12 Annette Wieviorka (2006b, 396) writes 'Each person has the right to fashion his or her own history, to put together what he or she remembers and what he or she forgets in his or her own way. . . . Each person has an absolute right to his or her memory, which is nothing other than his or her identity, his or her very being. But this right can come into conflict with an imperative of the historian's profession, the imperative of an obstinate quest for the truth.'

13 Scharf (1997, 215) argues, 'While there are various means to achieve an historic record of abuses after a war, the most authoritative rendering is possible only through the crucible of a trial that accords full due process.'

14 The ICTY continues in asserting that 'It is therefore imperative to document these "incredible events" in detail. However, the central issue in this case is the role that one man, General Krstić, played in the criminal acts and whether he is legally responsible for conduct that amounts to war crimes, crimes against humanity or genocide.'

15 Lawrence Douglas, while conceding that didactic trials as the Eichmann trial 'are not well equipped to render history in its complexity', and not denying 'that history and

law are governed by differing epistemological and evidentiary conventions', warns against over-exaggerating the differences (Douglas, 2006, 98, 101).

16 The Tribunal stressed that this exposé was exclusively based upon the evidence presented in court. Scharf concludes that the record of the Tadić trial 'provides an authoritative and impartial account to which future historians may turn for truth, and future leaders for warning' (Scharf, 1997, 215).

17 According to Booth (2006, 113–15), both the court and the historian depend on absence, on what is no longer present. However, justice, as Booth writes, seeks to act on the past by making it present.

18 Here Akhavan writes about 'the sacral aspect of remembrance' and the 'public ritual of atonement'.

19 White adds: 'Programmes for recovery from the disaster (or the reconstruction of the afflicted society) can thus be sublimated into public debates about the relative merits of different ways of construing the causes of the disaster.'

References

Dnevni avaz (2007) Sarajevo Joins Race For ICTY Archive, *Dnevni Avaz*, 20 November.

Nezavisne novine (2007) Discussion on the Fate of ICTY Archive, *Nezavisne Novine*, 24 November.

Nedeljni Telegraf (2008) Fighting for the Hague Documents, *Nedeljni Telegraf*, 19 March, 5.

Vecernji list (2008) The Archive Material of the Tribunal is of Crucial Importance, Our History will be Written Based On It, *Vecernji List*, 25 March.

Adami, T. A. and Hunt, M. (2005) Genocidal Archives: the African context – genocide in Rwanda, *Journal of the Society of Archivists*, **26**, 105–21.

Adler, N., Leydesdorff, S., Chamberlain, M. and Neyzi, L. (eds) (2009) *Memories of Mass Repression: narrating life stories in the aftermath of atrocity*, Transaction Publishers.

Akhavan, P. (1998) Justice in The Hague, Peace in the Former Yugoslavia? A commentary on the United Nations war crimes tribunal, *Human Rights Quarterly*, **20**, 737–816.

Allcock, J. B. (ed.) (n.d.) *The International Criminal Tribunal for the Former Yugoslavia: report by the Scholars' Initiative*, Research Group 10, www.cla.purdue.edu/academic/history/facstaff/ingrao/si/scholars.htm.

Arendt, H. (1977) Truth and Politics. In Arendt, H., *Between Past and Future: eight exercises in political thought*, Penguin Books, 227–64.

Atwood, B. and Magowan, F. (eds) (2001) *Telling Stories: indigenous history and memory in Australia and New Zealand*, Allen & Unwin Academic.

Balint, J. (2001) Law's Constitutive Possibilities: reconstruction and reconciliation in the wake of genocide and state crime. In Christodoulides, E. and Veitch, S. (eds), *Lethe's Law: justice, law and ethics in reconciliation*, Hart Publishing, 129–49.

Basic, S. (2007) Bosnian Society on the Path to Justice, Truth and Reconciliation. In Fischer, M. (ed.), *Peacebuilding and Civil Society in Bosnia-Herzegovina: ten years after Dayton*, 2nd edn, Lit Verlag, 357–85.

Bass, G. J. (2000) *Stay the Hand of Vengeance: the politics of war crimes tribunals*, Princeton University Press.

Bassiouni, M. C. and Manikas, P. (1996) *The Law of the International Criminal Tribunal for the Former Yugoslavia*, Transnational.

Bayard, F. (ed.) (2000) *Le génocide des Juifs entre procès et histoire 1943–2000*, Complexe.

Bevernage, B. (2008) Time, Presence, and Historical Injustice, *History and Theory*, **47**, 149–67.

Booth, W. J. (1999) Communities of Memory: on identity, memory, and debt, *American Political Science Review*, **93**, 249–63.

Booth, W. J. (2006) *Communities of Memory: on witness, identity, and justice*, Cornell University Press.

Borer, T. A. (ed.) (2006) *Telling the Truths: truth telling and peace building in post-conflict societies*, University of Notre Dame Press.

Cassese, A. (2004) The ICTY: a living and vital reality, *Journal of International Criminal Justice*, **2**, 585–97.

Chapman, A. R. and Ball, P. (2001) The Truth of Truth Commissions: comparative lessons from Haiti, South Africa, and Guatemala, *Human Rights Quarterly*, **23**, 1–43.

Christodoulidis, E. A. (2000) Truth and Reconciliation as Risks, *Social Legal Studies*, **9**, 179–204.

Corkalo, D. et al. (2004) Neighbors Again? Intercommunity relations after ethnic cleansing. In Stover, E. and Weinstein, H. M. (eds), *My Neighbor, My Enemy: justice and community in the aftermath of atrocity*, Cambridge University Press, 143–61.

Dembour, M. and Haslam, E. (2004) Silencing Hearings? Victim-witnesses at war crimes trials, *European Journal of International Law*, **15**, 151–77.

Djordjevic, D. (2002) *Summary Report Regarding Local, Regional and International Documentation of War Crimes and Human Rights Violations in the former Yugoslavia*, International Center for Transitional Justice, www.ictj.org/images/content/0/8/082.pdf.

Documenta (2007) *Conclusions from International Conference 'Establishing the Truth about War Crimes and Conflicts', Second Regional Forum on Transitional Justice*, Documenta: Centre for Dealing with the Past, www.documenta.hr/eng/index.php?option=content&task=view&id=29&Itemid=.

Donia, R. J. (2004) Encountering the Past: history at the Yugoslav war crimes tribunal, *Journal of the International Institute*, **11** (2–3), http://hdl.handle.net/2027/spo.4750978.0011.201.

Donia, R. J. (2006) The New Masters of Memory: libraries, archives, and museums in post-socialist Bosnia and Hercegovina. In Blouin, F. X. and Rosenberg, W. G. (eds), *Archives, Documentation, and Institutions of Social Memory: essays from the Sawyer seminar*,

University of Michigan Press, 393–401.

Donia, R. J. and Becirevic, E. (2008) *ICTY Archive Must Be Open To All*, www.ifimes.org/default.cfm?Jezik=en&Kat=10&ID=397.

Douglas, L. (2006) History and Memory in the Courtroom: reflections on perpetrator trials. In Reginbogin, H. R. and Safferling, C. J. M. (eds), *The Nuremberg Trials: international criminal law since 1945*, Saur, 95–104.

Edkins, J. (2003) *Trauma and the Memory of Politics*, Cambridge University Press.

Frijda, N. H. (1997) Commemorating. In Pennebaker, J. W., Paez, D. and Rimé, B. (eds), *Collective Memory of Political Events: social psychological perspectives*, Lawrence Erlbaum, 103–27.

Fuhrer, U. (2004) *Cultivating Minds: identity as meaning making practice*, Routledge.

Goldstone, R. J. (2000) *For Humanity: reflections of a war crimes investigator*, Witwatersrand University Press.

Gutmann, A. and Thompson, D. (2000) The Moral Foundations of Truth Commissions. In Rotberg, R. and Thompson, D. (eds), *Truth v. Justice*, Princeton University Press, 22–44.

Hafner, D. L. and King, E. B. L. (2007) Beyond Traditional Notions of Transitional Justice: how trials, truth commissions, and other tools for accountability can and should work together, *Boston College International and Comparative Law Review*, **30** (1), 91–109.

Hagan, J. (2003) *Justice in the Balkans: prosecuting war crimes in the Hague tribunal*, University of Chicago Press.

Harmon, M. B. and Gaynor, F. (2004) Prosecuting Massive Crimes with Primitive Tools: three difficulties encountered by prosecutors in international criminal proceedings, *Journal of International Criminal Justice*, **2**, 403–26.

Harris, V. (2000) *Exploring Archives: an introduction to archival ideas and practice in South Africa*, 2nd edn, National Archives of South Africa.

Harris, V. (2007) Contesting Remembering and Forgetting: the archive of South Africa's truth and reconciliation commission. In Harris, V., *Archives and Justice: a South African perspective*, Society of American Archivists, 289–304.

Haufek, S. (2006) *Reconciliation and the Expansive Archive: cultural memory and the legacy of the International Criminal Tribunal for the former Yugoslavia*. Master's thesis (unpublished), University of Amsterdam, Department of Media Studies.

Hoepken, W. (1999) War, Memory, and Education in a Fragmented Society: the case of Yugoslavia, *East European Politics and Societies*, **13**, 190–227.

Human Rights Watch (2004) *Justice at Risk: war crimes trials in Croatia, Bosnia and Herzegovina, and Serbia and Montenegro*, www.unhcr.org/refworld/docid/42c3bcf70.html.

Huttunen, L. (2005) 'Home' and Ethnicity in the Context of War: hesitant diasporas of Bosnian refugees, *European Journal of Cultural Studies*, **8**, 177–95.

Ignatieff, M. (1996) Articles of Faith, *Index on Censorship*, **5**, 110–22.

International Criminal Tribunal for the former Yugoslavia (1997) *Judgment IT-94-1-T*, www.un.org/icty/cases-e/index-e.htm, para.53.

International Criminal Tribunal for the former Yugoslavia (2001) *Judgment IT-98-33-T*, www.un.org/icty/cases-e/index-e.htm, para.2, 95.

International Criminal Tribunal for the former Yugoslavia (2006) *ICTY Rules of Procedure and Evidence*, www.un.org/icty/legaldoc-e/basic/rpe/IT032Rev38e.pdf.

International Criminal Tribunal for the former Yugoslavia (2007) *ICTY and the Legacy of the Past*, www.un.org/icty/pressreal/2007/pr1193e.htm.

Jelin, E. (1994) The Politics of Memory: the human rights movements and the construction of democracy in Argentina, *Latin American Perspectives*, **21** (2), 38–58.

Jorda, C. (2004) The Major Hurdles and Accomplishments of the ICTY: what the ICC can learn from them, *Journal of International Criminal Justice*, **2**, 572–84.

Ketelaar, E. (2001) Tacit Narratives: the meanings of archives, *Archival Science*, **1**, 143–55.

Ketelaar, E. (2003) Being Digital in People's Archives, *Archives and Manuscripts*, **31**, 8–22.

Ketelaar, E. (2005a) *The Legacy of the United Nations International Criminal Tribunal for the former Yugoslavia (ICTY): justice, reconciliation, and memory*, unpublished.

Ketelaar, E. (2005b) Sharing: collected memories in communities of records, *Archives and Manuscripts*, **33**, 44–61.

Ketelaar, E. (2006a) Access: the democratic imperative, *Archives and Manuscripts*, **34**, 62–81.

Ketelaar, E. (2006b) Writing on Archiving Machines. In Neef, S., van Dijck, J. and Ketelaar, E. (eds), *Sign Here! handwriting in the age of new* media, Amsterdam University Press, 183–95.

Ketelaar, E. (2008) Archives as Spaces of Memory, *Journal of the Society of Archivists*, **29**, 9–27.

Klarin, M. (2004) The Tribunal's Four Battles, *Journal of International Criminal Justice*, **2**, 546–57.

Kolanovic, J. (1996) Archives en temps de guerre: l'expérience de la Croatie, *Archivum*, **42**, 173–80.

Kovacevic, M. (1996) War Damage Suffered by the State Archives of Bosnia and Herzegovina, *Archivum*, **42**, 181–6.

Lazović, T. (2008) Tribunal's Archive of Truth, *Dnevni avaz*, 11 March, 3.

Lennon, H. (2005) A Witness to Atrocity: film as evidence in international war crimes tribunals. In Gaggith, T. and Newman, J. (eds), *Holocaust and the Moving Image: representations in film and television since 1933*, Wallflower Press, 65–73.

Leydesdorff, S. (2008) De leegte achter ons laten: een geschiedenis van de vrouwen van Srebrenica [*Leaving a Void Behind Us: a history of the women of Srebrenica*], Bert Bakker.

Macpherson, P. (2002) Theory, Standards and Implicit Assumptions: public access to post-current government records, *Archives and Manuscripts*, **30**, 6–17.

Maier, C. S. (2000) Doing History, Doing Justice: the narrative of the historian and of the truth commission. In Rotberg, R. and Thompson, D. (eds), *Truth v. Justice*,

Princeton University Press, 261–78.

Mason, P. (2000) *Report on the Impact of Electronic Media Coverage of Court Proceedings at the International Criminal Tribunal for the former Yugoslavia*, Centre for Media and Justice at the Southampton Institute (United Kingdom), www.un.org/icty/pressreal/final%20report%20_wp8_.pdf.

McKemmish, S. (1996) 'Evidence of Me . . .', *Archives and Manuscripts*, **24**, 28–45.

Menne-Haritz, A. (2001) Access: the reformulation of an archival paradigm, *Archival Science*, **1**, 57–82.

Miller, P. B. (2006) Contested Memories: the Bosnian genocide in Serb and Muslim minds, *Journal of Genocide Research*, **8**, 311–24.

Minow, M. (1998) *Between Vengeance and Forgiveness: facing history after genocide and mass violence*, Beacon Press.

Minow, M. (2000) The Hope for Healing: what can truth commissions do? In Rotberg, R. and Thompson, D. (eds), *Truth v. Justice*, Princeton University Press, 235–60.

Montgomery, B. P. (2004) Fact-Finding by Human Rights Non-Governmental Organizations: challenges, strategies, and the shaping of archival evidence, *Archivaria*, **58**, 21–50.

Morley, D. and Robins, K. (1995) *Spaces of Identity: global media, electronic landscapes, and cultural boundaries*, Routledge.

Moss, M. (2008) Opening Pandora's Box: what is an archive in the digital environment? In Craven, L. (ed.), *What are Archives? Cultural and theoretical perspectives: a reader*, Ashgate, 71–87.

Niemann, G. (2004) The Life and Times of a Senior Trial Attorney at the ICTY from 1994 to 2000, *Journal of International Criminal Justice*, **2**, 435–45.

Olick, J. K. (2007) *The Politics of Regret: on collective memory and historical responsibility*, Routledge.

Orentlicher, D. F. (2008) *Shrinking the Space for Denial: the impact of the ICTY in Serbia*, Open Society Institute.

Osiel, M. (1997) *Mass Atrocity, Collective Memory, and the Law*, Transaction Publishers.

Pennebaker, J. W., Paez, D. and Rimé, B. (eds) (1997) *Collective Memory of Political Events: social psychological perspectives*, Lawrence Erlbaum.

Peterson, T. H. (2005) *Final Acts: a guide to preserving the records of truth commissions*, Woodrow Wilson Center Press, Johns Hopkins University Press, www.wilsoncenter.org/press/peterson_finalacts.pdf.

Peterson, T. H. (2006) *Temporary Courts, Permanent Records*, www.usip.org/pubs/specialreports/sr170.html.

Pillemer, D. B. (2004) Can the Psychology of Memory Enrich Historical Analyses of Trauma?, *History and Memory*, **16**, 140–55.

Pimentel, D. (2004) Technology in a War Crimes Tribunal: recent experiences at the ICTY, *William and Mary Bill of Rights Journal*, **12**, 715–29.

Power, S. (2002) Stopping Genocide and Securing 'Justice': learning by doing, *Social*

Research, **69**, 1099–106.

Raab, D. (2005) Evaluating the ICTY and its Completion Strategy: efforts to achieve accountability for war crimes and their tribunals, *Journal of International Criminal Justice*, **3**, 82–102.

Riedlmayer, A. J. (2007) Crimes of War, Crimes of Peace: destruction of libraries during and after the Balkan wars of the 1990s, *Library Trends*, **56**, 107–32.

Robertson, G. (2006) *Crimes Against Humanity: the struggle for global justice*, 3rd edn, The New Press.

Sachs, A. (2006) Archives, Truth, and Reconciliation, *Archivaria*, **62**, 1–14.

Šajkaš, M. (2007) *Transitional Justice and the Role of the Media in the Balkans*, International Center for Transitional Justice, www.ictj.org/images/content/8/3/833.pdf.

Sax, J. L. (1999) *Playing Darts with a Rembrandt: public and private rights in cultural treasures*, University of Michigan Press.

Scharf, M. P. (1997) *Balkan Justice: the story behind the first international war crimes trial since Nuremberg*, Carolina Academic Press.

Schiff, B. N. (2002) Do Truth Commissions Promote Accountability or Impunity? The case of the South African Truth and Reconciliation Commission. In Bassiouni, M. C. (ed.), *Post-Conflict Justice*, Transnational Publishers, 325–43.

Schrag, M. (2004) Lessons Learned from ICTY Experience, *Journal of International Criminal Justice*, **2**, 427–34.

Škuletić, S. (2008) Sarajevo Major: the city of Sarajevo will request the ICTY archives on its own, *Dnevni avaz*, 28 February, 5.

Stover, E. (2004) Witnesses and the Promise of Justice in The Hague. In Stover, E. and Weinstein, H. M. (eds), *My Neighbor, My Enemy: justice and community in the aftermath of mass atrocity*, Cambridge University Press, 104–20.

Stover, E. (2005) *The Witnesses: war crimes and the promise of justice in The Hague*, University of Pennsylvania Press.

Stråth, B. (ed.) (2000) *Myth and Memory in the Construction of Community: historical patterns in Europe and beyond*, PIE-Peter Lang.

Teitel, R. G. (2000) *Transitional Justice*, Oxford University Press.

Teitel, R. G. (2005) Justice Seeks an Exit Strategy, *Taipei Times*, 7 January, www.globalpolicy.org/intljustice/tribunals/yugo/2005/0107justiceexit.htm.

Tolbert, D. (2004) Reflections on the ICTY Registry, *Journal of International Criminal Justice*, **2**, 480–5.

Truth and Reconciliation Commission of South Africa (1998) *Report*, vol. 1, www.doj.gov.za/trc/report/.

Twomey, C. (2003) 'Impossible History': trauma and testimony among Australian civilians interned by the Japanese in World War II. In Damousi, J. and Reynolds, R. (eds), *History on the Couch: essays in history and psychoanalysis*, Melbourne University Press, 155–65.

United Nations (2006) *Rules of Procedure and Evidence, IT/32/Rev. 37, 6 April 2006,* International Tribunal for the Prosecution of Persons Responsible for Serious Violations of International Humanitarian Law Committed in the Territory of the Former Yugoslavia since 1991, Rule 81, www.icty.org/x/file/Legal%20Library/Rules_procedure_evidence/ IT032_rev37_en.pdf .

United Nations Security Council (1993) *Resolution 827,* www.un.org/icty/legaldoc-e/basic/statut/S-RES-827_93.htm.

Wald, P. M. (2002) Punishment of War Crimes by International Tribunals, *Social Research*, **69**, 1119–134.

Wald, P. M. (2004) ICTY Judicial Proceedings: an appraisal from within, *Journal of International Criminal Justice*, **2**, 466–73.

White, H. (2000) Catastrophe, Communal Memory and Mythic Discourse: the uses of myth in the reconstruction of society. In Stråth, B. (ed.), *Myth and Memory in the Construction of Community: historical patterns in Europe and beyond*, PIE-Peter Lang, 49–74.

Wieviorka, A. (2006a) *The Era of the Witness*, transl. by J. Stark, Cornell University Press.

Wieviorka, A. (2006b) The Witness in History, *Poetics Today*, **27**, 2, 385–96.

Williams, P. (2007) *Memorial Museums: the global rush to commemorate atrocities*, Berg.

Wilson, R. (2001) *The Politics of Truth and Reconciliation in South Africa: legitimizing the post-apartheid state*, Cambridge University Press.

Wilson, R. A. (2005) Judging History: the historical record of the international criminal tribunal for the former Yugoslavia, *Human Rights Quarterly*, **27**, 908–42.

Zacklin, R. (2004) The Failings of Ad Hoc International Tribunals, *Journal of International Criminal Justice*, **2**, 541–45.

Zupan, N. (2006) Facing the Past and Transitional Justice in Countries of Former Yugoslavia. In Fischer, M. (ed.), *Peacebuilding and Civil Society in Bosnia-Herzegovina: ten years after Dayton*, Lit Verlag, 327–42.

8

Truth commissions and the construction of collective memory: the Chile experience

JOEL A. BLANCO-RIVERA

Introduction

Following the death of Augusto Pinochet in December 2006, Michelle Bachelet, the current President of Chile, reacted to the news. Herself a victim of torture from the Pinochet regime, President Bachelet stated, 'I'm not going to deny, in this moment, that I have a very fixed concept concerning a painful, dramatic and complex period that our country lived through . . . What we learn from the past ought to help us confront the future' (Reel, 2006).

Records became a powerful resource during this process of 'learning from the past'. In the US, the 24,000 documents produced by the Chile Declassification Project became strong evidence of the role of the US government during the overthrow of Salvador Allende and the establishment of the Pinochet dictatorship. In Chile, the National Commission on Truth and Reconciliation presented a report documenting 2279 cases of human rights violations. Organizations of victims' relatives and human rights groups along with the human rights programme of Chile's Ministry of Interior have played an important role in establishing memorials. Additionally, the Archbishopric of Santiago de Chile established an archive that is considered the main repository of materials documenting the repression during the Pinochet years. Pinochet's death also displayed the profound divisions among Chileans over his legacy. While one sector went into the streets to celebrate, others gathered to cry over the death of one whom they saw as Chile's saviour from communism. A fragmented and divided memory of the Pinochet years is still present in Chilean society.

This essay discusses the role of archives and records in Chile during its transition to democracy, with a focus on the work of the National Commission on Truth and Reconciliation. In addition, I will discuss the concept of memory from the Chilean experience, and the role played by archives in the shaping of the country's collective memory.

Transitional justice in Latin America

The period from the 1960s to the 1980s saw an unprecedentedly high level of violence and political repression in Latin America with the establishment of dictatorships in South America and civil wars in Central America. In the midst of the Cold War, Latin America went through a polarized and traumatic period during which gross atrocities took place.

Chile was one of the more stable democracies in Latin America. In 1970 Salvador Allende, running for the coalition Unidad Popular, became the first Socialist leader to be democratically elected as head of state. Yet, his administration also experienced a polarizing period between government and opposition that affected social, political and economic aspects of Chilean society. This led to the 11 September 1973 *coup d'état* that marked the beginning of 17 years of military rule led by General Augusto Pinochet.[1]

As has been widely documented, the Pinochet government was characterized by human rights abuses, although there are still sectors of Chilean society that dismiss these accusations. Following the coup, thousands of detainees were held in the national stadium of Santiago,[2] with many of them suffering torture and execution. The military rule was clear on searching for supporters of the Unidad Popular. On 18 June 1974, this task became the full responsibility of the newly created Dirección de Inteligencia Nacional (DINA; National Directorate of Intelligence) led by Colonel Manuel Contreras Sepúlveda (Constable and Valenzuela, 1991, 91). Its primary mission was to infiltrate and disrupt Marxist parties, including to eliminate party leaders. Torture and interrogations took place in more than a dozen detention centres, with Villa Grimaldi, on the outskirts of Santiago, becoming the most notorious. Today, Villa Grimaldi is a public memorial.

With the end of the Pinochet regime in 1990, Chile faced a similar series of complex issues that other countries transitioning from authoritarian rule to democratic leadership have needed to address. One of the main challenges is confronting past accounts of human rights violations. This question has been amply studied through the framework of transitional justice (Kritz, 1995; Teitel, 2000; Freeman, 2006; Roht-Arriaza and Mariezcurrena, 2006). Developed as a consequence of transitions to democracy around the world, transitional justice considers different strategies for dealing with the legacy of repression. Mechanisms like trials, investigative bodies, reparations and justice reforms are part of this framework (Freeman, 2006, 5–6). In addition, as Mark Freeman explains, transitional justice 'also intersects with other subjects such as amnesty, reconciliation, and the preservation of memory, as well as democratization and peace-building' (Freeman, 2006, 6).

Regardless of the mechanism, there is a general consensus over one aspect of these legacies: past atrocities cannot be forgotten. Guillermo O'Donnell and Philippe C. Schmitter exemplify this consensus when they recognize that no matter how difficult it is to deal with past accounts of human rights violations, ignoring the issue is the worst possible option. As the 'least worst' strategy, they propose imposing 'judgment upon those accused of gross violations of human rights' (1986, 30). In Latin America, the most common mechanism for accomplishing this was through the establishment of truth commissions.

Truth commissions in Latin America

The responsibilities of truth commissions go beyond investigating and documenting in detail the atrocities committed by past regimes. They also play a key role in the transition to a democratic government and do not allow the truth of past atrocities to be forgotten. And while records created by repressive regimes (when they are not destroyed) become evidence of their abuses, records about the truth commission (its minutes, case files, reports) become evidence for communities to construct and validate their memories.

Priscilla B. Hayner (2001, 14) discusses four main characteristics that define a truth commission. First, the work of a truth commission focuses on the past. Second, instead of a specific event, the commission investigates abuses over a period of time, usually an authoritarian rule or an internal war. Third, they are temporary bodies. And fourth, they have official authorization or sanction from the state. Freeman contends that although Hayner's definition is a good starting point, it does not include other vital attributes. He emphasizes that truth commissions are not equivalent to courts or tribunals, and thus their main function is investigative. In addition, truth commissions provide an analysis of the causes and consequences of the human rights abuses, they are '*victim-centered* bodies', and as such relatively independent from the state (Freeman, 2006, 14–17).

Freeman, expanding on the characteristics presented by Hayner, presents a more complex and complete definition of a truth commission when he states,

> A truth commission is an *ad hoc*, autonomous, and victim-centered commission of inquiry set up in and authorized by a state for the primary purposes of (1)

investigating and reporting on the principal causes and consequences of broad and relatively recent patterns of severe violence or repression that occurred in the state during determinate periods of abusive rule or conflict, and (2) making recommendations for their redress and future prevention.

Freeman, 2006, 18

Truth commissions are seen as alternatives to criminal trials in countries where trials are not politically viable. Historical justice is the commission's goal. Teitel highlights the importance of historical justice during regime transition and the struggle to construct a collective account of the authoritarian period. Through trials, official histories and truth commissions, society seeks to construct transitional histories that 'define the direction of political transformation' (Teitel, 2000, 72).

Although the implementation of truth commissions has been generally praised as a good mechanism of transitional justice, it has not been free of criticism (Moulian, 1998; Woods, 1998; Grandin and Klubock, 2007) and critics contend that truth commissions are not an acceptable option to justice (Phelps, 2004, 53). In her analysis of the South African Truth and Reconciliation Commission, Woods contends that by negotiating amnesties and setting the rules, political leaders 'precluded the people from freely choosing their own path to reconciliation' (Woods, 1998, 108). Moulian (1998), who analyses Chile's commission, indicates that although the 'merits of the Report are indisputable', it was nevertheless, 'a simulation of justice'.

Regardless of the debates about the effectiveness of truth commissions and their limitations in bringing justice, one aspect is clear: the documentary evidence gathered and created by these investigative bodies provides substantial accounts of human rights violations that communities need to confront as part of a healing process. It is here that the archive plays a significant role. During its investigative work, truth commissions examine records of the authoritarian regime and other documentation about the period. In addition, commissions develop their own record-keeping systems to manage the documentation gathered and created during their work. In Guatemala, the Comisión para el Esclarecimiento Histórico (CEH; Historical Clarification Commission) established a documentation centre to organize and classify the information gathered. This included the creation of a database to organize electronically the cases under investigation (CEH, 1999, 66–71).

The archive of a truth commission also experiences a transition, since the work of the truth commission does not end with the publication of the report. To the contrary, this is only a first step in a process that includes opening painful dialogue and also poses the challenge of harmonizing different memories. In Phelps' words, truth commission reports, 'instead of burying the past . . . help to exhume it' (2004, 120). In addition, records of truth commissions have been used as part of criminal investigations as in Argentina in 1985 (Grandin, 2005), and in criminal investigations against military officers in Chile (Roht-Arriaza, 2005). In sum, when the members of the truth commissions cease their work, the archive becomes responsible for accountability, memory construction and justice.

Truth commissions, archives and memory

Since the 1970s the world has experienced what Andreas Huyssen (2000) calls 'the culture of memory'. One of the major triggers of this culture of memory has been traumatic experiences of genocide, wars and dictatorships which have left profound wounds on individuals and countries, and where memory plays a role during the healing process and against forgetting (Jelin, 2003). The growing literature on memory, especially the memory of past atrocities and its role during democratic transitions (see Jelin, 2003; Bell, 2006; Olick, 2007), directly engages current archival discourse.

Recent literature from a number of archival theorists and practitioners has challenged the traditional conception of the archive as an institution preserving valuable historical documentation and has emphasized the power of archives in society (Hamilton, et al., 2002; Ketelaar, 2002; Schwartz and Cook, 2002; Blouin and Rosenberg, 2007; Harris 2007). For example, participants at the University of Michigan's Sawyer Seminar 'Archives, Documentation and Institutions of Social Memory' agreed that their 'point of departure was a conception of archives not simply as historical repositories but as a complex of structures, processes, and epistemologies situated at a critical point of intersection between scholarship, cultural practices, politics, and technologies' (Blouin and Rosenberg, 2007, vii).

This framework of analysing archives, records and record-keeping systems in relation to power, and social, cultural and political processes also provides the grounds for a deeper analysis of the concept of collective memory and its relationship to archives. Although the concept *collective memory* is often mentioned in archival discourse, I raise a serious concern that the true meaning and importance of this concept has not been fully addressed by the archival community. As Verne Harris explains, the phrase 'archives hold the memory of a nation' has become a 'stirring slogan' and 'also suggests a glibness about the complex processes through which archives feed into social memory' (2007, 173). As the case of Chile demonstrates, communities construct different memories of the same event or period of time. In addition, preservation, restriction of access and/or destruction of records directly affects memory construction and accountability.

The Chilean National Commission of Truth and Reconciliation

Following his compromise on addressing the issue of human rights violations under Pinochet rule, President Patricio Aylwin created by decree the Comisión Nacional de Verdad y Reconciliación (CNVR) on 25 April 1990. The decree established as the Commission's main responsibilities:

> a)   To establish as complete a picture as possible of those grave events, as well as their antecedents and circumstances; b) To gather evidence that may make it possible to identify the victims by name and determine their fate or whereabouts; c) To recommend such measures of reparation and reinstatement as it regards as just; and d) To recommend the legal and administrative measures which in its judgement should be adopted in order to prevent actions such as those mentioned in this article from being committed.   CNVR, 1993, 7

Eight people were appointed to be part of the Commission, including two former officials of the Pinochet government, and former senator Raúl Rettig was appointed as the Commission's chair. The CNVR had nine months in which to complete its work, presenting its final report to President Aylwin on 8 February 1991.

It is important to point out that limitations on Aylwin's presidency influenced the creation and responsibilities of the Commission. President Aylwin faced legal and institutional restrictions that led to the creation of the Commission by decree instead of through Congressional legislation (Zalaquett, 2006, 29). These limitations included the fact that Augusto Pinochet was still the commander of the armed forces. In addition, the National Congress had enough Pinochet supporters to veto any initiative from Aylwin. The CNVR did not have the judiciary authority to prosecute those who committed crimes. Related to this, José Zalaquett, former member of the Commission, explained during a lecture in 1991:

> At a societal level, the equivalent of penance is criminal justice. Yet the Chilean government's assessment of the situation led it to conclude that priority ought to be given to disclosure of truth. This disclosure was deemed an inescapable imperative. Justice would not be forgone, but pursued to the extent possible given the existing political restraints . . . The underlying assumption, which I share, was that if Chile gave truth and justice equal priority, the result might well have been that neither could be achieved. Fearing that official efforts to establish the truth would be the first step toward widespread prosecutions, the military would have determinedly opposed such efforts.
>
> Zalaquett, 1992, 1432–3

In addition, one of the main obstacles to seeking criminal prosecution in Chile was the amnesty law signed by Pinochet in 1978, which absolved military and police officials from being held accountable for their abuses (Constable and Valenzuela 1991, 129).

During its nine months of work, the CNVR examined a total of 4000 individual complaints. As part of the process of identifying possible cases of human rights violations, the CNVR released convocations in local newspapers asking relatives of the victims to solicit a hearing. The Commission also asked for lists of victims gathered by human rights organizations and government agencies such as the military branches. This process ended up with the identification of more than 3400 individual cases. In addition, the Commission extensively used records from the archive of the Vicaría de la Solidaridad (Vicariate of Solidarity), one of the leading human rights organizations during the dictatorship (CNVR, 1993, 15–16). The records gathered and created by the Commission, which included electronic data, were stored in their own documentation centre.

In order to organize the information obtained from the testimonies, each case had its own dossier, which included the formal request for an audience and evidence obtained from other sources. After hearing the testimonies – which took place behind closed doors – the Commission continued requesting new evidence and documentation to confirm the allegations. When the Commission requested records from the Chilean Police the response it mostly received was that the records had been legally destroyed. In addition, the military did not provide access to records documenting their activities, stating that the law prohibited the release of information about their intelligence activities (CNVR, 1993, 18–19).

The report of the CNVR is a three volume, 1800-page account of each case that the Commission concluded was a human rights violation. The Commission also concluded that 95% of these cases were the responsibility of the state, while 4% were the responsibility of 'politically motivated private citizens' (CNVR, 1993, 900). The report names and describes the fate of each of the individuals who suffered human rights violations. But it does not name the perpetrators of the abuses.

Part 4 of the report focuses on proposals for reparation and recommendations for preventing human rights violations. They include suggestions for symbolic reparations, and recommendations in the areas of social welfare (education, pensions, health care) and in the rule of law. In particular, two recommendations illustrate the importance of memory and the archive in the transition from authoritarian rule. First, as part of the recommendations for the reparation to victims of human rights abuses and their families, the Commission emphasized the importance of establishing symbolic reparations. Their report states

> It is to be hoped that as soon as it is prudently possible, the government will see fit to provide the means and resources necessary to set in motion cultural and symbolic projects aimed at reclaiming the memory of the victims both individually and collectively. Such projects would lay down new foundations for our common life and for a culture that may show more respect and care for human rights, and so provide us with the assurance that violations so threatening to life will never again be committed.   CNVR, 1993, 838

Currently, this responsibility lies in the Programa de Derechos Humanos (Human Rights Programme), which is under the Ministry of the Interior (www.ddhh.gov.cl). During the period 2002 to 2006 the programme supported the construction of 18 memorials (www.ddhh.gov.cl/ proy_construidos.html).

Second, the Commission recommended the creation of a public law foundation, which was to be responsible for the archives of the records of the CNVR. In addition, the report states that there is 'a need for an office to centralize the files and evidence on cases and to maintain a library devoted to this topic. People could have access to this office under conditions to be laid down by law' (CNVR, 1993, 888). The public law foundation was not created, and the archive of the CNVR is under the control of the Ministry of the Interior (Stern, 2006, 487). Additional records related to the truth commission are also housed at the archive of the Corporación Justicia y Democracia (Corporation Justice and Democracy), a non-governmental organization created by former President Aylwin (Peterson, 2005, 64).

The report was accepted by the majority of Chile's political and social sectors. Pinochet and his military leaders rejected it, but did not contest any of the cases presented in the report (Zalaquett, 2006, 28). In addition, in 1992 the National Congress passed legislation to create the Corporación Nacional de Reparación y Reconciliación (CNRR; National Corporation for Reparation and Reconciliation). The CNRR was responsible for continuing the work initiated by the CNVR. The CNRR identified 899 additional cases of human rights violations and released its report in 1996. In her description of Chile's truth commission, Hayner indicates that despite the release of the reports, in the following years the general public and the press in Chile felt uncomfortable discussing the issue of past abuses (2001, 37). This is clearly evidenced by the struggles over memory, which today are still unresolved.

A fragmented memory

'Memory and forgetting are recurrent issues. Is like the positive and the negative of human action, and the reflection the man does about life and events.' These words are spoken by Chilean painter José Balmes portrayed in Patricio Guzmán's documentary *Chile: obstinate memory*. Following Balmes' words, the film shows former members of Allende's security personnel looking at pictures of what took place in La Moneda Presidential Palace on 11 September 1973. While identifying the persons in the pictures, they were naming names and recounting their fates – many of them were among the 'disappeared'. Photographs became the medium for remembrance.

However, limiting the discussion of memory, collective memory and Chile just to the perspective of Guzmán's film does not offer a complete picture of how Chilean society has dealt with this period of time. A research study carried out in 2003, 30 years after the coup, showed that, although the events of 11 September 1973 remain relevant to Chilean society, there are still different perceptions about it (Manzi et al., 2003). The study also shows that these differ-ences are highly influenced by the ideological position of the surveyed. For example, when asked about their perception about the events of 11 September 1973, 47.3% responded that it was unjustified while the rest believed it was somewhat or completely justified. Almost 60% of persons identified with the right believed the events had justification, while almost 75% of the people from the left believed the events were unjustified (Manzi et al., 2003, 185–6).

One of the most complete explanations about memory struggles in Chile comes from historian Steve J. Stern in his three-book series *The Memory Box of Pinochet's Chile*. Stern argues against what he calls the 'memory-against-forgetting dichotomy', which he considers 'too narrow and restrictive', as is the characterization of Chile 'as a culture of oblivion, marked by a tremendous compulsion to forget the past and the uncomfortable' (2004, xxvii). Although Stern recognizes the fight of human rights organizations against forgetting as 'powerful and legitimate', he calls for a 'study of contentious memory as a process of competing selective remembrances, ways of giving meaning to and drawing legitimacy from human experience' (2004, xxvii). Political ideologies, and economic and societal status, among other aspects, influence the way people remember specific events, as is demonstrated in the survey results presented above. So it is too simplistic to just define the struggles for memory as a fight between those who want to remember and those who want to forget.

In the first book of the series, Stern presents human stories of Chileans who experienced Allende's government, the coup and the Pinochet dictatorship as a way to develop a theoretical framework of memories in Chile. Stern's main purpose, in his own words, is to 'offer a human portrait of Chile's memory division and drama' (Stern, 2004, 2). To help understand these narratives, Stern used the concept of 'emblematic memory'. This concept encompasses a broad spectrum of collective memory, and it is a framework in which different kinds of memories reside. Stern explains that the Chilean experience has been constructed by four main emblematic memories: memory as salvation, memory as an unresolved rupture, memory as persecution and awakening, and memory as a closed box (Stern, 2004, 104–13). People who recall memory as salvation see the period of Allende's government as the real trauma that caused economic and social crisis. So, the advent of Augusto Pinochet to power was seen as the salvation of the country. Memory as an unresolved rupture sees the Pinochet regime as a brutal dictatorship that used violence and torture as a means to try to destroy the opposition. For those who see memory as an unresolved rupture, the experience of suffering repression from the government, or the loss of a relative or friend, is still latent in their lives. Memory as persecution and awakening recalls the military rule as a period of repression, but that eventually led to a social awakening against the regime. The social movements like the Vicaría de la Solidaridad in the 1970s, and other movements that arose during the 1980s, leading to the transition back to democracy in the 1990s, can be considered as part of this framework. Finally, memory as a closed box offers a framework for those who choose forgetting as the process for social reconciliation. Stern concludes:

> It was as if Chileans lived in a house whose living room was dominated by a giant truth box . . . The truth box was a memory chest, filled with scripted photo albums ('emblematic memory') and scattered prints and messages ('lore'). These served as guides of understanding and misunderstanding, reminder and revelation, debate and agreement, that explained the destiny of everyone who lived in the house. Those who opened the box sometimes found themselves pulled into agreeing or arguing with an album, pondering a stray picture, perhaps contributing a picture or a message.   Stern, 2006, 245

Alexander Wilde (1999) explains that collective memory in Chile since the 1990s has been characterized by what he calls 'irruptions of memory'. These irruptions of memory played a role in the political transition to democracy. As Wilde explains, after the first years of the transition, the government assumed a defensive attitude, responding to issues of memory as specific events erupted. These 'irruptions of memory' have been latent through the years of transition. The arrest of Pinochet in 1998 and his death in December 2006 are examples of these irruptions. They opened again the wounds of the fragmented memories in Chile.

Similarly, Chilean sociologist Dr Manuel Antonio Garretón (2003) reflects on this issue by explaining the importance of facing the legacy of what he calls *hitos* (milestones). These milestones, historical events that had profound effects in Chile, are the failure of the proposed social changes by the Allende administration, the *coup d'etat*, Pinochet's dictatorship and the transition to democracy. Garretón explains how there is no national collective memory of these historical events, but a fragmented memory that has divided the Chilean society. This fragmented memory, Garretón argues, affects how the country builds its future. Although he recognizes that there are multiple collective memories, he also states that there should be a national collective memory with a shared core of ideas about these events. Chile, Garretón concludes, has not yet built this core national memory (Garretón, 2003, 224).

There is one voice that was systematically silenced by the regime, but which has played an essential role in shaping the collective memory of Chile: the *desaparecidos* (disappeared). In fact, the memory of the *desaparecidos* has filled the gaps that exist because of the destruction of records by the military government. Michael J. Lazzara explains,

> I would like to propose the figure of the *desaparecido* as a locus for articulating a series of tensions – tensions among presence and absence, visibility and invisibility, life and death, humanity and inhumanity, speech and silence, memory and forgetting. It seems possible to argue that absence (even more than presence) characterizes post-dictatorial experience. I say this because the reality of state sponsored repression has left us to deal [with] considerable gaps in the collective archive that cannot (and will not) ever be filled.
>
> Lazzara, 2006, 101

How is the absence of the disappeared transformed into a voice of remembrance? Here is where Lazzara sees the role of art, in all its manifestations, as playing a unique role in the shape of collective memory. For this matter, Lazzara presents in his book different types of art, from documentary to literature. Nevertheless, I would like to comment on one artistic manifestation that closely relates to the importance of documents and archives as a medium for remembering: the *Muro de la Memoria* (Wall of Memory) (Lazzara, 2006, 111–17).

The *Muro de la Memoria* was prepared in 2002 by visual artists Claudio Pérez and Rodrigo Gómez and is located in Puente Bulnes. It consists of 950 photographs of the *desaparecidos*, with each photo listing the name of the person and the date of his/her disappearance. The location of the monument also holds symbolism because during the dictatorship bodies were found floating on Mapocho River, which passes below Puente Bulnes. Among the sources from which Pérez and Gómez obtained the photos were the archives of the Vicaría de la Solidaridad and the CNVR. The wall was intended to display the photos of the 1192 *desaparecidos* named in the Commission's report, but the artists were unable to obtain photos of 242 persons. Empty spaces were left in the monument for the missing photos in case they eventually surface.

This example demonstrates the importance of archives and documents beyond their practical purpose and research value. It speaks of the power that archives have as symbolism of past events. In his essay about the symbolic aspect of archives, James O'Toole discusses the case of records created by repressive regimes, like the Stasi in East Germany, and how for democratic movements these records 'had been transformed, at least temporarily, into something else: symbols of all that was wrong with the regimes they were knowingly overthrowing' (O'Toole, 2000, 71). In the case of the photos used for the *Muro de la Memoria*, they were not records created by the regime; most are family photographs which were initially taken for personal remembrance (weddings, pictures at the beach, and so on), but they became strong symbols of what the dictatorship did.

Conclusion

Records are evidence that play key roles in shaping the memories of communities, and, as archivists, we have the responsibility to see that these records are preserved and made accessible to researchers. Understanding the importance of records in shaping memories should make archivists realize how essential our responsibility is not only to the archive, but to society. Traumatic historical events like the dictatorship in Chile and the central roles of records created by the regimes, as well as those created during the processes of seeking truth and justice, call attention to the importance of archivists as key players, and even leaders, in these transitions. This call for leadership applies not only to advocacy for open governments, but even more, to the key role that archivists should play in different archival institutions. In other words, archivists need to come to realize that archives and power are at the same level of discussion. Through appraisal, archival representation and access archivists have 'control of the archive', which 'means control of society and thus control of determining history's winners and losers' (Schwartz and Cook, 2002, 4). At the core of the broad perception of our profession as passive and neutral lies the refusal, consciously or unconsciously, by archivists to recognize or accept the intrinsic relation between archives and power.

The Chile experience, just like the work of other truth commissions around the globe, provides an example of the challenges and struggles that different communities face in coming to terms with the memory of a traumatic period. In terms of communities of records, this case also shows the close connection between the creation, use, preservation and destruction of records in shaping a community's collective memories. Furthermore, the trend of trials against perpetrators of human rights violations in Latin America that have followed the Pinochet arrest in 1998, and the work done by the National Security Archive providing support in these trials (see Blanton, 2008), also show the function of archives not only as memory institutions, but also as vehicles for accountability and justice.

Jeannette Bastian states that a 'community of records may be further imagined as the aggregate of records in all forms generated by multiple layers of actions and interactions between and among the people and institutions within a community' (2003, 5). In Chile, the work of the truth commission in documenting a dark period in Chilean history, along with the memory struggles that have surfaced in Chilean society, show these multiple layers of actions and interactions. Furthermore, the creation, use, destruction and access restrictions to records directly affect these dynamics of memory. Within this context, the archive becomes, more than merely a repository for memory, part of the struggle for collective memory, accountability and justice.

Notes

1   A detailed discussion about the Allende presidency, and the events and causes that
    led to the coup in 1973 is beyond the scope of this essay. A comprehensive
    discussion of these issues and the Pinochet years is presented in P. Constable and A.
    Valenzuela, *A Nation of Enemies: Chile under Pinochet*, W. W. Norton & Company,
    1991. Part 2 of the Chilean Truth Commission report also provides a historical
    background of this period, see *Report of the Chilean National Commission on Truth and
    Reconciliation*, Notre Dame, published in co-operation with the Center for Civil and
    Human Rights, Notre Dame Law School, by the University of Notre Dame Press,
    1993, 47–98. For a discussion about the role of the US Administration in the plans
    to disrupt the Allende administration and their support to the military regime, see P.
    Kornbluh, *The Pinochet File: a declassified dossier on atrocity and accountability*, New Press,
    2003.
2   Santiago is the capital of Chile.

References

Bastian, J. (2003) *Owning Memory: how a Caribbean community lost its archives and found its history*, Libraries Unlimited.

Bell, D. (ed.) (2006) *Memory, Trauma and World Politics: reflections on the relationship between past and present*, Palgrave Macmillan.

Blanton, T. S. (2008) Recovering the Memory of the Cold War: forensic history and Latin America. In Joseph, G. M. and Spenser, D. (eds), *In From the Cold: Latin America's new encounter with the Cold War*, Duke University Press.

Blouin Jr, F. X. and Rosenberg, W. G. (2007) *Archives, Documentation and Institutions of Social Memory: essays from the Sawyer Seminar*, University of Michigan Press.

Comisión Nacional de Verdad y Reconciliación [Chile] (1993) *Report of the Chilean National Commission on Truth and Reconciliation*, trans. Phillip E. Berryman, Notre Dame Press.

Comisión para el Esclarecimiento Historico [Guatemala] (1999) *Guatemala: memoria del silencio*, CEM.

Constable, P. and Valenzuela, A. (1991) *A Nation of Enemies: Chile under Pinochet*, W. W. Norton & Company.

Freeman, M. (2006) *Truth Commissions and Procedural Fairness*, Cambridge University Press.

Garretón, M. A. (2003) Memoria y Proyecto de País, *Revista de Ciencia Política*, **23** (2), 215–30.

Grandin, G. (2005) The Instruction of Great Catastrophe: truth commissions, national history, and state formation in Argentina, Chile, and Guatemala, *American Historical Review*, **110** (1), 46–7.

Grandin, G. and Klubock, T. M. (2007) Truth Commissions: state terror, history, and memory, a special issue of *Radical History Review*, 97.

Hamilton, C., Harris, V., Pickover, M. and Reid, G. (eds) (2002) *Refiguring the Archive*, Kluwer Academic Publishers.

Harris, V. (2007) *Archives and Justice: a South African perspective*, Society of American Archivists.

Hayner, P. B. (2001) *Unspeakable Truths: confronting state terror and atrocity*, Routledge.

Huyssen, A. (2000) Present Pasts: media, politics, amnesia, *Public Culture*, **12** (1), 21–38.

Jelin, E. (2003) *State Repression and the Labors of Memory*, University of Minnesota Press.

Ketelaar, E. (2002) Archival Temples, Archival Prisons: modes of power and protection, *Archival Science*, **2** (3–4), 221–38.

Kornbluh, P. (2003) *The Pinochet File: a declassified dossier on atrocity and accountability*, The New Press.

Kritz, N. J. (ed.) (1995) *Transitional Justice: how emerging democracies reckon with former regimes*, US Institute of Peace Press.

Lazzara, M. J. (2006) *Chile in Transition: the poetics and politics of memory*, University Press of Florida.

Manzi, J. et al. (2003) El Pasado que nos Pesa: la memoria colectiva del 11 de septiembre de 1973, *Revista de Ciencia Política*, **23** (2), 177–214.

Moulian, T. (1998) A Time of Forgetting the Myths of the Chilean Transition, *NACLA*

Report on the Americas, **32** (2), 16–21.

O'Donnell, G. and Schmitter, P. C. (1986) *Transitions from Authoritarian Rule: tentative conclusions about uncertain democracies*, Johns Hopkins University Press.

Olick, J. K. (2007) *The Politics of Regret: on collective memory and historical responsibility*, Routledge.

O'Toole, J. (2000) The Symbolic Significance of Archives. In Jimerson, R. C. (ed.), *American Archival Studies: readings in theory and practice*, Society of American Archivists.

Peterson, T. H. (2005) *Final Acts: a guide to preserving the records of truth commissions*, Johns Hopkins University Press.

Phelps, T. G. (2004) *Shattered Voices: language, violence, and the work of truth commissions*, University of Pennsylvania Press.

Reel, M. (2006) In Death, Pinochet Continues to Divide, *Washington Post*, 12 December, A16.

Roht-Arriaza, N. (2005) *The Pinochet Effect: transitional justice in the age of human rights*, University of Pennsylvania Press.

Roht-Arriaza, N. and Mariezcurrena, J. (2006) *Transitional Justice in the Twenty-first Century: beyond truth versus justice*, Cambridge University Press.

Schwartz, J. and Cook, T. (2002) Archives, Records and Power: the making of modern memory, *Archival Science*, **2** (1–2), 1–19.

Stern, S. J. (2004) *Remembering Pinochet's Chile: on the eve of London, 1998*, Duke University Press.

Stern, S. J. (2006) *Battling for Hearts and Minds: memory struggles in Pinochet's Chile, 1973–1988*, Duke University Press.

Teitel, R. G. (2000) *Transitional Justice*, Oxford University Press.

Wilde, A. (1999) Irruptions of Memory: expressive politics in Chile's transition to democracy, *Journal of Latin American Studies*, **31** (2), 473–500.

Woods, J. M. (1998) Reconciling Reconciliation, *UCLA Journal of International Law and Foreign Affairs*, **81**, 81–127.

Zalaquett, J. (1992) Balancing Ethical Imperatives and Political Constraints: the dilemma of new democracies confronting past human rights violations, *Hastings Law Journal*, **43**, 1425–38.

Zalaquett, J. (2006) La Comisión de Chile y su Misión Moral e Histórica, *Hechos del Callejón*, (November), 26–30.

Part 4

Online communities: how technology brings communities and their records together

9

From Yizkor Books to weblogs: genocide, grassroots documentation and new technologies

ANDRÁS RIEDLMAYER AND STEPHEN NARON

Introduction

In the aftermath of World War 1, the journalist Aram Antonean, a survivor of the Armenian genocide of 1915–16, collected testimony from other survivors and published it, along with photographs and other documents, in a book entitled *Mets ochire* [The Great Crime] (Antonean, 1921). Antonean, and others, recognized the urgent necessity of capturing these stories. In the introduction to his book, he wrote: 'Many times, I thought that a volume needs to be written for each [survivor] in order to encompass, at least in a schematic way, the overall picture of the terrible horrors. And there were a hundred thousand of these survivors, each one of whom had a story to fill a volume' (Slyomovics, 1998, 4).

By telling their stories, these survivors added their 'volume' to a collective effort to defy the attempt to efface their people, the Armenians of the Ottoman Empire, from history. Of course, Antonean realized that this effort, important as it was, was destined to be incomplete. Presaging David Boder's interviews[1] with survivors of the Holocaust decades later, Antonean knew that the 'colossal endeavor would still fall short of the stories of those who had perished, taking with them more than a million volumes' (Slyomovics, 1998, 4).[2] Sadly, this dynamic of destruction and communal reconstruction would not end with the Armenian genocide. In fact, it was an omen of things to come. Genocide and forced exile has been the 20th century's terrible and consistent companion. But despite the staggering loss of human lives and cultural heritage, communities of survivors – bound by ethnic, religious and social relations – have found remarkable ways to collectively reconstruct and remember what was lost. And despite the unique contexts and circumstances of each genocide or persecution, the survivors' responses are similar in substance and aim. Of course, communal commemoration of the dead and of victims of national tragedy is nothing new – its visible signs, from ancient burial grounds to national war memorials to today's high-tech memorial museums and hyperlinked online documentation centres, are all around us. But each group of survivors, each generation, reinvents the process by which their lost community is commemorated. And in doing so, survivors employ those technologies most prevalent at the time.

The goal of this essay is to explore three iterations of such efforts to document communities destroyed by genocide in the 20th century: Yizkor books, video testimonies of Holocaust survivors, in particular those held by the Fortunoff Video Archive for Holocaust Testimonies, and weblogs built by Bosnian survivors in the diaspora. These three examples share many characteristics. In fact, they can be looked at as three nodes on a continuum of collective efforts to commemorate a community lost. Above all, they are usually grassroots efforts – and as such these acts of remembrance by and for members of the survivor community share similar structures, narrative components and forms of documents.

Yizkor books as grassroots documentation

Although the terms 'genocide' and 'ethnic cleansing' are of relatively recent vintage, the phenomena they describe – systematic attempts to destroy or forcibly remove from a territory groups of people, targeted on the basis of their ethnicity or religion – are unfortunately nothing new. If we take Jewish history as our point of departure, we see a past punctuated and shaped by the memory of catastrophic events. The call to 'remember and forget not' echoes throughout the Hebrew Bible and the religious obligation to commemorate the dead plays a central role in Jewish tradition. It has been noted that in some ways memory, or at least the constant 'reference to a sequence of historical events', is at the very 'core of the Jewish identity' (Yerushalmi, 1996, 113). The Hebrew verb for remember, זכר (zakhar), appears in the Hebrew Bible no fewer than 169 times, 'usually with either Israel or God as the subject, for memory is incumbent on both' (Yerushalmi, 1996, 5). This emphasis on remembrance and commemoration extends to specific catastrophic events as well. The Book of Lamentations, traditionally attributed to the Prophet Jeremiah, is one example. A series of poems bemoaning the destruction of Jerusalem by the Babylonians in 586 BCE, the Book of Lamentations is usually read on Tisha b'Av, a holiday mourning the destruction of both

Hebrew temples (Lewis, 1975, 45).

The compilation and codification of the Mishna[3] could also be considered an important example of Jewish response to and commemoration of national tragedy – the destruction of Jerusalem and the Second Temple in 70 CE by the Romans. During the siege, thousands of Jews were killed, and many thousands taken as slaves.[4] It was the total and final loss of Jewish sovereignty, and the destruction of the Temple, the centre of the Hebrew religion. After the sack of Jerusalem, Rabbi Yochanan ben Zakkai obtained permission from the Roman commander Vespasian to establish a rabbinical school in Yabneh. The college at Yabneh became Judaism's 'fortress against oblivion' after the destruction of the 'most pivotal of all Jewish places of memory' – the Jewish Temple. At Yabneh, 'tradition was salvaged, studied, and recast' in written form, so that it could be preserved for posterity (Yerushalmi, 1996, 11). Sigmund Freud expressed the significance of this event best in a message to his daughter in 1938, in which he wrote:

> The political misfortune of the [Jewish] nation taught them to appreciate the only possession they had retained, their Scripture, at its true value. Immediately after the destruction of the Temple by Titus, Rabbi Yochanan ben Zakkai asked for permission to open at Yabneh the first school for the study of the *Torah*. From now on it was the Holy Book and the intellectual effort applied to it that kept the people together.   Yerushalmi, 1996, 11

Yabneh marks an important turning point in the development of Judaism, and an emphasis on the written word as a form of preserving and commemorating communal loss and traditions. In fact, the Mishna contains an entire section that recounts detailed rituals and rites performed in the destroyed Temple. It was, as Freud suggested, a means of preserving the holy Temple, which had been the centre of Hebrew faith, in text.

The Jewish tradition of commemorating loss in text re-emerges with *Memorbücher* and Yizkor books. During Europe's Middle Ages, Ashkenazic communities compiled *Memorbücher* with the intention of preserving the names of famous rabbis and communal leaders, as well as to produce 'records of persecution and lists of martyrs to be read aloud periodically in the synagogue during the memorial services for the dead' (Yerushalmi, 1996, 45). The most famous of these texts is Isaac ben Samuel of Meiningen's Nuremberg *Memorbuch*, which was started in 1296.[5] The Yizkor books of the 20th century, in turn, are considered a revival or extension of the medieval tradition of *Memorbücher*. Yizkor books are compilations of material related to the history of a particular Jewish community in Eastern Europe destroyed during the Holocaust. Although Yizkor books take their name from the

Jewish memorial service for the dead, these books also fulfil a secular purpose, and they are mainly used outside a liturgical context.

The story of Yizkor books began immediately following the Second World War as Jewish survivors gathered in displaced persons' camps, primarily in Germany, where they waited to emigrate to Israel or to other destinations, such as the US, Canada or South America. While in these camps, survivors compiled Yizkor books to commemorate their lost communities. The work was done while memory was fresh, with few resources, and with the knowledge that the survivor communities in the Displaced Persons (DP) camps would soon be scattered around the globe in their new countries of residence. Once survivors settled in their new homes, the task of memory work continued. As in the DP camps, survivors from a particular town or *shtetl* formed networks and mutual aid organizations, known as *landsmanshaftn* (home town associations). These *landsmanshaftn* provided emigration aid and organized efforts to commemorate the murdered relatives and inhabitants of their former towns. These efforts took many forms, from erecting communal tombstones at local cemeteries to planting memorial forests in Israel. Another important component of this memorial work was the production of Yizkor books. These books were private publications, printed in limited presses in Hebrew or Yiddish, and primarily intended for use by members of the *landsmanshaftn* and their families. In many ways, these Yizkor books were meant to serve as virtual communal tombstones in book form for relatives lost in the Shoah, many of whom had neither proper Jewish burials nor headstones. And, as with the sacred scriptures, the Mishna and the Torah, and unlike a physical tombstone, Yizkor books were portable. But they were much more than simple memorial markers. The books include not only lists of those killed during the Holocaust, but also complete documentation of a town's history, a recreation 'on paper of the community of the past' (Kugelmass and Boyarin, 1998, 10).

There are hundreds of Yizkor books. YIVO Institute for Jewish Research's library alone has more than 750 books in its collection. They vary greatly in scope, content and organization. Yet, despite their variety, most Yizkor books share the following elements:

- A complete history of the Jewish community in a given town or region;
- Personal recollections of events and personalities before the War, often accompanied by photos;
- Eye witness accounts of life in the ghettos, deportations and mass murders;
- A list of all the townspeople who were annihilated, intended to serve as a tombstone for people whose final burial place is unknown.

YIVO, n.d.

Yizkor books is a collective effort from the bottom up, a model of what one could call grassroots commemoration and documentation. Usually, *landsmanshaftn*, once they had decided to embark on this effort, would send out a bulletin to their members asking for assistance. For instance, in 1963, the Ostrolenka *landsmanshaft* sent a request to its members for all means of documentation, including 'photographs, documents, newspapers, periodicals, proclamations, announcements, letters, descriptions, etc.' about any of the following topics: '1) A history of Ostrolenka . . . 2) Ostrolenka its suburbs and surroundings . . . 3) Cultural and social life . . . 4) Personalities and types . . . 5) In Memoriam – pictures of our sainted departed . . . 6) The life of the survivors in the State of Israel and in the Diaspora' (Kugelmass and Boyarin, 1998, 9).

Figure 9.1

The shul (synagogue) in Czestochowa, Poland, before its destruction by the Nazis (source: Waga, 1949)

The editors of Ostrolenka's Yizkor book took this body of evidence, reproduced it for publication, and arranged it accordingly. The original documents were then returned to the contributors 'in good condition' (Kugelmass and Boyarin, 1998, 9), as the bulletin had promised. Thus, for a brief time, the editors had gathered together a provisional communal archive for a community that no longer existed. Then, after their editorial work was complete, this archive of this Jewish community, comprising perhaps some of the last traces of Ostrolenka and of the lives of its inhabitants, was dismantled and returned to its owners. This was an understandable conclusion to a project of this kind, considering that in many cases these photographs and documents were the last remnants of these survivors' families, and surely most were reluctant to part with them permanently.

Holocaust testimonies: a new medium

The testimonies held at the Fortunoff Video Archive for Holocaust Testimonies (FVAHT) in many ways built on the legacy of Yizkor books. Both Yizkor books and testimonies are products of survivor communities, and they both share many of the same goals. But whereas Yizkor books were conceived to tell the story of a town, *shtetl*, or Jewish community collectively, through the narratives of individuals who lived there, video testimonies focus exclusively on one individual's life story and experiences. For the most part, as with Yizkor books, these are the stories that may never have been heard outside the family or community. Survivors that choose to give such testimony are often 'common' people who would never publish a memoir. They are individuals whose life stories, more real and compelling than any film, will never become the basis for a screenplay. Moreover, like the Yizkor books, these survivors' testimonies were primarily produced by and for the individuals themselves, their families and their communities, although they also have enormous value as primary sources for researchers from a wide range of disciplines.

Although such testimonies capture one individual's story, when viewed in their entirety as a corpus, they do also tell the stories of entire communities. Thus, in an abstract sense, they have the potential to be used as building blocks for the creation of audiovisual Yizkor books. All that is required is a researcher, who collocates testimonies from a particular town and compiles the material. In fact, researchers do something very similar when they search through the FVAHT's catalogue records in Yale's online public access database (www.library.yale.edu/). Every testimony is represented in the catalogue by bibliographic records that contain a brief 200-word summary of the testimony, as well as dozens of topical and geographic Library of Congress headings assigned to it by the FVAHT's cataloguers. Researchers can conduct keyword searches to locate testimonies related to particular places, such as villages or concentration camps, descriptive categories such as the age and gender of the speaker, and the language of the testimony, interactions with historical figures, or specific experiences, such as fighting in the resistance, or the psychological effects of life in the camps. By searching in the catalogue, researchers can collocate testimonies with shared qualities, and in doing so create a virtual audiovisual 'collection' of evidence for use in their research. For example, a researcher interested in viewing testimonies that describe life in the Polish town of Łódź before, during and after the war could develop search strategies with the help of the archivist to locate those testimonies in the online catalogue.

One important difference between these video testimonies and the Yizkor books is that testimonies do not have editors. The FVAHT's testimonies are unedited and in some ways loosely structured. There are no set questions, and survivors can speak as long as they like. The concept is to provide a free space where survivors feel comfortable telling their stories the way they want, with as little outside intervention as possible. Interviewers are there to serve as empathic listeners, and to help locate the survivor in time and place, if necessary, but not to steer the taping. Experience has shown that if survivors are allowed this free space to recount their experiences as they choose, more of the individual's overall experiences are revealed in the end. Memory works in peculiar ways, and people do not necessarily remember events in strict chronological order. A memory of a place or moment in time can trigger another memory, and so forth. The result is often a complex, non-linear audiovisual document.

At the beginning of a testimony, interviewers ask the survivor to state his or her name, date and place of birth, and then to recount their life story from their earliest memories up until the present. As they do so, as with the Yizkor books, a full picture of life before, during and after the war can emerge. Obviously, this sets the FVAHT's testimonies apart from many similar projects, particularly from oral history projects that are designed to examine a specific historical issue, as they often employ a set of predetermined questions, and are carried out within defined time limitations. These video testimonies, by contrast, are often recorded over several days, even months, and may vary in length from less than one hour to over 30 hours. They are then processed and catalogued in their unedited form. The archive's obligation is to catalogue, manage, provide access to and preserve the unedited testimony as *the* document. It is the researchers who will make their own 'editorial decisions' when they select excerpts and quotes from these recordings for use in their research.

Despite the lack of an editor, video testimonies share a great deal in common with Yizkor books in terms of content. Like Yizkor books, these individuals describe various aspects of their town's history. There are vignettes of daily life, of interactions between various groups, both within the Jewish community as well as between Jews and non-Jews. Survivor testimonies provide illuminating descriptions and anecdotes about members of the Jewish community, such as rabbis, butchers, local characters, neighbours and friends. These testimonies, like the personal accounts contained in the published Yizkor books, often preserve information that may never be found in any other source. They are unique, personal documents. Moreover, during the recordings, survivors frequently show photographs and documents relevant to their life stories, and the stories of their towns. These items, and the context that the survivors provide for them, are similar in nature to the visual materials reproduced in most Yizkor books. And, like most of the ad hoc organizations established to compile and publish Yizkor books, the video archive usually does not retain the original documents, but reproduces or captures them for its purposes – in this case as on-screen images that are part of the video recording. Finally, as with Yizkor books, these individuals often provide a necrology of their family members, friends and neighbours who were killed during the war. Unlike the pages in Yizkor books with their well ordered lists of names, the necrology sections of a video testimony are spoken, spontaneous and often have ambiguous boundaries, since murdered relatives may be discussed at different points throughout the testimony.

Whereas the content and purpose of Yizkor books and video testimonies of survivors are very similar, the technology differs dramatically. Yizkor books, for the most part a product of the immediate postwar period, employ a traditional means of recording and disseminating information – the codex. Printing a book was also the most logical and relatively inexpensive medium available at that time. The FVAHT, on the other hand, was born in the late 1970s, and to a certain extent it reflects the most prevalent media of the day, television and film. Indeed, many see the FVAHT as a reaction to one particularly important media event: the television broadcast of *Holocaust*, starring Meryl Streep, which aired in 1978 on NBC, and was later broadcast to millions more around the world. Although this was hardly the sole impetus behind the creation of the FVAHT,[6] it was an event that evoked strong, mixed reactions from survivors. Many survivors felt it was an unrealistic, Hollywood-style portrayal of the Holocaust that failed to capture the variety and authenticity of actual events as they had experienced them. Survivors sought a means of telling their own stories – to provide a counter-narrative to what they feared could become *the* official narrative of the Holocaust in the public's imagination.

This is perhaps one explanation of why the FVAHT's precursor organiz- ation, the Holocaust Survivors Film Project (HSFP), embraced video as its medium. Furthermore, one of the founders of HSFP, Laurel Vlock, worked in television, and was familiar with the use of video and video production. But in this context it is also important to recognize that the founders of the archive saw video, a relatively new medium, as a way of 'fighting fire with fire'. The choice of an audiovisual medium was the recognition of an important change in society and how it consumed information – that is the rapid drift from the written word to audiovisual representations. Moreover, video had become a less expensive and more readily available alternative to film, and with Vlock's knowledge of television production, it proved to be the best technological medium to accomplish the project's original goals – capturing, disseminating and commemorating the stories of a local survivor population. Like the publication of Yizkor books before them, the choice of video for recording these testimonies was both a practical decision, as well as a choice that reflected the importance and pervasiveness of a new medium.

As we will see, the development of this type of grassroots documentation continues, building on new media and technology. In the 1990s survivors of the Bosnian genocide created similar bodies of documentation, but this time they employed the popular medium of the time, the internet.

Bosnian refugee weblogs

In the last decade of the 20th century, just as the cold war came to an unexpectedly peaceful end, a series of wars engulfed the former Yugoslavia. The bloodiest of these conflicts was the 1992–5 war in Bosnia-Herzegovina. It led to the deaths of over 100,000 people and the 'ethnic cleansing' of millions more, singled out for persecution, dispossession and exile because of their ethnic and religious identity. Half a century after the Holocaust ended, genocide had returned to Europe (Riedlmeyer, 2001; International Court of Justice, 2007).

More than half of Bosnia's population of four million was turned into refugees. Many were forced to flee the country. By the time the war ended in December 1995, some 1.5 million Bosnian refugees had been scattered across Europe, North America, Australia and other parts of the world. Like their counterparts in the Displaced Persons camps 50 years earlier, these survivors of the Bosnian genocide responded to the multiple traumas of war, exile and loss by trying to locate fellow refugees from the home towns and villages they had been forced to leave behind. In addition to looking for lost friends and neighbours, they were also trying to establish who had died and who was still unaccounted for, to share information about what had happened, and to try to reforge some of the broken bonds of community.

Even before the war ended, formal and informal associations of exiled Bosnian survivors began to compile this kind of documentation systematically. A number of these projects have resulted in the publication of printed books. One such memorial book was published in 2000, by an association of refugees from the eastern Bosnian town of Zvornik (Hudović, 2000). On the eve of the war in 1991 the municipality of Zvornik had been home to 81,000 residents, three-fifths of them (48,102) Bosnian Muslims. In the spring of 1992 Zvornik was overrun by Serb nationalist militiamen, who blew up the town's mosques, killed hundreds of Muslim residents and expelled the rest. By the following year, Zvornik's new Serb mayor, Branko Grujić, was telling reporters that 'the demographics are different now' – only five Bosnian Muslims were left in Zvornik (International Court of Justice, 2007).

The years of the Bosnian war also coincided with another development: the birth of a new form of communication, the world wide web. Almost from the beginning, Bosnian refugees made use of the internet, communicating via e-mail newsletters (such as BosNet, founded in 1993 by a group of young Bosnians in the US, first as a bitnet list and later as a web-based listserve), as well as through a growing number of home-town websites.

These websites have served not only as online, 'virtual memorial books' commemorating lost home towns, relatives and neighbours, but also as a dynamic means of compiling, exchanging and disseminating information among the scattered survivors – a virtual community. Like the memorial books issued by Armenian and Jewish survivors in earlier decades, many of these Bosnian memorial books and websites share certain features in common:

• Most of these are collective undertakings, sponsored by a group of Bosnian refugees who hail from a particular town or village in Bosnia.

- They usually include a history of that community, concluding with an account of its tragic fate in the 1992–5 war.
- A necrology, a list of all the people from the community who died or disappeared during the war, often accompanied by photographs and other data, is a feature of both printed and online Bosnian memorial books.
- Many include collections of photographs showing people, places and events in the community as they were before the war, along with hand-drawn 'memory maps' and sketches of the lost home town, its houses and landmarks.[7]
- Information, photos and other documentation posted on these sites often consists of material contributed by members of the group, but some of it may be copied (with or without indication of the source) from other websites, or from printed publications, postcards and ephemera. The content is not fixed, but tends to be dynamic and constantly evolving as new items are introduced, as information is added to items already posted (for example, as site visitors post comments and identifying information for persons and events in old photos), as sites are redesigned or change webmasters. Some of these sites are not maintained and eventually disappear from the web, but others become institutionalized, with many active members.
- Most Bosnian refugee websites also feature an *adresar* – a directory listing the current locations and e-mail addresses of fellow survivors from that community, now scattered across the globe – as well as interactive forums, where members can share and discuss not only stories about the old days and the war, but also news and information about the present.

Over time, many of these websites have become more elaborate, as members started posting photographs and accounts of their first tentative visits to their former homes in Bosnia, as they debated the prospects for return and rebuilding, and as they began to use the website as a base for communal projects, such as raising funds for the reconstruction of a school or a mosque back in the home village.

Thus the memorial website has become not only a place of commemoration, but also an active link between the diaspora and the village back in Bosnia. At the same time, it has also become a 'virtual village', where the dispersed members of a diaspora community can come together to share news and gossip. Many websites now regularly feature reports on diaspora events, such as engagements, weddings, funerals and holiday celebrations, as well as annual picnics and get-togethers organized by former residents of a Bosnian village who over the past 15–20 years have built new lives in Scandinavia, North America or Australia.

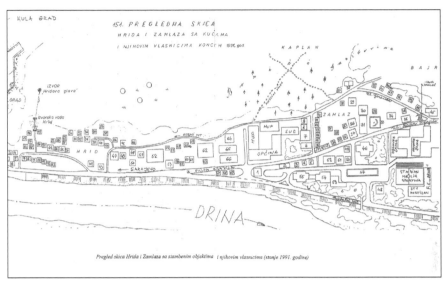

Figure 9.2 'Memory map' of a formerly Bosnia Muslim-majority neighbourhood in the town of Zvornik, hand-drawn by a former resident, now a refugee; the numbers on the houses are keyed to the names of the families that lived in them before the war; the crescent and star mark the mosque, blown up in 1992 (source: Hudović, 2000)

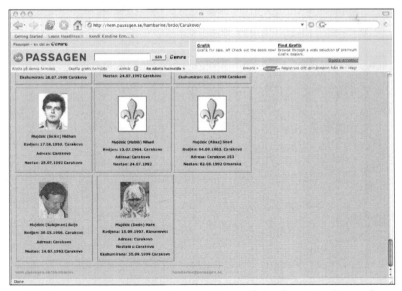

Figure 9.3 Memorial webpage, listing residents of the Bosnian village of Čarakovo still missing from the 1992–5 war (source: http://hem.passagen.se/hambarine/brdo/carakovo.htm)

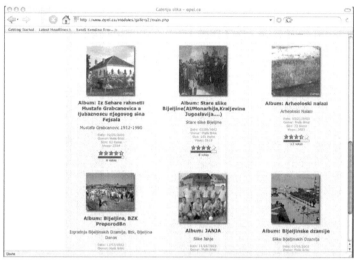

Figure 9.4 A page from a home-town website created by Bosnian Muslim refugees from the town of Bijeljina, with collections of photos (galerije) showing the town and its people before and after the 1992–3 'ethnic cleansing' drove most of its 30,000 Muslim residents into exile (source: www.opel.ca)

Figure 9.5 Excerpt from an online directory (adresar) showing the e-mail addresses and locations of exiled Muslim former residents of the northwest Bosnian town of Bosanski Novi, now living as refugees in St Louis, Mo.; Tromsø, Norway; Seattle, Wa.; and Zizers, Switzerland (source: www.bosanskinovi.com)

One example of such an online memorial is a relatively simple website, based in Sweden, maintained by Bosnian refugees from the village of Čarakovo, near Prijedor: http://hem.passagen.se/hambarine/brdo/carakovo.htm. The home page opens with a note thanking all those who have helped, or will help by contributing photos and information to the site. One of the links at the top of the page points to a text describing the village and its recent history. Another points to a page of pictures (*slike*) showing the village and its people both before and after the 1992–5 war. Some of the photos show former village residents returning from abroad, for events such as the annual memorial prayers held for the villagers who died or disappeared during the war (*dan šehida* means day of the martyrs), held each year in the third week of July, the anniversary of the week the village was overrun by Serb forces in 1992.[8] The middle link atop the Čarakovo home page is entitled 'the missing' (*nestali*). It leads to a series of pages of names and photographs, arranged alphabetically, recording the people from the village who were recorded as missing at the end of the war. For each missing person, the information below the photo gives the name, father's name, last known address, the date and place where the person was last seen alive (whether in the village, or in one of several Serb-run concentration camps in the area), and if the body has since been found and identified, the date and place where it was exhumed.

A more elaborate memorial website is the one for the small town of Bosanski Novi, in northwestern Bosnia (www.bosanskinovi.com). This is a site that has progressively grown since it first appeared on the web in February 2003. Its current version shows excellent web-design skills, featuring interactive maps, and an elaborate section for news (*vijesti*), featuring events such as:

- a May 2008 reunion of Bosnian refugees from Bosanski Novi in St Louis, Missouri
- erection of a monument in Bosanski Novi commemorating the missing
- a daring jewellery-store robbery in Bosanski Novi on 9 May 2008.

Also on the top menu bar are profiles of noteworthy people from Bosanski Novi (*Novljani*); an elaborate section of texts and images on the town's history (*istorija*); image galleries (*galerija*) including prewar and postwar photos of Bosanski Novi; a bulletin board, with items such as appeals for assistance; appeals for help in locating people from Bosanski Novi; want-ads for buying and selling goods and real estate; announcements of new births, engagements, marriages and deaths at home and in the diaspora; a section on sports; a section on the municipal government of Bosanski Novi, in which a Bosnian Muslim returnee recently got elected vice-mayor; and a contact page (*kontakt*). Earlier versions of the site can be found in the Internet Archive (www.archive.org). From the beginning, it featured an address directory (*adresar*) with e-mail addresses and locations for former Bosanski Novi residents who now live dispersed across four continents as a result of the war.

There are scores of websites such as these, some more ambitious than others, each representing the memory of a Bosnian community shattered by war and genocide, as well as its will to endure. Unfortunately, there is no central registry – one has to find them one by one, through trial and error, and by following web links. While these sites are deeply meaningful for the individuals and groups that create them, and an invaluable tool for research, in practice they can also be frustratingly elusive. Many websites turn out to be short-lived, as key individuals in the project that created the site move on, return to Bosnia, no longer maintain them, or fail to renew their accounts with the ISP that hosts the site. Sites optimized for older browsers that are no longer supported may have features that have ceased to work, or multiple broken links. The websites that remain active also keep on changing and evolving; tracking the additions and deletions to the site's content can be difficult. The Internet Archive's web crawlers visit each site just a few times a year. When they do, they often capture only the site's 'top layer'. If images are embedded in the top page, they may be archived; if they are linked from other parts of the server, all one might see in the archived version are broken icons. After years of experience, librarians and archivists have developed well-established protocols for preserving works on paper. But the standards for archiving and preserving material in these new media are still evolving.

Conclusion

These forms of commemoration pose new challenges to librarians and archivists who intuitively understand their importance as resources for scholarly and community research. One of the greatest challenges, particularly with modern media and formats such as video testimony and websites, is their 'physical' preservation. Unlike most books and documents, materials in these new formats are inherently unstable. In the case of video testimonies, this is a result of 'inherent vice' and technological obsolescence. In the case of video, the cause of this inherent vice is often the videotape binder. The binder is added to the magnetic coating to keep the magnetic particles attached to the basefilm. It is this magnetic coating that contains the recorded information. If that binder deteriorates, the recording can be damaged or lost entirely. Unlike many collections of video materials, the FVAHT's tapes have been housed under ideal climate conditions. But the spectre of technological obsolescence is even more menacing. The archive consists of thousands of three-quarter-inch U–Matic tapes recorded as early as 1979. U–Matic was once a video broadcast standard, but it is now obsolete. There is a finite number of playback decks in existence. At some point, we simply will no longer be able to cobble together video machines to play these tapes anymore. Digitization is clearly the only solution to ensure long-term preservation of these testimonies. But digitization, while solving some problems, creates new challenges. For instance: which of the dozens of digital video file formats is the right one? How can we be sure that these files will remain accessible to users decades from now? What are the costs and risks of digital storage? And what will be required to maintain and migrate these files moving forward? In many cases, there is still no consensus on the answers to some of these questions. There are many institutions and organizations dedicated to advancing the preservation of audiovisual archives, and they are making progress, and standards are emerging. But the clock for legacy video is ticking, and funding for these projects, which are generally very expensive and time consuming, is tight.[9]

With the Bosnian weblogs, the dangers are more related to the ephemeral nature of websites and internet providers and the dynamics of their creation and maintenance over time. Another challenge to librarians and archivists is how to treat these collective documents, which do not neatly fit into our traditional categories of primary and secondary materials. Often, they are a confluence of various primary and secondary materials, many of them unique or ephemeral, compiled from multiple sources for the production of these works, and then returned to the original owners. As a result, in many cases, these projects preserve the only known copies of documentation that may no longer exist, or has been scattered to the four corners of the earth. In a sense, these weblogs, like the Yizkor books, represent the virtual communal archives of survivor communities, brought together to build a metaphysical archive, memorial, and virtual reconstruction of a village or town and of life stories now lost, and as a dynamic means of preserving the bonds of a community dispersed by 'ethnic cleansing'. How do we as information professionals deal with such materials, which are not archival documents in the traditional sense, but something else, equally important? Certainly, their informational and historical value warrant a serious debate, and, more importantly, immediate action to prevent these ephemeral cultural materials from vanishing forever.

Notes

1   The title of D. P. Boder's work, *I Did Not Interview the Dead*, published in 1949, echoes Antonean's words.

2   More than 125 Armenian memorial books (called *hishatakaran*, derived from the classical Armenian root for memory, '*hush*') were published by home-town associations of exiled survivors of the 1915-16 genocide; for further discussion and bibliography, see Slyomovics (1998), 2-5, 222-3. Among the few that have been translated into English is M. Dzeron, *Village of Parchanj: general history*, Fresno, 1984, first published in Armenian in Boston, 1938.

3   The Mishna, or *Torah be-Peh*, is the oral law given on Mt Sinai and passed down from Moses to Joshua, from Joshua to the Elders, and so on. It is not a commentary on the Bible per se, but rather a separate, related code of laws.

4   In his chronicle *The War of the Jews*, the first-century Jewish historian Josephus puts the number of casualties at close to one million.

5   New York Public Library's Dorot Jewish Division refers to Isaac ben Samuel of Meiningen's Memorbuch as the first Yizkor book, and the model for subsequent books. See www.nypl.org/research/chss/jws/aboutyizkor.html.

6   The confluence of reasons and events resulting in the founding of the FVAHT are too complex to explore in this article; for more information visit www.library.yale.edu/testimonies/ and www.library.yale.edu/testimonies/about/Local_to_global.pdf.

7   For the use of 'memory maps' and sketches in Armenian, Jewish and Palestinian Arab memorial books, see S. Slyomovics, 1998, 7-9, and 224 n. 24.

8   For the fate of Čarakovo and the Prijedor region during the war, see: Helsinki Watch, 1993, 81-2; and I. Wesselingh and A. Vaulerin, 2005.

9   A more in-depth discussion of these challenges, while essential, goes far beyond the scope of this article. For more information on audiovisual preservation and the challenges of maintaining digital collections, see http://prestospace.org/ and www.digitalpreservation.gov/.

References

Antonean, A. (1921) *Mets ochire: Haykakan verjin kotoratsnere Taleat Pasha: Pashtonakan heragirner bnagimeru storagruteanbew baznatiw patkernerov*, Tparan Pahaki.

Boder, D. P. (1949) *I Did Not Interview the Dead*, University of Illinois Press.

Helsinki Watch (1993) *War Crimes in Bosnia-Hercegovina*, vol. 2, Human Rights Watch, 81-2.

Hudović, M. (2000) *Zvornik: slike i bilješke iz prošlosti* [Zvornik: pictures and notes from the past], Udruženje Gradjana Opštine Zvornik.

International Court of Justice (2006) *Application of the Convention on the Prevention and Punishment of the Crime of Genocide (Bosnia and Herzegovina v. Serbia and Montenegro)*, public sitting, 1 March, www.icj-cij.org/docket/files/91/10493.pdf.

International Court of Justice (2007) *Application of the Convention on the Prevention and*

Punishment of the Crime of Genocide (Bosnia and Herzegovina v. Serbia and Montenegro), judgment, 26 February,
www.icj-cij.org/docket/files/91/13685.pdf.

Kugelmass, J. and Boyarin, J. (1998) *From a Ruined Garden: the memorial books of Polish Jewry*, Indiana University Press.

Lewis, B. (1975) *History: remembered, recovered, invented*, Princeton University Press.

Riedlmayer, A. (2001) Convivencia under Fire: book-burning and genocide in Bosnia. In Rose, J. (ed.), *The Holocaust and the Book: destruction and preservation*, University of Massachusetts Press, 266-91.

Slyomovics, S. (1998) *The Object of Memory: Arab and Jew narrate the Palestinian village*, University of Pennsylvania Press.

Waga, S. (1949) *Hurbn Tshenstochov*, Buenos Aires, Tsentral-farband fun Poylishe Yidn in Argentine.

Wesselingh, I. and Vaulerin, A.(2005) *Prijedor: laboratory of ethnic cleansing*, Saqi Books.

Yerushalmi, Y. H. (1996) *Zakhor: Jewish history and Jewish memory*, University of Washington Press.

YIVO Institute for Jewish Research (n.d.) Introduction to Yizkor Books: about holocaust memorial books,
www.yivoinstitute.org/library/index.php?tid=46&aid=254.

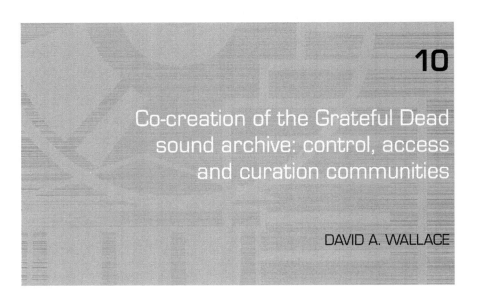

10

Co-creation of the Grateful Dead sound archive: control, access and curation communities

DAVID A. WALLACE

A lot of what we are selling is community. That is our main product . . .
Band lyricist John Perry Barlow, quoted in McNally, 2002, 386

Introduction[1]

The Grateful Dead[2] ('Dead') represents a 30-year travelling experiment in improvisational music and audience-band co-creation. Between 1965 and 1995 the band performed over 36,000 songs during 2317 concerts in nearly 300 cities. Beyond band member commitment, the Dead's longevity and yield also resulted from the loyalty of an ever-expanding base of supporters ('Deadheads') who symbiotically fuelled the band's renowned creative process. Hand in glove with this performative arc was the creation of 'two' complementary archives of enormous size, scope and distribution: the band's official recordings, and a much larger body of permitted *and* illicit in-concert audience recordings. Over the decades the band was forced to evolve its position on audience recordings. Initial disinterest and hostility gave way to a tentative acceptance, and finally to the sanctioning of an 'Official Taper's Section' (OTS) in 1984.

Early audience recordings were made on reel-to-reel tapes and traded hand-to-hand and through the postal system. These humble beginnings sparked ever-expanding systems of reproduction through sharing that occurred alongside the shift from analogue to digital to network technologies.

All contributed to an aggregated-disaggregated taper and trader community that was in full flourish when the band disintegrated in 1995 with the death of co-founder Jerry Garcia. The rise of the internet and the world wide web caused and continues to cause seismic shifts in the scale, availability, reproduction and curation of the band's formal and informal sound archive. Nearly 15 years after the band's demise, the ongoing voluntary efforts of the taping and trading community ensure unprecedented access to performances and their metadata.

This chapter charts the history and continuing evolution of the taping and trading community, now in its fifth decade. It briefly describes the band's performance philosophy and the taping and trading sub-culture it triggered within the broader Deadhead community. A discussion of the band's institutional audio recording and archiving is followed by a more detailed analysis of the taping and trading community and its practices. This leads to an examination of the revolutionary impact of the internet and the world wide web on trading, documentation and curation. The chapter closes with a consideration of this case study's lessons regarding the value of non-commercialized sharing and co-operation and alternative intellectual property configurations. At its core the co-creation and curation of the band's official archive and the audience-taped corpuses represents a story of conflict, innovation and creative co-operation among intersecting interests within the larger Grateful Dead community.

The Grateful Dead and Deadhead taping and trading sub-cultures

The Dead evolved their musical-philosophical approach to performance and audience connection at the coalface of nine 'Acid Tests' throughout 1966, when LSD was still mostly legal. Traditional distinctions between audience and performer were rendered quasi-invisible and replaced with formlessness and communal participation. While a more structured performer–audience approach would later emerge, concerts never fully lost this fundamental building block of joint production. Primacy was given to co-creation through improvisation and the continuous evolution of the music – keeping alive the potential for transcendence for both band and audience. To help achieve these ends, the band continuously innovated new technologies for amplified sound. A 1984 business meeting green-lighted a projected $1 million research project for a digital system that could be adjusted to any performance space. The band's organization also reviewed venue engineering drawings and would use a transit to determine optimal equipment layout to ensure the best possible aural experience for the audience (Shenk and Silberman, 1994, 4–5,

305–6; Getz and Dwork, 1998, 38; Getz and Dwork, 2000, 19; McNally, 2000, 171; McNally, 2002, 58; Selvin 2007).

These commitments were always motivated towards the integrity of the music and elevating the shared 'experience' between the band and the audience. Able to draw upon a corpus of over 100 songs, the band created a unique experience with each performance. Official biographer Dennis McNally called this band-audience collaboration a form of 'communication . . . that constitute[d] a true communion' anchored in Carl Jung's concept of synchronicity. For bassist Lesh, it is 'hard to overemphasize the importance of the Deadheads . . . to the core values that made the music so unique. . . . The enthusiasm, openness, and, more important, the burning desire of our audience to be astonished . . . transported and transformed . . . was truly what closed the circuit to create the music.' An ironical elemental component of this communionism was an understanding and acceptance of inter-subjectivity over how the music was produced and received. Legitimacy of alternating perceptions and reactions was part of the system. Garcia himself noted in the mid-1970s that he could discern 'no relationship that I've ever been able to hear on tapes between the way I feel and the way it went down . . . Doesn't matter how I feel . . . I haven't been able to *hear it matter*' (McNally, 2000, 386–8, 619; Grateful Dead Productions, 2004; Lesh, 2005, 265).

In 1971 the band initiated a communications channel with the burgeoning Deadhead community via an album insert that read: 'Dead freaks unite. Who are you? Where are you? How are you? Send us your name and address and we'll keep you informed.' By 1980 this invitation generated a mailing list of over 90,000 names. By the early 1990s it contained over 200,000 names (Shenk and Silberman, 1994, 57; McNally, 2000, 606). Deadheads have largely been characterized by popular culture as throw-back hippies pining for a time past. In actuality, they are drawn from a much greater cross-section of US society:

> Left-of-center, white middle-aged professionals, young working-class Americans, strait-laced students, preppies, yuppies, some elderly citizens, and, often, dozens of children. [They] hold responsible positions in law, medicine, computer science, education, and other highly skilled fields. Stockbrokers, salesmen, entrepreneurs, actors, writers, artists, carpenters, craftspeople, and cab drivers . . . [All constitute the Deadhead community].
>
> Trager, 1997, 86

While Sutton (2000, 125) hypothesizes that the Deadhead community maintains characteristics of a 'nontraditional religious community' such as creed, codes and rituals that has helped it to survive and thrive even beyond the band's existence, it must ultimately be understood as an American cultural phenomenon. As highlighted by Ritzer (2000, 261) the Dead were simply a 'rock 'n' roll band that became wildly successful working within the capitalist system' where Deadheads were somewhat 'bound by conventions, economic and social, of the dominant society'. But Deadhead culture also offered 'oppositional meanings' to the prerogatives of the dominant culture, mainly through communitarianism, drug use and the non-commercial sharing of the music. Elements of Deadhead culture and its oppositionalist tendencies hark back to forms of 'collective joy' amply documented throughout human history by Ehrenreich (2005).

And it was the tapers who produced the 'sacred talismans' that circulated into the wider Deadhead community that helped bind it together (McNally, 2002, 385). As indicated by Marshall (2003, 61–2), tapers and traders helped the wider community develop the awareness of the music as an 'ongoing process' of creativity, which offered the possibility to produce and elaborate an environment outside the industry standard commodification model of production and consumption. They offered the opportunity for Deadheads to 'document their participation in mass cultural events on their own terms and for their own purposes . . . as a source of social memory and authenticity, and to mediate the events of their lives through means of technological reproduction'. The taping and trading community that evolved out of this context has made the Dead the most recorded and traded act in music history (Neuman and Simpson, 1997, 319, 323; Herman, 2005, 22).

The key philosophy driving practices within taping and trading networks was the proviso that no monetary exchange be associated with trades. Recording, copying, duplication and trading were always voluntary non-commercial efforts and were expected to be so. For-profit endeavours were taboo and in violation of the intellectual property rights that the band wished to retain. This 'trading ethos' was central to the practices of trading within networks of reproduction and central to the development and elaboration of the Deadhead community (Tanen, 1995; Pattacini, 2000, 7–8; Whitman, 2005, 27). Commenting on receiving his first Phish – a 'jam band' descendant of the Dead – concert recording on tape, Matranga perfectly captures the motivations and satisfactions of taping and trading:

> From the first moment that I received unpaid for music, I knew that I was acting in a larger context, one that I did not yet understand . . . . I knew that in my hands was something more than just music or a piece of plastic. There was a culture within this transaction, this practice, and this product. . . . I could listen to music in my home, free from the concert, but still fully able to reconnect with that moment of creation. This also meant that I had one person, sometimes a few people, to thank for that ability.   Matranga, 2002, 11

However, as noted by Belk (2007), while 'sharing can foster community', it is complex. The potentially shareable item can intersect with feelings of 'possessiveness and attachment', especially if the item is seen as part of our 'extended self'. The development of the taping and trading community reflected this paradox. While sharing was encouraged and expected, there were also hoarding and intense trading hierarchies controlling access to the best sources, creating, in the words of co-editors of the multi-volume *Deadhead's Taping Compendium*, John Dwork and Michael Getz, a 'moral grey zone' characterized by broken promises, misrepresentation, leaks and even outright theft. More commonly and positively, sharing opened up new social configurations around the music. It provided Deadheads with, in the words of Dwork, 'seemingly endless opportunities to engage in research, archiving, documentation, and communication with others' (Nash, 1988, 56; Getz and Dwork, 1998, xii–xiii, xiv; Belk, 2007, 126–7, 131, 135–6).

The Grateful Dead's institutional audio concert archives

The degree of intellectual and physical control the band was able to muster over its live performance corpus has evolved over time. This evolution witnessed shifts from the early years of informal management, to an era of an informal/formal archive susceptible to unauthorized massive leaking, to its current manifestation as a highly formalized and professionally run archive from which little, and more likely nothing, ever leaked again. However, the ease of duplication and evolving trading networks ensured that the band could never control dissemination of what had been leaked. By 2001 the *Deadhead's Taping Addendum* (Getz et al., 2001, 7) surmised that the taping and trading community circulate and curate copies of 'around 98%' of the contents of the band's vault.

During its formative years, 1965–7, the band lived communally and had meagre earnings. Very few performances survive from this period. Towards the end of the 1960s, supported by a rising, though shaky solvency, the band developed and continued a relatively strong commitment to record performances, primarily to evaluate and improve aesthetics and the aural experiences of the audience. While there are hints that a longer-term view was also a factor, that the recordings had some vague historical-ness, this appears to have been a tertiary factor at best. And while tapes from this era were labelled inconsistently and haphazardly cared for, recording of performances remained a serious commitment. Throughout the band's first decade, recording responsibilities shifted among various members of the road crew who also simultaneously managed other performance related tasks. As time went on the band became more diligent in recording and documenting the growing volume in a changing technological environment (from analogue magnetic tape until 1982 to fully digital with DAT by 1987) (Getz and Dwork, 1998, 8–9, 16–18, 40, 43, 44; Getz and Dwork, 1999, 18, 24–5; Getz, Dwork and Dyke, 2001, 286–7; Wild, 2001, 30; Gans, 2002, 117, 327, 332; Lesh, 2005, 174; Jackson, 2006, 3, 9).

As a consequence of lax custodianship and inattentive recording, the band's institutional sound archive is by no means comprehensive. Missing are most of 1966–7, the vast majority of 1968, almost all of June 1970 through February 1971, and a small portion of 1972. For 1976–8 36% of shows are missing and for 1979–82 60% are missing. The last significant gap is 1987, with 70% missing. The remaining years, 1988–95, are comprehensive. Despite these absences the vault still contains well over 10,000 tapes documenting the band across three decades. And remarkably, as noted in 1988 by then-band archivist Dick Latvala, 'things surface all the time' both from inside the Dead organization and outside it. This phenomenon continues up to the present day, making the story of the Dead's official audio archive open-ended (Dick's Picks FAQ, n.d.; Getz and Dwork, 1998, 17, 48; Cobb, 2001).

A semi-formalized tape vault was located at the band's Front Street studio in San Rafael, California, from the mid-1970s until the early 1990s. It was initially overseen by Willy Legate, the studio's superintendent and maintenance manager. In 1985 Latvala was appointed as keeper of the vault. A long time Deadhead who had seen his first shows in January 1966, Latvala had been an avid tape trader from the early 1970s. His impact on the vault was transformational. He spent years assiduously listening to, cataloguing, documenting and preserving the vault's contents. These efforts enabled the band to increase commercial releases dramatically. These, however, paled in comparison to the volume of recordings he informally leaked into the taping and trading community. While the band seemed to be vaguely aware at the time that tapes were being leaked and that it was Latvala doing the leaking, they appear to have been unaware of the scope. During his 14-year tenure, until 1999, Latvala circulated substantial amounts of the vault's holdings into the trading community, revolutionizing the availability of high quality soundboard recordings. Throughout the band's career and beyond it, leaking from the vault and distribution of copies into the widening tape trading community was a persistent feature. Uncontrolled access to the vault, access to soundboard patches during performances, lax custodianship of masters during and after tours, gifting and even theft all contributed (Shenk and Silberman, 1994, 30; Getz and Dwork, 1998, 18, 45, 48, 51; Getz and Dwork, 1999, 16, 24–5, 64–7; Getz and Dwork, 2000, 41–3; Legate, 2000, 86; Getz, Dwork and Dyke, 2001, 229, 253–6, 282, 286–8, 292–5, 311, 317–18, 342–3; *Grateful Dead: The Illustrated Trip*, 2003, 307).

With Latvala's unexpected death in the summer of 1999, David Lemieux was tapped to be the new vault archivist. Lemieux came to the band as its first formally trained archivist, holding a master's degree in film archiving. Similar to Latvala, Lemieux was a long time Deadhead, albeit from the later 1980s–1990s generation. Ever since his appointment the vault has been tightly controlled to prevent additional unauthorized leaks. As of early 2009 Lemieux remains the Dead's sound archivist and he spends most of his time on commercial audio and video releases, hosts a daily satellite radio show – 'Today in Grateful Dead History' – on Sirius/XM's Grateful Dead Channel, and continues to make the music accessible through other official outlets (Getz and Dwork, 2000, 43; Cobb, 2001; Opening the Dead's Vault, 2004).

Towards the very end of their career the band moved to new office space in Novato, California, and constructed a tape vault compliant with professional standards for room temperature and relative humidity. The new facility also maintained a fire-suppression system, an alarmed security system, and thick five-layer walls. While the band entertained different distribution models over the years for making the vault available to Deadheads, including cassette mail orders and plans for full-scale digitization and downloading, none ever came to fruition. This absence was eventually overcome through the taping and trading community's harnessing of emergent internet and web-based technologies after 2000. In 2007 the band entered an agreement with Sirius satellite radio for a channel dedicated to recorded performances. And in 2006 surviving core band members entered into a ten-year licensing agreement with Rhino Entertainment that saw the vault's contents re-located to Burbank, California, for ongoing live performance commercial releases (Shenk and Silberman, 1994, 300; Getz, Dwork and Dyke, 2001, 253–4; Wild, 2001, 30; Jackson, 2006, 273; Libertore, 2006).

Taping: practices and community development

As previously noted, the efforts of tapers and traders offered the most meaningful connective tissue of the Deadhead community as a whole: captured performances. Over time the band evolved a 'legal loophole for tape-trading' by factoring it into their studio contracts. They also lent support to audience taping at venues hostile to the notion. This fragile legal and practice equilibrium enabled the band to survive as a corporation while remaining faithful to its values as an 'anti-establishment, countercultural musical group' (Whitman, 2005, 6).

There is ample evidence that band members were sympathetic to the philosophical motivations of audience tapers. In the early 1960s Weir would record entire performances of Jorma Kaukonen (later of Jefferson Airplane and Hot Tuna) in San Francisco area coffeehouses. Garcia's immersion in bluegrass at the same time saw him collecting and trading tapes of performances. In a 1993 interview Hart noted that he had been 'making remote recordings since 1967'. His involvement with the US Library of Congress's 'Endangered Music Project' has released indigenous music from Africa, The Caribbean, South America and Indonesia. Beyond decades-long affinity for personal taping, band members have also encouraged tapers at performances. At the Hollywood Palladium in August 1971, Weir and Lesh suggested to a taper close to the stage that he would have to move back about 40 feet to 'get a decent recording' (Weir), 'where it will [sound] a lot better' (Lesh) (Nash, 1988, 54; Greenfield, 1997, 37, 43; Trager, 1997, 168; Jackson, 1999, 61; *Grateful Dead: the illustrated trip*, 2003, 412).

In 1975 Garcia offered the following perspective on tapers and traders: 'If people like it they can certainly keep doing it. I don't have any desire to control people as to what they're doing and what they have. There's something to be said for being able to record an experience you've liked, or being able to obtain a recording of it . . . . My responsibility to the notes is over after I've played them. At that point I don't care where they go' (Jackson, 1999, 277).[3]

In his autobiography, Lesh (2005, 192) declared that permitting Deadhead taping and trading was the 'best decision we *never* made' (emphasis added): 'Every friend or sibling of a Deadhead that weaseled a copy of a favorite tape and passed it on was contributing to the growth of the community (and to the size of our audience)'. Band lyricist Barlow agrees, pointing to taping and trading as 'probably the single most important reason' for the band's popularity (McNally, 2002, 386).

The earliest documented undisputed audience recording was 15 September 1967. Db.etree.org, an authoritative source tracking known master recordings, identifies two audience recordings from that year, eight for 1968, and 16 for 1969. From 1970 onwards taping increased steadily and dramatically. This spiralling growth often resulted in acrimonious interactions between tapers and members of the band's organization. Restrictions on taping contracted with their record company, Warner Bros, in line with standard industry practice, probably drove the band's organization to make some effort at curtailing taping. By 1972 a sustained effort to stop tapers was reported under way. However, by 1974 mounting tensions and hassles associated with this strategy had grown so unbearable that the band appeared to have taken a decision to tolerate audience taping. In late October 1974 the band entered an 18-month hiatus from its demanding touring schedule. With their re-emergence in June 1976, they met an expanding taping community, encouraged by the circulation of performances through growing trading networks. It is believed that from June 1976 until the band's final performance in July 1995, an audience taper captured almost every single performance. Over these years the number of individual tapers increased continuously. This evolution was made possible in part by ongoing advances in field recording technologies: superior sound capture, miniaturization and cost reduction (Nash, 1988, 58; Shenk and Silberman, 1994, 278–9; Getz and Dwork, 1998, 33–5; Getz and Dwork, 1999, 35).

Beyond contending with the multifaceted responses from the band's organization and harvesting new technologies, tapers also developed and refined methods to smuggle their gear into venues and elude event security. These challenges were linked to additional ones such as access to a good tape deck and quality microphones, a microphone stand, tapes, batteries and cables; then getting tickets and, once successfully inside, locating and setting up in a prime spot sound-wise, then monitoring recording levels and equipment to capture the best possible recording (Nash, 1988, 56–7; Getz and Dwork, 1999, 35–6). Taper Les Kippel highlights the combined efforts Deadheads would undergo to succeed: '[O]ne person would bring in the tape machine and two people would bring in the microphones, a few people would bring the batteries and a few people bring in tapes. We'd sit in a cluster, and friends would always protect the person who was taping' (Getz and Dwork, 1998, 33).

In order to setup where the sound was best – the 'pit' or 'mouth' – tapers regularly established themselves in front of the soundboard (FOB). Taper Mike Yacavone noted that, by the early 1980s, the pit had become quite a 'scene . . . the intensity of the compulsive behavior about mic[rophone]s and cords and the space around the mic[rophone]s, and no talking and no clapping . . . . It was a whole different world . . . .Very male, somewhat macho' (Shenk and Silberman, 1994, 225–6).

The seeming truce between the band's crew and tapers was fragile and at times broke down completely. Bob Wagner recalled that: 'If [band sound engineer Dan] Healy saw people taping near the soundboard, he would run out into the crowd and cut their wires. I recall that as being a major turning point. . . . He'd always supported the taping scene' (Getz and Dwork, 1999, 54).

A 1984 band business meeting raised the issue of tapers. Recognizing the tapers' preference to be in the pit, they nevertheless entertained the prospect of 'set[ting] aside a section for them behind' the soundboard in consideration of others in the audience. Audience sight lines to the stage were being interfered with by the multiplying microphone stands and there was a rise in overly aggressive behaviour by *some* tapers. Under the guidance of Healy a decision was taken to launch an 'Official Taper's Section' (OTS) *behind* the soundboard. Tapers needed to purchase a special taper's ticket to use the

OTS. The OTS remained a staple of performances for the band's remaining 11 years (Nash, 1988, 59–60; McNally, 2002, 59; Lesh, 2005, 265–6).

An early taping section sign explained the new parameters: 'There will be a special taping section located behind the soundboard . . . . This will be the only place taping will be allowed and you must have a tapers ticket to tape. If you tape anywhere else you will be told to leave the concert . . . . Taping is for non-commercial home use only! Unauthorized duplication, distribution, broadcast or sale is forbidden!!! Absolutely no video equipment of any kind!!!' (reproduced in Getz and Dwork, 1999, 64).

The clause 'for non-commercial home use only!' was key to the Dead's ongoing tolerance of taping. The band's legal team spent enormous resources identifying and suing bootleggers who mass-produced and sold performance recordings. By and large, though, tapers honoured the band's request. In fact, well before the taping section was established, trading and non-commercialized distribution was the expected and standard norm – in effect the foundational ethos – of the taping and trading community (Hill and Rifkin, 1999, 44).

For many experienced tapers the OTS proved insufficient. They found it to be pressed with novices and, most importantly, the location of the OTS behind the soundboard could not match the sound quality available in the pit. This dynamic launched a new struggle over taping. Dougal Donaldson explains the rationale motivating FOB tapers who violated band policy: 'You needed to get the best recording possible, for posterity. That was the point . . . .To sit in the tapers' section and get a terrible recording wasn't even worth going to a show or trying to tape . . . . [T]o ghettoize all tapers like that was almost punishment' (Getz and Dwork, 1999, 56–7).

With the Dead's first commercially successful album – *In the Dark* in 1987 – a horde of new fans emerged who fundamentally reshaped the scale of the concert and taping experience. It has been estimated that, by the early 1990s, every set of microphones was patched into multiple decks and that there were roughly 100 hardcore tapers who captured almost all shows and roughly 20 who captured all of them (Shenk and Silberman, 1994, 278–9; Getz and Dwork, 2000, 46).

Digital recording entered the taping community sometime between 1982 and 1983. Initially costly and bulky, digital technologies quickly evolved with miniaturization and cost reduction and, despite their finickiness and upkeep, became widely employed by tapers. Digital technology captured a wider sound spectrum; digital tapes ran considerably longer than analogue cassettes; and digital recordings did not suffer from generational loss when copied. Tapers would continuously and rapidly adopt and adapt new technologies. At one point, noticing the band had switched to an in-ear monitor system, some started bringing scanners to record directly from individual band member mixes that reflected interior band dynamics (Getz and Dwork, 1999, 25, 58–9; Getz and Dwork, 2000, 50–1).

From bulky reel-to-reel decks to sophisticated compact digital recording setups costing over $10,000, tapers continuously contributed to the stream of available performances that surged into the ever-growing trading community, believed to be the 'largest co-operative taping network in the music world' (Jackson, 2000, 162–3).

Trading: practices and community development

As with taping, trading emerged from humble beginnings – face-to-face and through the postal system. And as with taping, trading grew in scale as a result of tremendous individual and co-operative efforts (in time, energy and money) designed to cultivate and develop the trading community.

The birth of the 'First Free Underground Grateful Dead Tape Exchange', the earliest formalized trading mechanism for performance recordings, was in 1971. At this time most collectors claimed barely one dozen recordings. Motivated principally by a desire to 'mobilize taping activity', this effort sought to increase the number of in-concert tapers and traders to ensure ever-widening circulation of newly captured performances. The tape exchange concept expanded and it has been estimated that between 1971 and 1973 20 to 30 exchanges had been established throughout the US. The governing rules of the 'Hell's Honkies Grateful Tape Club', formed in the New York City area in 1972, outlined typical operating principles. Members had complete access rights to any other member's collection and newly acquired recordings were to be made equally available to all exchange participants. Trading developed further with the appearance of the publication *Dead Relix* (later *Relix*) in 1974, just as the Dead entered their 18-month touring hiatus. *Dead Relix* offered show and tape reviews, interviews, advice on field recording and trading classifieds. As a result, the band returned to the stage in mid-1976 amid a burgeoning trading network (Shenk and Silberman, 1994, 105, 245, 265–6, 271, 277, 323, 335; Trager, 1997, 316; Getz and Dwork, 1998, 20–3, 28, 37; Getz and Dwork, 1999, 30–1, 39; Abraham, 2000, 28; Getz et al., 2001).

Despite assumptions of reciprocity and transparency, not all trading was open. Intensely competitive trader hierarchies developed alongside the sharing ethos. According to the *Deadhead's Taping Addendum* (Getz et al., 2001, 7–8), this paradox frequently resulted in 'paranoia, suspicion of friends, avarice, and lost or strained relationships'. Donaldson explains this broader environment as well as a specific instance of how it operated in the Baltimore, Maryland area:

> Every city had its group of tapers or tape collectors . . . [w]here I was, Mitchell Ash
> was the top of the tree. And then there was a layer of five or six guys below him.
> Mitchell had everything there was to get. . . . It was very much a hierarchical setup.
> And for most people it was not that easy to get tapes out of those at the top of the
> hierarchy. . . . The taping hierarchy, who got soundboards, who got all the good
> quality tapes, basically was centered around California and New York. . . . It was
> very competitive. . . . You'd have to keep up with it, and if you didn't, then you'd
> drop out of it. And once you started falling by the wayside, it was a steep downhill
> slide from there.   Getz and Dwork, 1999, 30

These hierarchies and their efforts at stockpiling and control were ultimately
broken by significant leaks of official master and first generation
soundboards. The 'Betty Boards' were recordings made by long-term official
band sound engineer Betty Cantor Jackson. After working for the band
throughout the 1970s until the early 1980s she entered into a prolonged
dispute over royalties and expenses. After losing her house she stored her
belongings, including her vast collection of master tapes, in rented storage
space. Her storage unit went into default and in 1987 the tapes went on the
auction block. The band knew about these tapes but decided not to pursue
them. As noted by long time crew member Kidd Candelario, the 'feeling
about [these] . . . tapes at that point was that they were unimportant, that they
had no value . . . . I remember it came up at a meeting and the vote was not
to go ahead and support [recovering them].' The tapes totaling several
hundred hours were sold in multiple blocks at auction. Many of these
recovered tapes made their way into wide circulation and helped mute the
influence of hierarchies within trader circles wherein 'upper echelon' traders
dominated 'lower echelon' traders by refusing to part with high quality and
rare recordings. The Betty Boards project was purposely designed to
democratize trading.

In 2000 a 'Mysterious Molly' surfaced another enormous stash of
previously unavailable recordings. Her efforts surfaced notable 'tape hoarders'
who were forced to share from their collections. Emergent digital recordings
also played a role in eroding long-standing trading hierarchies as older more
established traders, eager to discern for themselves the value of the new
technology, entered into trades with newer digital recordists. In combination,
these efforts resulted in the wide dissemination of previously hoarded and
unavailable master recordings, enabling new traders with no roots or power
to easily amass a sizeable body of high quality soundboard recordings (Getz
and Dwork, 1999, 16–18, 61; Getz and Dwork, 2000, 33–41; Getz, Dwork
and Dyke, 2001, 7–8, 287, 296; Dick's Picks FAQ, n.d.).

As taping and trading networks expanded so did the necessity for more accurate and reliable documentation. Traders maintained detailed holdings lists to facilitate reliable exchanges. Such lists normally included date, location, venue and a sound quality 'grade' (A+ to F). These early efforts were complicated by the absence of a performance master list. Though the first known effort to better document the Dead's touring history emerged in Chicago in 1981, it would take until 1987, with the creation of the independently published *DeadBase* (and *DeadBase, Jr* in 1995), for comprehensive date, venue and setlist data to be accurately compiled and made widely available. Initiated as a computer science masters programme project, it drew from several other efforts and even received formal band approval and assistance. Printed volumes ran from 1987 to 1999 before moving online. The *Deadhead's Taping Compendium*, published from 1998 to 2001, which comprises four volumes totalling 2400 pages, took documentation to the next level by providing reviews of every known recorded performance (Getz and Dwork, 2000, 43).

The networked computer revolutions: trading, documentation and curation

The taper and trader community was an early adopter of networked computing. E-mail, bulletin boards, newsgroups and later websites provided unprecedented access to trading 'trees' (networks of sequential individuated copying), metadata-rich collector lists, authoritative performance databases, compilations of tapes in circulation and their versioning (including sophisticated digital post-processing) and trader resource portals. These offerings were later complemented by sites enabling the downloading and streaming of entire concerts, both those created by audience tapers and others alienated, 'liberated' or heisted from the band's official sound archive. By December 2005 the presence of thousands of audience and soundboard recordings on the Internet Archive surfaced tensions between surviving core band members, the Grateful Dead Productions parent company, and the taping and trading community. At issue was control over both the band's official archive and the one created by Deadheads.

The roots of these transformations date from 1973, when band-related content first appeared on ARPANET, the embryonic internet. Hosted by Stanford University's Artificial Intelligence Lab, a locally oriented mailing list allowed those few with online access to share basic ticketing information. By 1975 this had evolved to an unmoderated mailing list, and by the early 1980s, when there were a mere 60 hosts on ARPANET, traffic volume forced a split into two groups: 'Dead-flames', a cornucopia of Dead related topics, such as setlists, lyrics decipherment, rumours, the history of the band and so on, and

'Dead-heads', for sharing information on upcoming shows and ticketing. In 1985 these lists were folded into the budding Usenet discussion forum net.music. Somewhat controversially, Deadheads decided to collectively seize this broadly constituted group by inundating it with band-related discussions. This led to the brokered birth of net.music.gdead (later rec.music.gdead), the first Usenet newsgroup dedicated to a single band. By the early 1990s some 70,000 Deadheads were making use of this forum (Shenk and Silberman, 1994, 56; Getz and Dwork, 2000, 54–6).

The mid-1980s also saw the emergence of the 'WELL' (Whole Earth 'Lectronic Link), a networked computer update to Stewart Brand's counter cultural *Whole Earth Catalog*. According to Howard Rheingold (1994, 73), though it catered to a diverse range of 'utopians . . . solar power enthusiasts, serious ecologists and the space-station crowd, immortalists, Biospherians, environmentalists, [and] social activists', Deadheads were to become a central presence. By the late 1980s the 'Grateful Dead Conference' evolved into the WELL's 'single largest source of income'. By 1990 a formalized tape trading conference – the 'tree conference' – was formed. It was designed to systematically arrange postal-based trades of new performances during the band's final years. This practice represented an electronic network update to established trading practices. The WELL was even tapped by band archivist Latvala to initiate an invitation-only high-level discussion on the band's corpus. Despite these benefits, the WELL also evidenced some of the more unsavoury aspects of online communication. Band publicist and biographer McNally has pointed to gossip, rumour and competitiveness. The WELL was followed by a slew of online trading fora that formalized online trading even more. They also altered the nature of long-established trading patterns. Performances became more readily obtainable beyond the constraints of competitive trader hierarchies. Long time taper and trader, Jeff Tiedrich noted that his collection tripled within a year of joining online trading groups. Over time, guidance and formalized processes were documented and made available to ensure consistency with online community trading standards. 'Netiquette' evolved for turnaround times, tape stock and transparency regarding problems arising with source recordings and copying logistics. Fears about dishonesty and unreciprocated trades were understandable but appear to have been insignificant in comparison to the number of successfully organized online trades amongst geographically dispersed individuals who had never met face-to-face (Brightman, 1998, 312–13; Getz and Dwork, 2000, 56–8; Getz, Dwork and Dyke, 2001, 282–3; Gans, 2002, 285).

The mechanisms for trades arranged online and conducted through the postal system, 'tape trees' and 'cyber-vines', were active while the band was still performing, ensuring that recent shows rapidly entered into wide circulation. With tape trees, an individual with a tape to trade made an online announcement followed by a sign-up to participate. Their original 'seed' tape – ideally a low generation high fidelity recording – was copied and provided to different branches who themselves made and offered multiple copies to others in the tree, who then duplicated the process. A few short iterations could result in the production and dissemination of hundreds of copies of the original seed. This also ensured a high quality 'gene pool' of tapes in circulation. By the late 1990s some websites completely automated the process of sign-up and distribution chaining. Cyber-vines were similar with the exception that they were smaller and more private, with the original seed tape sequentially sent out to each individual who made their own copy and then forwarded the seed to the next person in the vine. The band's own official website has long hosted tape tree and cyber-vine discussion forums, offering formal sanction to these community practices (Shenk and Silberman, 1994, 293–4; Getz and Dwork, 2000, 59).

A substantial component of co-creation in the networked computer era were efforts by the taping and trading community to develop authoritative setlists and recording documentation on circulating recordings. In 1993 Eric Doherty's list of known 1969–70 performances quickly morphed and 'pushed' him 'into a role of a record keeper . . . people started coming forth with more information. . . . I became a central repository for information'. Subsequent efforts provided greater specificity and accuracy. The database-driven 'Deadbase' shifted from print to online and offered search, retrieval and browsing of setlists, venues and locations. Through a collective distributed effort, the 'Deadlists Project' additionally included individual song timings, posters and links to downloadable performances. The 'Grateful Dead Collection', hosted by the Internet Archive's Live Music Archive, and Etree provide even more detailed genealogies on tapes in circulation to help differentiate versions of the same performance.

Current community-wide documentation practices of performances include, when known: date, venue, setlist, track timings, recording gear (decks and microphones), recording location, recordist and format transfers. This final category can note transfer sequences from, for example, open reels to cassette to DAT to a digital lossless file format (typically SHN – Shorten and FLAC – Free Lossless Audio Codec). They can even specify which production software was used. Over time, Deadheads have post-produced recordings to improve sound quality or piece together a complete performance from multiple sources. Some even mix audience and soundboard recordings together to create manufactures ('matrix' tapes) that retain audience ambience while preserving the clarity of soundboards. Such efforts have generated 'brands' associated with particular recordists, collectives, or post-production editors (Getz and Dwork, 2000, 60–1).

As early as 1997 the band issued a policy cognizant of this new and rapidly changing landscape. It permitted non-commercial downloading and sharing of performances in the low fidelity MP3 file format. The 'non-commercial' clause prohibited receiving payment for downloads, selling any information gathered about users, and advertising (Moore, 2007, 629–30). This embrace of the new sharing potential of the web resulted in the legitimation of trading and streaming sites such as Gdlive.com, Sugarmegs.org and Nugs.net. A 2005 analysis of 20 Dead trading websites found that these sites 'state or imply that everyone is welcome. . . .' Other identified characteristics include: a primacy placed on sound quality; the creation and use of extensive performance and recording metadata; willingness to help a 'newbie' to start building their own collection; and strict observance of the ethos of non-commercial sharing. As a result, trading community members have been able to amass sizeable collections without purchasing the music *and* without resort to the 'theft' of intellectual property so commonly highlighted in discussions of online music sharing. As noted by Herman, the net result of these initiatives created opportunities for 'fan creativity [that] goes beyond poaching and moves toward (if not achieving) co-creation' (2005, 10–19, 22–3).

Through the efforts of individuals and collectives in the taping and trading community, this past decade has witnessed dramatic growth of the Dead's online presence. Today, access not only to documentation about the band's performance corpus, but also to the actual performances themselves, extends far beyond previous manifestations in size and scope. The ability to make a perfect copy with no generational loss through affordable and accessible blank CD-ROMs, external hard drives, copying and burning hardware and software, high-speed access to the world wide web, and high fidelity file formats (such as SHN and FLAC) has revolutionized trading and collecting. Downloading, streaming and file sharing technologies offer on-demand access to many thousands of individual performances (Shenk and Silberman, 1994, 52; Getz and Dwork, 2000, 54).

Out of this context emerged the Internet Archive's Grateful Dead Collection. Launched in March 2004 it witnessed ongoing rapid growth, hosting over 3000 audience and band recordings by the end of 2005. Beyond offering streaming and downloading in low and high fidelity formats, it also provides Web 2.0 'ratings' where listeners can post their own commentaries, observations and reminiscences. The Live Music Archive was created in 1996 to enable online trading of live performances of bands that assented to this distribution mechanism. The Dead were approached and agreed to participate, in line with their 1997 decision to allow online sharing and trading as a practice parallel to earlier tape trading. However, in late November 2005, the band requested the Live Music Archive to remove *all* recordings of its performances. After this request was complied with a vigorous debate arose online. Removing soundboards leaked from the band's institutional archive appeared reasonable, but to include audience recordings in the take down proved to be too controversial. It appeared to many that the band, after having affirmatively granted a 'right' of audience taping and trading across the years, had overreached its own intellectual property rights by attempting to control audience recordings.

By early December, Deadheads generated a 5200-signature petition threatening a boycott of band-related merchandise. Within days, for various reasons, the band relented. A compromise settlement continued to allow the downloading of audience recordings but only the streaming of soundboards. Soundboards of commercially released performances would be removed in their entirety. Surviving core band members – Hart, Kreutzmann, Lesh and Weir – differed on the wisdom of pulling the site with Lesh in the minority for allowing continued access. He had come to value the Live Music Archive while doing research for his 2005 autobiography. One very real fear was that uncontrolled access would limit the band's ability to merchandise its own recordings, including its recent move offering selected downloads from its own website. One legal question unanswered by this compromise was whether, over the years, the band had already implicitly granted a licence to audience recordings that would place control of them beyond their intellectual property claims. Also untested was whether the band could again decide to remove the re-instituted recordings at any point in the future (Leeds, 2005; Mayshark, 2005; Pareles, 2005; Moore, 2007, 625, 630–2).

Since reinstatement, the band's presence on the Live Music Archive has continued to experience dramatic growth, nearly doubling between January 2008 and January 2009 (from roughly 3300 items to over 6300 items, respectively). In many instances multiple versions of individual performances are available and have been widely copied. For example, a run of three shows in Alaska in June 1980 lists 22 sources that have been downloaded over 131,000 times. Another highly regarded May 1977 three-show run from New York and Massachusetts offers 20 sources that have been downloaded over 1.1 million times. The 15 most popular performances have been downloaded over 3.74 million times. This unprecedented ability for collectors to capture their own individual copies on this scale represents magnitudes of increase in duplication and dissemination.

The associated ability to comment and review individual concerts allows Deadheads not only to evaluate performances critically, but also permits them to offer observations to the wider community on sound quality and share stories ranging from their attendance to experiences with trader hierarchies to reminiscences on themselves and the community as they look backwards in time. This mechanism offers an additional new layer of community creation and interpretation – both aesthetic, social and biographical – related to the band's sound archive. However, such ubiquitous access at the desktop level has altered trading from a person-to-person relationship to more of a person-to-computer relationship. While such dynamics can manifest online and even in face-to-face connections, it more commonly results in a solitary anonymous endeavour. So though it affords the ability to amass an enormous collection quickly and cheaply without having to navigate taper politics and hierarchies, it significantly corrodes the sentient human relationships that long formed the foundation and essence of the trading community (Matranga, 2002, 6).

The rise of peer-to-peer networks and file sharing bit torrent software represents the latest development of widened availability and community development. While not always dedicated solely to the Dead, sites such as Furthurnet.org, The-zomb.com, Gdvault.iforumer.com, Dimeadozen.org, Thetradersden.org and Shnflac.net have thousands of registered members and offer thousands of performances. The most significant of these is Etree.org.[4] Launched in 1998, Etree describes itself as a: 'Community committed to providing the highest quality live concert recordings in a losslessly-compressed, downloadable format. All of the music on etree.org is free, and 100% legal to download, trade, and burn. We also assist new traders in learning to trade online through our extensive guides.'

As noted by Jones (2005, 651), this 'contributor run archives' requires 'people of shared interests and of varied technical competencies'. This includes server technicians, mailing list administrators, web designers and an army of volunteers to create and maintain metadata and seed performances for sharing (Matranga, 2002, 81). By 2005 there were three individuals who oversaw hardware administration and site databases, nearly 300 individuals who were granted administrator privileges, and over 100,000 registered accounts permitting additions and corrections. In essence, the site functions as a giant wiki. It serves as an exemplar of distributed user-generated 'quality assur[ed]' metadata. Etree maintains the most comprehensive and detailed documentation on individual source recordings with links to versions available online via bt.etree.org (Matranga, 2002, 81; Jones, 2005, 657, 659).

Bt.etree.org regularly links to over 1000 Dead performances available for bit torrent downloading and sharing, many of which represent newly surfaced recordings or Deadhead remasterings of previously available recordings. Many have been served hundreds and even thousands of times. Db.etree.org permits registered users to create their own personalized lists and submit 'want list' requests to the community for shows missing from their collection, thereby allowing users to create their own personal collection space within the same framework and community that manages authoritative lists and metadata.

In combination these efforts, enabled by a sizeable decentralized volunteer community, supersede anything the band's organization has been able to muster. The internet and the world wide web currently provide access to just about every known performance through streaming and/or downloading. In this sense the continuity of Deadhead culture owes a great debt to the efforts of the online trading community. They have completely shattered the legacy of the trading hierarchies. More fundamentally, this unprecedented duplication and dissemination of the Dead's performance corpus renders it invulnerable to loss with prospects of tremendous persistence. All made possible by the individual and collective efforts of thousands of volunteers contributing to a common pool and motivated by a community-bred philosophy of non-commercial sharing and curation.

Conclusion

Following Whitman (2005, 4–5), this chapter offers 'depth and complexity' for understanding the 'interaction between music technology and cultural practices', specifically 'on the way music fans listen to, distribute, and consume music'. By charting the rise of the Deadhead taping and trading community from its humble beginnings in the late 1960s to its current online incarnation as something akin to a wiki-based universal library, two key findings emerge: the values of non-commercialized sharing and co-operation, and reconsideration of traditional intellectual property configurations. Both have provided key features for community building. Both have also made substantial contributions to the likely persistence and widening dissemination of the co-created Grateful Dead performance sound archive. It also underscores how online environments changed the dynamics of the community and the collective ownership it produced.

The values of non-commercialized sharing and co-operation.

The advent of online sharing, downloading and curation have made the band's performances more widely available than ever before, in both its quality and comprehensiveness. The shift from personal to disintermediated anonymous trading, and the interactive capabilities of Web 2.0 technologies (such as show ratings and reviews) have, in combination, challenged long-held traditions, standards and etiquette of the taper and trading community as well as laying the foundation for new formulations. The connecting thread between these two eras is the continuation of the foundational ethos of non-commercialized sharing and co-operation.

This foundational ethos has, over the decades, resulted in the finest curated and documented distributed sound archives in existence. The internet continues to offer an unprecedented elaboration of this ethos far beyond what anyone could have forecast in the late 1960s when taping and trading started. These values triggered and sustained the co-creative experience between the band and the Deadheads and the attendant 'collective joy' it incarnated. The archive as a locus of joy and transcendence remains one of the fundamental aspects of this archive and, therefore, must feature prominently in any explanation as to why it has received so much curatorial care largely outside the support of or legitimation from formal organizational structures. It also helps to partly explain why so many individuals were willing to leverage considerable voluntary effort and personal resources (both materially and temporally) to create something that, in effect, was required to be shared to be meaningfully valued as a community resource. It was from within the taping and trading community itself that sustained campaigns were launched to eradicate entrenched efforts to 'control' the music through hierarchies and hoarding. Such efforts were helped in no small measure by the community's willingness and adeptness in adopting emerging networked computer and digital technologies.

Through the adoption of Web 2.0 technologies for user participation via collaborative authoring, tagging and sharing, the trading community itself continues to actively and deeply enrich the knowledgebase on performances and source recordings. User contributed and collaboratively assured content and metadata generation via the Internet Archive and Etree vividly demonstrates how values of sharing and co-operation have powerfully augmented the Grateful Dead sound archive. Distributed production, curation and documentation management has resulted in an online archive – actually several online archives – that provide far more content and context than could ever be possible in a traditionally configured institutional or collecting archival setting. This harnessing of expertise outside the formal archive hints at the types of emergent theory and praxis of user collaboration indicated by Light and Hyry (2002), Duff and Harris (2002) and, more recently, by Krause and Yakel (2007).

Reconsideration of traditional intellectual property configurations

By sanctioning audience recordings and ultimately audience co-curation, the band itself initiated an alternative to traditional intellectual property configurations that on face value appeared to run contrary to their own financial solvency. However, over time the band came to recognize that their ongoing success rested in large part on the decision to see their performances as something beyond the normative model of commodification of music and performance – the dominant mode staked out by the music industry. The band recognized that their performances were in effect collaborations made possible only through the audience's presence. In effect, the audience became a part of the band itself. The recordings of those co-created performances were therefore logically seen as something beyond property that were true to the counter cultural values out of which the band emerged. Through this consciousness the traditional boundaries of author and audience, of producer and consumer, eroded. Each taper could be granted credence as an author or producer. In the online environment, individuals have continued to render themselves as author and producer by aurally enhancing and remixing extant recordings. This current is in wide evidence across the internet.

The band also came to understand that the community which supported them financially and artistically was able to be built on the scale it achieved only through the ongoing circulation and reproduction of their performances. The power of the copy, in contradiction to all fears normally resulting from 'unauthorized' duplication, in effect rendered continuity to the community and solvency for the band far beyond what would have been otherwise achievable. The band did not abolish its intellectual property rights. Rather, it chose to implement some of those rights and not put into effect others of those rights. Contrary to dominant intellectual property discourse, the key lesson here is that just because property rights exist does not mean that they all have to be aggressively adhered to. The band gave up certain property rights while strongly protecting others. The central taping and trading ethos of non-commercial duplication and distribution honoured the band's property rights that they did wish to retain and enforce, namely the anti-piracy right to exclusively profit from their work.

These innovations have been adopted by hundreds of bands, evidencing that efforts to control the 'archive' may in fact be detrimental to sustainability. The culture of the copy and duplication sanctioned by the Dead is likely to ensure the ongoing persistence and preservation of the band's corpus far beyond anything it could achieve through its own institutional archive. Although not constituted within the framework of institutionalized archives or professional archival description, the lessons from the Internet Archive and Etree.org offer much to contemplate and act on.

While the transfer of these guiding principles to formalized archival settings remains unrealized, what is undeniable is that, in this instance, they have resulted in the successful curation, documentation and access to a substantial archive. An all-volunteer network framed within non-commercial collaborative cultural production has resulted in a distributed archive that resides in the hands of many thousands of individuals who value it, collect it, use it. If the Dead teach us anything, it is that the impulse to control obviates other social and cultural configurations that may instead arise that offer opportunities for more meaningful engagement with archives. Such practices elegantly lend themselves as a model quite sympathetic to Evans' (2007, 387, 395) recent call for 'commons-based peer-production', wherein archives see themselves as 'common and public good rather than as the protected property of an institution'.

This mutually beneficial symbiosis, developed though community-bred commitments and values, sometimes fragile, sometimes controversial, is still evolving. Its patterns of innovation and creative co-operation and collaboration are likely to successfully guide ongoing persistence and elaboration. The taping and trading community, in exercising its own agency and 'rights', amply demonstrates how other communities centred around archives can organize themselves and thrive.

Notes

1 Acknowledgements: The multi-volume *The Deadhead's Taping Compendium* provided invaluable and essential primary source data. Peter Alegi, Jeanette Bastian, Verne Harris, Anthea Josias and David Lemieux offered insightful comments on an earlier draft. All extant shortcomings remain mine.
2 Jerry Garcia – lead guitar, vocals (1965–95); Bill Kreutzmann – drums (1965–95); Phil Lesh – bass, vocals (1965–95); Ron 'Pigpen' McKernan – keyboards, harmonica, vocals (1965–72); Bob Weir – rhythm guitar, vocals (1965–95); Mickey Hart – drums (1967–71, 1975–95); Robert Hunter – lyricist (1967–95); Tom Constanten – keyboards (1968–9); John Perry Barlow – lyricist (1971–95); Donna Jean Godchaux – vocals (1971–9); Keith Godchaux – keyboards (1971–9); Brent Mydland – keyboards (1979–90); Bruce Hornsby – keyboards (1990–2); Vince Welnick – keyboards (1990–5).
3 This attitude stands in stark contrast to the position staked out on audience taping by other well established touring musicians, most notably Bob Dylan.
4 According to Jones, 'The Etree site is really several sites with several different, but interrelated, functions. . . . Forums.etree.org offers threaded discussion groups to members. . . . News.etree.org offers a syndicatable blog and announcement area. . . . Etree.org/irc gives access to real-time chat among etree-ers via Internet relay chat. Db.etree.org . . . is the database that describes in extreme detail the music that etree members have to share' (2005, 657).

References

Abraham, L. (2000) The History of Relix: music for the mind, *Relix Magazine*, (3) May/June.

Belk, R. (2007) Why Not Share Rather Than Own?, *ANNALS of the American Academy of Political and Social Science*, **611** (1), 126–40.

Brightman, C. (1998) *Sweet Chaos: the Grateful Dead's American adventure*, Pocket Books.

Cobb, C. (2001) What a Long, Strange Trip it's Been, *Ottawa Citizen*, March, http://mysite.verizon.net/cmp1163x/vault.htm.

Dick's Picks FAQ (n.d.).

Duff, W. and Harris, V. (2002) Stories and Names: archival description as narrating records and constructing meanings, *Archival Science*, **2** (3–4), 263–85.

Ehrenreich, B. (2005) *Dancing in the Streets: a history of collective joy*, Metropolitan and Henry Holt and Company.

Evans, M. (2007) Archives of the People, by the People, for the People, *American Archivist*, **70** (2), 387–400.

Gans, D. (2002) *Conversations with the Dead: the Grateful Dead interview book*, Da Capo.

Getz, M. M. and Dwork, J. R. (1998) *The Deadhead's Taping Compendium, Volume I: an in-depth guide to the music of the Grateful Dead on tape, 1959–1974*, Henry Holt and Company.

Getz, M. M. and Dwork, J. R. (1999) *The Deadhead's Taping Compendium, Volume II: an in-depth guide to the music of the Grateful Dead on tape, 1975–1985*, Henry Holt and Company.

Getz, M. M. and Dwork, J. R. (2000) *The Deadhead's Taping Compendium, Volume III: an in-depth guide to the music of the Grateful Dead on tape, 1986–1995*, Henry Holt and Company.

Getz, M. M., Dwork, J. R. and Dyke, B. (2001) *The Deadhead's Taping Addendum*, Pepper Tonic.

Grateful Dead: the illustrated trip (2003), DK Publishing.

Grateful Dead Productions (2004) *Grateful Dead Movie*.

Greenfield, R. (1997) *Dark Star: an oral biography of Jerry Garcia*, Broadway Books.

Herman, B. (2005) Dead Traders: a textual analysis of websites trading in Grateful Dead bootlegs, paper presented at the annual meeting of the International Communication Association, New York, www.allacademic.com/meta/p13888_index.html.

Hill, S. and Rifkin, G. (1999) *Radical Marketing: from Harvard to Harley, lessons from ten that broke the rules and made it big*, Harper Business.

Jackson, B. (1999) *Garcia: an American life*, Penguin.

Jackson, B. (2000) Introduction to We Want Phil! an interview, and In Phil We Trust: a conversation. In Dodd, D. G. and Spaulding, D. (eds), *The Grateful Dead Reader*, Oxford University Press.

Jackson, B. (2006) *Grateful Dead Gear: the band's instruments, sound systems, and recording sessions, from 1965 to 1995*, Backbeat Books.

Jones, P. (2005) Strategies and Technologies of Sharing in Contributor-Run Archives, *Library Trends*, **53** (4), 651–62.

Krause, M. and Yakel, E. (2007) Interaction in Virtual Archives: the Polar Bear Expedition digital collections next generation finding aid, *American Archivist*, **70** (2), 282–314.

Leeds, J. (2005) Deadheads Must Be Satisfied With 1,300 Audience Tapings, *New York Times*, 2 December.

Legate, W. (2000) Liner Notes to Europe '72. In Dodd, D. G. and Spaulding, D. (eds), *The Grateful Dead Reader*, Oxford University Press.

Lesh, P. (2005) *Searching for the Sound: my life with the Grateful Dead*, Little, Brown and Company.

Liberatore, P. (2006) Only the Memories Remain: Grateful Dead's recordings moved, *Marin Independent Journal*, 4 August, www.marinij.com/ci_4136208.

Light, M. and Hyry, T. (2002) Colophons and Annotations: new directions for the finding aid, *American Archivist*, **65**, 216–30.

Marshall, L. (2003) For and Against the Record Industry: an introduction to bootleg collectors and tape traders, *Popular Music*, **22** (1), 57–72.

Matranga, A. J. (2002) The Folk Devil Goes Digital: taping and trading live music in the digital age, Master's thesis, Syracuse University, http://anize.org/ajm/The%20Folk%20Digital%20Goes%20Digital.pdf.

Mayshark, J. F. (2005) Downloads of the Dead are Not Dead Yet, *New York Times*, 1 December.

McNally, D. (2000) Meditations on the Grateful Dead. In Dodd, D. G. and Spaulding, D. (eds), *The Grateful Dead Reader*, Oxford University Press.

McNally, D. (2002) *Long Strange Trip: the inside history of the Grateful Dead*, Broadway Books.

Moore, C. A. (2007) Tapers in a Jam: 'trouble ahead' or 'trouble behind'?, *Columbia Journal of Law & The Arts*, **30** (3–4), 625–53.

Nash, M. (1988) Grateful Tapers: an informal history of recording the dead, *Audio*, **72** (1), 54–62.

Neumann, M. and Simpson, T. A. (1997) Smuggled Sound: bootleg recording and the pursuit of popular memory, *Symbolic Memory*, **20** (4), 319–41.

Opening the Dead's Vault: David Lemieux (2004) *Jambase*, 16 December, www.jambase.com/headsup.asp?storyID=5914.

Pareles, J. (2005) The Dead's Gamble: free music for sale, *New York Times*, 3 December.

Pattacini, M. M. (2000) Deadheads Yesterday and Today: an audience study, *Popular Music and Society*, **24** (1), 1–14.

Rheingold, H. (1994) A Slice of Life in My Virtual Community. In Harasim, L. M. (ed.), *Global Networks: computers and international communication*, MIT Press.

Ritzer, J. (2000) Deadheads and Dichotomies: mediated and negotiated readings. In Adams, R. G. and Sardiello, R. (eds), *Deadhead Social Science: you ain't gonna learn what you don't want to know*, Altamira Press.

Selvin, J. (2007) For the Unrepentant Patriarch of LSD, Long, Strange Trip Winds Back to Bay Area, *San Francisco Chronicle*, 12 July, www.sfgate.com/cgi-bin/article.cgi?file=/ c/a/2007/07/12/MNGK0QV7HS1.DTL.

Shenk, D. and Silberman, S. (1994) *Skeleton Key: a dictionary for Deadheads*, Doubleday.

Sutton, S. C. (2000) The Deadhead Community: popular religion in contemporary American culture. In Adams, R. G. and Sardiello, R. (eds), *Deadhead Social Science: you ain't gonna learn what you don't want to know*, Altamira Press.

Tanen, B. (1995) Recorded Live Music and Alternative Intellectual Property Protection, paper prepared for Massachusetts Institute of Technology course entitled Ethics and Law on the Electronic Frontier (Fall), http://groups.csail.mit.edu/mac/classes/6.805/student-papers/fall95-papers/tanen-taping.html.

Trager, O. (1997) *The American Book of the Dead: the definitive Grateful Dead encyclopedia*, Fireside.

Whitman, M. L. (2005) When We're Finished With It, Let Them Have It: jamband tape-trading culture, Master's thesis, University of Chicago, http://66.102.1.104/scholar?hl=en&lr=&client=safari&q=cache:Nmk9r_QNSVMJ:www.livemusicmusings.com/2006/09/Marc_Whitman_MA_Thesis_May_2005.pdf+Grateful+Dead+tapers.

Wild, D. (2001) Raiding the Dead's Vault, *Rolling Stone*, 8 November, 30.

Part 5

Building a community archive

11

'All the things we cannot articulate': colonial leprosy archives and community commemoration[1]

RICARDO L. PUNZALAN

Are there cases in which records contain practical information, but in which the real significance is larger and more symbolic?   O'Toole, 1993, 238

Introduction

In recent years archival scholars have pondered the complex association between archives and collective memory (see, for example, Taylor, 1982; Foote, 1990; Brown and Davis-Brown, 1998; Brothman, 2001; Craig, 2002; Schwartz and Cook, 2002; Jimerson, 2003; Piggott, 2005a; Piggott, 2005b; Rosen, 2008). Some have examined this relationship in a critical fashion, emphasizing the inherent problems of the claim while dispelling the almost automatic and often unexamined assertion of their synonymity. Calls for more nuanced characterization of archives' relationship with memory and their communities have gained much attention. Assertions of the archives–memory relationship vary from the critical – 'connecting archives with memory is, of course, in one important respect, misleading' (Harris, 2001, 5; Craig, 2002, 278) – to the convinced – 'Memory, like history, is rooted in archives. Without archives, memory falters, knowledge of accomplishments fades, pride in a shared past dissipates' (Schwartz and Cook, 2002, 18). The various articulations of the problematic contexts and apparent limitations of records, archives and archivists either as evidence, sources, inspiration, shapers or mediators of memory prompt further reflection. They also underscore the need to find more evidence of how archives (as both social institutions and collections of records), archivists and record-keeping functions might figure in the construction and remembrance of the past by societies, groups or communities.

A few terms have been suggested in the attempt to illustrate this association. Among these are Laura Millar's (2006) 'touchstones' which refers to how records function to trigger memories and the recollection of past events. Margaret Hedstrom uses 'interface', a term often associated with computing technology, to describe the capacity of archivists as intermediaries between documents and their users that 'enable, but also constrain, the interpretation of the past' (Hedstrom, 2002, 22). Similarly, Robert McIntosh puts forward the notion of archival 'authorship' to emphasize the mediating role of archivists in memory creation as they 'practice a politics of memory, a determination of what will be remembered' (McIntosh, 1998, 18). Reflecting on the archival experiences in South Africa in its transition from apartheid to democracy, Verne Harris concludes that records comprise mere 'archival slivers' of the events and processes that they are supposed to embody and reveal. In her discussion of the records of the US Virgin Islands, Jeanette Bastian proposed the notion of a 'community of records', as a framework for understanding the dynamic between archives, memory and community while expanding notions of provenance and ownership of records (Bastian, 2003). 'Memory text' is another concept in the list of ideas that some have used to illustrate the dynamic between archives and community memory. While Bastian and Eric Ketelaar have separately tackled 'memory text', both use the concept to emphasize the need to transcend the limits of traditional archival records and formats to embody cultural performance (Bastian, 2006) and distributed remembering (Ketelaar, 2005).

This paper will not propose yet another term to illustrate the relationship between archives and collective memory. Instead, I wish to account for how this dynamic manifests itself in specific communities within specific moments, or occasions, of public remembering. I shall provide an interpretive discussion of my experiences in organizing the archives on the island of Culion, a former segregation colony for people afflicted with leprosy in the Philippines. The arrival of the first contingent of patients on the island on 27 May 1906 was identified as the community's historical beginning. The project of organizing the archives of Culion was clearly bound up with reflections not only on beginnings, but also on community origins, stirred up by the approaching centennial. The archives thus officially opened at the height of a major public remembrance.

The observations presented in this paper took root during my experiences as archivist and curator of the Culion Leprosy Museum and Archives (CLMA) from April 2005 to May 2006. Using a range of sources (colonial accounts of the island from existing archival records, personal observations and interviews with people in the community, its local elites, centennial organizers and funding agencies), I wish to describe how one community interpreted the organization of its records and the establishment of archives within the centennial rhetoric of hope and healing and the politics of observance and commemoration. Through this 'thick description' (Geertz, 1973), I show how members of the Culion community came to regard a body of colonial medical records as 'their' archives.

My goal is to provide a case that illustrates how records and the establishment of archives figure at a moment of remembrance and commemoration. I propose to examine an occasion of community remembrance and how archives assume a particular meaning in the process. In my discussion, I focus on how the conduct of the larger Philippine national centennial commemoration coincided with Culion's own centenary and thus became the framework for the remembrance of leprosy, the island and its community. I also identify the key actors in Culion's centennial by placing these in a 'web of interests' of competing and complementary visions and interpretations. I show how the archives were used to support differing claims about the meaning of the past, and I suggest some possibilities as to what allows for competing interpretation and meanings of the Culion archives. In telling the stories Culion residents 'tell themselves about themselves' (Geertz, 1973, 448). I depict a duality of interpretation that divides the insider and the outsider and the way in which this influences the collective understanding of the archives. In my position as an outsider 'expert' archivist, I learned that my vulnerabilities in the community also provided an opportunity to act more as a co-witness in the construction of the collective meaning of archives.

Centennial fever

The current period of Philippine history might be characterized as an era of centennial celebrations memorializing the fateful events of about a century ago, specifically the forming of the nation and the revolution that inspired the country's liberation from Spanish colonial domination.[2] The role of heritage institutions in crafting narratives of national history, representing the colonial experience in exhibitions, and displaying a national identity for the general public has been greatly amplified with the centennial of the Philippine revolution against Spain in 1996, the commemoration of the proclamation of national independence in 1998, and the various centennials that followed.[3] This heightened, state-instigated desire for celebratory commemoration of colonialism and nationhood may be described as centennial fever. The centennial fever has indeed engulfed the nation, inspiring various sectors and institutions to situate their centenaries as points of reckoning, as key moments of collective reflection, affirmation and celebration of heritage and identity.[4]

The hospital on the island of Culion, established in 1906, is yet another important site that recently marked its own centennial.[5] The facility was at one point the world's largest leper colony, primarily because of an American colonial legislation that mandated segregation and literally criminalized leprosy.[6] Given its patient population, budget appropriation and modern hospital infrastructure and facilities, Culion was regarded as among the leading institutions in leprosy research and experimental treatments in the 1920s. This prominence attracted the world's leading leprologists to the island (Carpenter, 1926, 178). Numerous accounts claimed that the island supplied the largest number of patients who were depicted to be willing volunteers of various experimental treatments.[7] The compulsory segregation of lepers was an American colonial legacy that remained decades after the colonial era came to an end. Culion is no longer a segregation colony but a municipality populated largely by former patients and their second- or third-generation descendants. In Philippine contemporary memory, Culion still connotes affliction and banishment to an 'island of no return'. It also gained a more sinister reputation as an 'island of the living dead'.

Among the highlights of Culion's centennial commemoration in 2006 was the inauguration of a leprosy archives and museum, one of the few existing in the world. Asked about the significance of the archives at the centennial, one doctor responded, 'It will be our ultimate homage. The archives will be both a testament and a monument to the dedicated doctors, nurses and the religious, numerous volunteers whose personal sacrifices transformed this inaccessible island into a shelter for lepers. This is also a remembrance to the early settlers of this island who chose to make this land their home.'[8] The chair of the centennial celebrations, an influential doctor on the island, described the importance of the records: 'These are remnants of our past. While those records may seem outdated, they mean something powerful. But I cannot explain why they are powerful. For now, the archives is the symbol of all the things we cannot articulate about our past, about our need to heal in the present and about our desire to foresee a great future.' These statements made clear that the referent for Culion's centenary was the national centennial commemorations of the revolution.

Visible acts of state remembrance of identifying heroes and pioneers, homage and testimony, and monuments and statues served as the example that the Culion community emulated. In 'Symbiotic Commemoration', cultural historian Carolyn Strange illustrates how the remaining residents of Kaluapapa in the island of Molokai, also a former leprosy segregation site, negotiate with the 'state's framing of the past' (Strange, 2004, 87). Using the characteristically responsive and adaptive biological model of symbiotic organisms, Strange depicts how contemporary Kaluapapans 'selectively incorporated, adapted to and externally generated representations of the past' (Strange, 2004, 89). As an interpretive community, Culion manifests its understanding and interpretation of the past not by wholly incorporating grand state narratives, but by using them to frame their commemoration and remembrance of their local history within broader narratives.

A web of interests

The often competing, sometimes complementing, entities and interests under the commemorative mode of the centennial fever served as the backdrop for the community to understand its archives. The creation of the Culion archives occurred within a web of overlapping contexts and values: the foreign benefactor providing financial assistance; the hospital bureaucracy that claimed ownership of the records; the archivist who is not a member of the community rendering expertise on how the records could be kept, organized and preserved; and the municipal government composed of public officials who were struggling against the sanitarium to exercise greater influence over the community. Planning for the Culion centennial took place within this web of 'interest groups', all aiming to achieve various missions, visions, programmes and agendas that mediated the establishment of the archives.

Most prominent among these was a Japanese humanitarian foundation that funded community aid, livelihood projects and campaigns for the eradication of leprosy and its stigma across the globe. It also provided funding for the establishment of leprosy museums and archives not only in Culion, but in other developing countries such as India and China. Stories of Japanese atrocities in Culion during World War II were alive in the collective consciousness of the community. Mere mention of 'the Pacific war' elicited memories of starvation, hardship, torture and death, especially among the elderly who survived those onerous years. As one senior resident recalled, 'I was a boy during the war. Many patients died of hunger and disease because the Japanese cordoned off the island knowing that American doctors worked here. Food and medicine did not come. Now they're back to help. Perhaps because they're trying to correct past wrongs.' Thus, actions of the humanitarian agency were largely seen as a gesture of restitution despite the fact that its motivation had nothing to do with the Pacific war. Japanese aid to the community was willingly accepted, appreciated and never turned away but this was not without any recollections of the painful war. The attitude of many was, therefore, largely oblivious to the foundation's altruistic mission as the act of giving was almost automatically interpreted as some form of compensation for an irrevocable and overdue debt.

The municipal government and hospital administration occasionally clashed over authority and influence in the community. The elected municipal officials saw the centennial as a moment to assert a new era of public governance and independence from the hospital administration that had influenced the island since its establishment as a leper colony. When Culion was declared a local government unit in 1992, the former seat of the leper colony, the sanitarium, was reclassified as a regional hospital. The newly formed local government saw the centennial as the celebration of its own history of transformation and empowerment and thus saw itself as the chief organizer of the commemoration. This differing conceptualization of influence and control between the local government and the sanitarium was manifested through their conflicting debates over the interpretation and administration of the centennial activities and the ownership of the archives. According to one elected official, 'Why call it "the Culion" Museum and Archives if it will be owned by the hospital and not by the municipality and managed through the elected people of the community? Maybe they should call it "the sanitarium" museum since it is obvious that the doctors want control over it.'

I came to the island as an outsider, the 'expert' consultant archivist to organize the records through the initiative of the hospital and largely funded by the Japanese foundation. In a diary entry for November 2005, I wrote, 'It is obvious that people are monitoring what I'm doing from a distance. After months of work in the island, some started to be more comfortable in expressing some of their thoughts about why I am here: my work in the archives and the exhibition. One even asked if I intend to seek help from the municipal government.' At that point, I was not aware of the ongoing tension between the hospital and the local government. It was only weeks before the archives opened (in May 2006) that I realized the conflict. In my diary for May 2006 I wrote,

> I observed that elected officials did not come to the opening. The [Japanese] Foundation representatives were there. The Department of Health representatives were there. The Catholic nuns and parish priest were there. More importantly many from the 'community' were there. From my conversation with [a clerk from the municipal office], I was told that she did not expect the local government officials to be there given the contention over who owned the records.

A community like no other

At the height of the American occupation of the Philippines (1898–1904), there were about 126,000 American soldiers stationed throughout the islands (Gillett, 1990). The possibility of soldiers contracting leprosy and subsequently bringing the disease with them into the mainland US was among the concerns that deeply disturbed the colonial bureaucracy. Leprosy was probably the most dreaded of all tropical diseases, perpetually feared for possible importation to central North America from some largely unknown, primitive and foreign land. Cholera (Rosenberg, 1967), influenza and tuberculosis may have continually plagued the US in this era, but leprosy was regarded as a biblical and medieval disease that was no longer present in the 'civilized' western world. While there were leper colonies in the US, they were located in the island of Molokai, Hawaii and the fairly isolated town of Carville, Louisiana: places regarded as relatively recent colonial possessions. As historian Michelle Moran argues, leprosy was a 'foreign menace' located in what 'Americans imagined as primitive places' that perpetually threatened to invade the mainland (Moran, 2007, 5).

The American presence in the islands was in part justified through the rhetoric of health and sanitation, with leper segregation in Culion as the ultimate embodiment of colonial success. According to early 20th century American geographer and travel writer Frank G. Carpenter, 'I have heard it said that even if we had failed in all else here in the Philippines, what we have done in Culion would justify the American occupation' (Carpenter, 1926, 178). With its policy of 'benevolent assimilation',[9] many regarded the US as different from other colonial orders in the tropics, such as the Spanish who pursued conquest for their material gain and neglected the welfare of the Filipinos. This view was expressed in a 1901 essay by L. Mervin Maus, MD, first Director of the Board of Health, entitled 'The Sanitary Conquest of the Philippine Islands': 'The watchword of American activity in Cuba and the Philippines was "Cleanliness", and in our fight against diseases and sanitary conditions all rancor of battle and strife was lost' (Maus, 1912, 1017). For Maus, US conquest was justified by a moral imperative and was best implemented through sanitary policies that brought about 'priceless victories over tropical diseases and conditions which for centuries had hovered over those favored isles of the southern seas as angels of death, and converted them into a charnel house both for native and foreign born' (Maus, 1912, 1017).

Culion is a community bound by its association with disease and segregation. Past practices of forced isolation produced a population with an ethnic makeup unique from other communities of the Philippines. Culion was assembled through a series of countrywide expeditions, or 'leper collections' as they were described in various reports, that rounded up individuals' suspected of having leprosy. A majority of the present-day inhabitants of the island – numbering about 20,000 – can directly trace their lineage to former patients, if are not former patients themselves. Others link their roots to the pioneer doctors, nurses, staff or administrators of the former leprosarium. Segregation thus created a community that comprised a diverse array of cultural and ethno-linguistic groups from the various regions of the Philippines.

The colonial policy on compulsory medical segregation from 1906 to 1952 produced a community like no other in the Philippines. As a form of social classification, forced segregation identified a population not by its kinship, ethnicities, region or other cultural affinities, but by its medical and health conditions. Segregation on Culion island gathered Filipinos from various regions and ethno-linguistic communities on the basis of a disease: as lepers who were taken from their homes and families based on a state-sponsored medical programme. Culion was often referred to as a microcosm of the Philippines: a site not only dedicated to leprosy treatment or cure, but a social laboratory where notions of citizenship and civic duties were inculcated in a population. Historian Warwick Anderson describes this as 'biomedical citizenship', a medically oriented approach to identity and social labelling (Anderson, 2006).

The implementation of sanitation and segregation policies tells at least as much about colonial thought as it does about the administration of public health. The segregation of lepers was not only an attempt to contain the disease physically, but also metaphorically confirmed the prevailing values of public health at the time. As anthropologist Mary Douglas argues about the relationship of cleanliness with order, 'dirt is essentially disorder . . . [and] exists in the eye of the beholder . . . In chasing dirt, in papering, decorating, tidying, we are not governed by anxiety to escape disease, but are positively re-ordering our environment, making it conform to an idea' (Douglas, 2002, 2).

Active segregation embodied American ideas of modern, sanitary science of the early 20th century. The colonial Bureau of Health, for instance, once declared: 'The difference between an ordinary barrio and a sanitary barrio is the difference between order and chaos' (Bureau of Health, 1911, 21). This approach promoted personal hygiene, environmental sanitation and combinations of medical treatment practices as the solution to a plethora of public health concerns. The emerging field of 'tropical medicine' was largely organized within these ideas. At first concerned with the survival of the white race in the new colonial possessions, it gradually moved its focus to investigate the immunities and vulnerabilities of the natives. Practices of quarantine and segregation were rooted in, and at the same time reinforced, the prevailing belief in the first half of the 20th century that diseases were mainly caused by the exposure of vulnerable hosts to filthy and unclean environments.

The segregation of people with leprosy created a social taxonomic system that is not only conceptual but also grounded in actual practice.[10] Colonial health and sanitation policies are widely recognized as one of the techno-scientific mechanisms exercised by the colonial state on a population in order for them to be monitored, dominated and controlled. As sociologist Nikolas Rose notes: 'To differentiate is to classify, to segregate, to locate persons and groups under one system of authority and to divide them from those placed under another. Placing persons and populations under a medical mandate – in the asylum, in the clinic, in an urban space gridded by medical norms – exposes them to scrutiny, to documentation and to description in medical terms' (Rose, 1995, 58). In the case of Culion, the bureaucratic act of documentation produced innumerable files and data that became the basis of colonial knowledge and administration. Thus, as historian Penelope Papailias observes, 'archival categories and conventions' always reveal 'imprints of governance, traces of imperial imaginaries, and products of discourses and technologies of documentation (statistics, demography, ethnology, law, etc.) marshaled by the state to describe, manage, and rule various 'problematic' populations' (Papailias, 2005, 7–8). In this sense, archives become prospective subjects, sites of knowledge production suitable for ethnographic inquiry (Stoler, 2002).

Records as control, archives as remembrance

'Colonial administrators', anthropologist Ann Laura Stoler remarked in her most recent book, 'were prolific producers of categories' (Stoler, 2009, 1). In the era of leper segregation, various records were systematically created and used in the imposition of social exclusion as well as physical segregation. The Segregation Law of 1907 (Act No. 1711, 1907) offered a legal mandate that effectively criminalized leprosy, a view that is inscribed and embodied by the voluminous records, and the categories that they contain, that were produced and utilized for the purpose of documenting and classifying the people in the island. The records in the archives of Culion thus bear old categories used in classifying and documenting the segregated patients of the former colony, tangible remnants of the intangible past, of colonial practices and ideas. In their individual record, patients were referred to as 'inmate', and any subsequent release from the facility was termed a 'pardon'. The moment a patient was admitted in the island, his or her name, age and place of origin was entered in the Patient Registry, which also tracked down their status as either pardoned, escaped or dead. A separate registry was in use for children born of leprous parents who were immediately segregated from their parents and brought to a nursery, and later on, adoption. Information was recorded about every patient on the island in regular bacteriological reports; gratuity cards recorded the small allowances they received from the government in exchange for their mandatory labour; and when a patient died a necropsy report was made.

Visual records are perhaps the most 'visible' remnants of the leper segregation era in the archives of Culion. Photographs of patients were taken before and after they received experimental chaulmoogra oil-based treatments (Figure 11.1). Silent films and photography were also circulated within the medical field to provide a visual index of the various manifestations and stages of leprosy in the body. Visual records were made with the intent of being distributed as campaign materials – images showing the day-to-day affairs of the colony and its modern treatment facilities, the various leisure and social activities, and the clean and orderly community where the lepers were happy and free. Such images represent the island as an

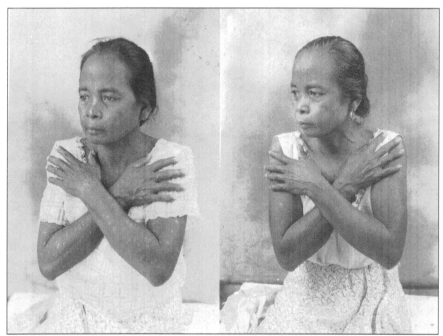

Figure 11.1 Photographs illustrating the before and after treatment of an unknown female patient taken in the 1920s; papules present on the patient's arms (left) were almost completely eradicated after a series of chaulmoogra oil injections (right) (courtesy of the Culion Leprosy Museum and Archives)

idealized 'haven' for lepers. In his memoir, Victor G. Heiser, then Chief Quarantine Officer and later Director of Health of the Philippines, proudly revealed, 'I wanted to popularize Culion so that the lepers who were at large would come there willingly. I had photographs taken of the colony, and even moving picture reels made, a great achievement in those days, showing how attractive it was' (Heiser, 1936, 230).

Canadian archival thinker Hugh Taylor once argued in favour of the necessity to understand records, especially during their active lives, as powerful 'instruments' or tools used in the conduct of bureaucratic affairs and social relationships. 'Our documents', he contends, 'have, in one way or another, made an impact on the lives of people to whom they were directed' (Taylor, 1995, 9–10). Recording and record keeping were embedded in socio-medical practice that controlled people's lives and mobility on Culion. Records were more involved in ensuring the seamless implementation of segregation than simply passive containers of data. From each patient's arrival at the colony until their death or 'parole', all forms of records were used to document and monitor their status and condition. Records not only recorded but inexorably defined the communities for which they were created.

Records served the goals of mandatory isolation. In this light, I argue that records have a rather precarious relationship with the community that they were meant to document and regulate. Created and consumed by the old colonial institutions of public health and medicine, documents were inextricably connected not only to their makers, but also to the population that they classified, labelled or described. Moreover, the current generation, which desires to come to terms with its past, has revived its connection to these surviving documentary artefacts.

Culion's leprosy archives now assumes two simultaneous functions: first, as evidence and former tools of community dismemberment and segregation by a former colonial regime; and second, as the embodiment of the archives' newly acquired and contemporary purpose as the symbol of community heritage and a common collective past. The transformation of a body of forgotten records into archives enabled a collection of documents, the very evidence of segregation and colonial control, to become the tangible manifestation of community heritage and identity. The archives of communities like Culion, with histories of isolation, displacement and segregation, can help us to better understand the nature of records; moreover, they offer a point of reflection to think about the function of archives in collective commemoration and remembrance.

Archives and the affirmation of community memory

According to one sanitarium employee who was born to former patients of the leprosarium: 'What's a centennial without a monument to erect? The Philippine centennial was about the statues of our national heroes. Since the whole island is already a monument, we are erecting a museum full of records about our ancestors who are our heroes.' Archives are among those 'boundary stones of another age, illusions of eternity' identified by the French historian Pierre Nora as *les lieux de mémoire* – sites that are 'fundamentally remains, the ultimate embodiments of a memorial consciousness' (Nora, 1989, 12).

Reflecting on the work of establishing the archives of Culion, the administration and application of archival rules and processes, I noted a kind of ritualistic performance that rendered and symbolically transformed a body of records into archives. This transformation begins when an archivist enters the community to organize records, and culminates in the inauguration of the collection as archives. Somewhere between its nascent beginnings in a roomful of 'old' papers and its inauguration during the centennial commemoration as 'the archives', the Culion community observed and interpreted the actions implemented and applied on this body of documentary artefacts as constituting a set of legitimating practice. When I asked one schoolteacher what she thought about the archives, she replied:

> Since I was a child, I was aware that the old laboratory [now the archives building] had old documents, papers left behind by the American doctors. Now they are neatly organized in boxes and carefully arranged. I never realized their importance until I saw how meticulously they were cared for and handled for the centennial. It is embarrassing to realize that I did not know then that our heritage was in those papers.

In her eyes, archival acts of arranging, boxing, labelling and exhibiting rendered the dormant records into meaningful archives that embodied heritage and identity. 'We are glad that we now have people helping us bring the needed expertise to transform our paper scraps into archives,' said one doctor on the eve of the centennial. This statement perhaps best represents the prevailing idea among the community that a professional archivist has the legitimate power of transforming documents into archives.

Though far removed from the actual act and experience of compulsory isolation, the records in the archives of Culion are remnants of the past practices of segregation. As members of the community internalize the centennial message that spoke of healing and closing the darkest chapter of their history, they chose to refashion and reinterpret the records in the archives in agreement with the rhetoric that dominated the centennial commemoration. According to Yael Zerubavel: 'The performance of commemorative rituals allows participants not only to revive and affirm older memories of the past but also to modify them' (Zerubavel, 1995, 5–6). If there was a period in time that could be regarded as the moment that transformed the meaning of leprosy records from remnants of a bygone era towards an attitude of respect for artefacts of heritage and identity, it would be Culion's centennial commemoration in May 2006. From their dormant status as papers bundled and wrapped to be forever forgotten in storage, the Culion Leper Colony records became the centre of attention for a community seeking for something tangible that could articulate and embody its collective heritage and symbolize its hundred years of existence. In this moment of heightened sensitivity and search for meaning, the community repurposed the records of leprosy into archives.

What makes it possible for a community to collectively embrace remnants of an oppressive colonial past as its heritage and identity? Interpreting the fate of the archives of Hawaiian hula and its relationship with contemporary hula performance, ethnomusicologist Amy Stillman, quoting Antze and Lambek (1996, xi–xxxviii), underscores the relationship between memory and the construction of identity: 'Memory serves as both a phenomenological ground of identity (as we know implicitly who we are and the circumstances that have made us so) and the means for explicit identity construction (as when we search our memories in order to understand ourselves or when we offer particular stories about ourselves in order to make a certain kind of impression)' (Stillman, 2001, 188). For Stillman, archival sources of the hula comprise a poetics 'dismembered' from its contemporary performance. Dismemberment here means the dislocation of textual evidence from actual performance of the hula as a ritual and as an embodied act of cultural memory.

The act of archiving and keeping of records in institutional repositories consequently limits the presence of documents in the outside world. In a similar vein, the records kept in archives become so far removed from the utilitarian transactions and day-to-day lives of the people that they acquire a different status in the collective imagination. Archives then become fertile ground for the interpretation and inscription of symbolic meaning. Historian Antoinette Burton has argued that 'we must concede the fundamental liminality of the archive: its porousness, its permeability, and the messiness of all history that is made by and from it. We might even think of it as a kind of "third space": neither primary nor secondary because it participates in, and helps to create, several levels of interpretive possibility at once' (Burton, 2003, 26).

Culion taught me to understand archives not as mere collections of documentary artefacts, but as a storehouse for and affirmation of community memory where the archivist facilitates as mediator, but not the final arbiter, of evidence and remembrance. Reflecting on the recent calls for archivists to recontextualize and be 'self-conscious' about the interpretive aspects of their work – such as appraisal, arrangement, description and exhibitions (Hedstrom, 2002; Yakel, 2003; Nesmith, 2005) – I came to realize the role of archives in collective remembrance and representation. In this context, the challenge is to understand how a community perceives archives and how it comes to terms with the documentation of its past. I argue that by renaming records as archives within the context of commemoration, archivists mediate the production of collective memory – the realm of selective remembering or forgetting and the affirmation of community identity.

Co-witnessing: becoming a 'vulnerable archivist'

Records, according to Wendy Duff and Verne Harris, are

> always in the process of being made . . . 'their' stories are never ending, and . . .
> the stories of those who are conventionally called records creators, records
> managers, archivists, users and so on are (shifting, intermingling) parts of bigger
> stories understandable only in the ever-changing broader contexts of society.
>
> Duff and Harris, 2002, 265

In the context of a commemorative event, practices of representation and commemoration are largely mediated by the decisions made by a few members of the community, the elite who assume the representative voice for the rest of the community. As Laura Millar observes, 'if social memory is forged and refashioned through a process of pick and choose, then the vehicles of memory will be subject to the inevitable partiality and bias of those in society with the power to do the picking and choosing' (Millar, 2006). The irony in the creation of Culion's archives was that the path towards constructing the archives of this displaced and segregated post-colonial community is through the decisions made by archivists, leaders of the community and funding agencies.

I am inspired by anthropologist Ruth Behar's notion of the vulnerable observer, which emphasizes that field researchers cannot be absolutely objective as they both shape and are shaped by their research encounters (Behar, 1997). Similarly, archival work in Culion was a rare opportunity to be a 'vulnerable archivist': to experience and witness how a community comes to terms with its past by repurposing its archives. Vulnerability also helped me to understand my own position as part of a larger web of interests that both limits and influences the interpretation of archives.

It was obvious that there was an outsider/insider divide that was operating in Culion at the time of its centennial and beyond. Perhaps nothing best exemplifies this than the stark difference in the narratives about the meaning of the seal of the Philippine Health Service. This seal is prominently displayed on a high slope of the island and is particularly visible when approaching Culion from the sea (Figure 11.2). Outsiders, mainly reporters, tourists and even academics normally interpreted this as a warning for those approaching the island that they were entering the dreaded leper colony. The seal, built in 1926 to commemorate the colony's 20th anniversary, was in fact made of coral stones carried to the edge of the mountain and constructed by the patients themselves. For residents of Culion, the seal was a testament to the achievements of their ancestral predecessors, a triumph of the human spirit to overcome the most deforming and debilitating of all diseases. For the community today, the seal is not a mark of fear or stigma, but symbolizes hope and pride.

Figure 11.2 Built in 1926 by the patients themselves, the seal of the Philippine Health Service – also known in Culion as 'Aguila' or Eagle – is a prominent landmark seen when approaching the island from the sea

Another contrast between outsider interpretation and the insider narrative is the notion of the island as a site of banishment versus a shelter for the patients. Early accounts of segregation produced numerous reports of the most unwilling patients being forcibly taken into the island. However, there have been instances of voluntary segregation, and stories of those who found the island a haven where patients could be free to be themselves without fear of humiliation and stigma also abound. The current generation understands the island to be a shelter.

This was apparent from the centennial motto (Figure 11.3), prominently painted on walls near the hospital entrance: 'Culion: Nurtured and Blessed for a Hundred Years; Yesterday a Shelter; Today Hope and Unity; Tomorrow Stability and Prosperity'.[11] From a reputation of being diseased, desperate and debilitated, the current generation emphasizes their ancestors' exercise of agency through labour and being able to take control of their environment. Patients were usually depicted as deteriorating, degrading and dying by the outside world. But for the community, the presence of structures still standing on the island built through compulsory labour, attests to the fact that

Figure 11.3 The centennial motto was written in Filipino on a wall leading to the hospital entrance; it reads 'Culion: Nurtured and Blessed for a Hundred Years; Yesterday a Shelter; Today Hope and Unity; Tomorrow Stability and Prosperity'

not all patients in Culion were brought there to die. Many lived almost normal lives, got married, had children, and were productive citizens who contributed to the development of the community.

Although everyone agreed on the importance of Culion's records, outsiders and community members understood their meanings through different interpretive frames. As an outsider specialist, my difficulty lay in the irony that our project was to 'bestow' a heritage status on a body of hospital records that documented the bodies of those who had been incarcerated under the Segregation Law. These records were conduits to the isolation of individuals and documented a mechanism of subjugation and control based on colonial medico-scientific knowledge. However, many in the community understood these records as the only evidence of their departed descendants and predecessors, the ancestral lineage for much of their community. 'I opened one of the boxes', said one respondent, 'and saw the old Gratuity Cards. I immediately searched for [my uncle's name] but I did not see it. But I saw another name [of a family that] still resides in this island. I immediately went to tell them about my discovery. It made me happy.' Most of the records provided the only remaining traces and proofs of the existence of people otherwise unknown to have existed who were in danger of being forever forgotten given their marginal status. Thus, the record's legacy of colonial society did not inhere in the community's prevailing narrative – the 'story they tell themselves about themselves' – about what the archives kept (Geertz, 1973, 448). As Liam Buckley observes, 'In the archive, colonial categories continue to work at shaping social relations even though the world outside is living in the time of independence' (Buckley, 2005, 255).

'All the things we cannot articulate . . . '

Two views of archives seem to be most prominent. On the one hand, archives are sources of evidence about the past suitable to be harvested or mined by historians and other arbiters of knowledge about the past. On the other hand, there are an increasing number of claims that archives are the embodiment of and repository for society's collective memory. Perhaps now is the time to establish a rapprochement between these two viewpoints and reflect on how archivists could respond to the needs of both popular memory and history in various contexts and profound ways. We can begin by acknowledging that we could serve both memory and history and that both have equal importance to communities that we all serve. In this regard, historian of American slavery Ira Berlin provides a compelling argument about the interdependence of history and memory:

[T]hey desperately need one another. . . . If memory is denied and history is allowed to trump memory, the past becomes irrelevant to the lives of all. . . . But if history is denied and memory is allowed to trump history, then the past becomes merely a reflection of the present with no real purpose other than wish fulfillment or, at best, myth with footnotes: a source of great satisfaction to some, but of little weight beyond assertion. . . . Indeed, only by testing memory against history's truths and infusing history into memory's passions can such a collective past be embraced, legitimated, and sustained. And perhaps . . . by incorporating . . . memory into . . . history and vice versa . . . [we] can have a past that is both memorable and, at last, past.   Berlin, 2004, 50–1

Brien Brothman suggests two types of archivists that echo the memory and history relationship: 'history's archivist' and 'memory's archivist'. History's archivist is primarily concerned with 'finding records and, in them uncovering evidence to develop a linear narrative about a past. . . . Memory's archivist is interested in the past's residue as material promoting integrated knowledge, social identity, and the formation of group consciousness' (Brothman, 2001, 62). If we consider archives a set of records adopted by the community as their own, it will be helpful to account the meanings and values that people ascribe to archives and the context for which these values are employed. Once more, archivists are challenged to be more self-reflective and to account for their decisions. Archivists should view their actions as 'co-witnessing' and not only as expert authors in the construction of archives as heritage and collective memory of a community. We make archives more meaningful by being aware that, as we perform archival tasks, we participate in, and to some extent mediate, the communal re-membrance of the past.

Whenever we perform our mediating functions on records, we ourselves become the 'interface' (Hedstrom, 2002) between the past embodied in archives and the community who access them. I would say that while I satisfied the perceived need for expertise to transform records into archives in the eyes of many in the community, my role was more an element within a larger commemorative ritual of what historian and geographer Kenneth Foote characterized as 'sanctification', or the process by which something is erected and designated as a memorial site (Foote, 1990, 387). In the case of Culion, the designation of a body of colonial medical records into archives constitutes an act of memorialization. Understanding this relative position of archives in commemoration helps us situate the limited place of archives and archivists in collective memory. In the contemporary and memorializing function of Culion's colonial archives, the records are collectively repurposed to embody contemporary desires and aspirations regardless of their actual contents and what they documented. Archives in Culion were 'touchstones'

(Millar, 2006) not only because they evoked memory, but also because, to repeat my earlier quote from one doctor, they were used as tangible representations of 'all the things we cannot articulate about our past, about our need to heal in the present and about our desire to foresee a great future'.

Notes

1   The term 'leper' has been widely recognized as stigmatizing and because of this it is advocated that its use be discontinued. My use of the term is mainly to recreate past perspectives and conditions associated with the disease but not to endorse them. Ideas for this paper were first articulated at the Fourth International Conference on the History of Records and Archives (ICHORA 4), 3–5 August 2008, Perth, Western Australia. I am grateful to Jo Robertson of the Global Project on the History of Leprosy (www.leprosyhistory.org) at Oxford University for introducing me to Culion and for inspiring me to embark on this research. I have tremendously benefited from the insightful conversations and comments from my mentors, colleagues and friends at the University of Michigan School of Information, particularly my adviser Margaret Hedstrom as well as David Wallace, Anthea Josias, Trond Jacobsen and members of the interdisciplinary workshop on Archives and Collective Memory. Thanks to Fatma Müge Göçek, whose course on culture, memory and history provided much encouragement. I owe special thanks to Jesse Johnston for the many hours spent patiently listening to my ideas for this paper.

2   This period also saw the transfer of colonial powers from Spanish to American. The years surrounding 1898 are significant in Philippine history as they mark the transition from one colonial government to another. Filipinos hailed their victorious revolution against 333 years of Spanish rule, the US entered into an agreement with Spain to purchase and annex the islands through the Treaty of Paris in 1898. Thus, although 1898 marks the year when the Spanish colonial regime ended in the country, it is also the moment when the US commenced its 48-year occupation of the islands.

3   Such as the Philippine-American War of 1899 to 1902; see A. Velasco Shaw and L. H. Francia (eds) (2002) *Vestiges of War: the Philippine-American War and the aftermath of an imperial dream, 1899–1999*, NYU Press.

4   Following America's annexation of the Philippines, numerous agencies were created to implement programmes for public health and sanitation, which also upheld modern and scientific ideals of their time. These institutions have commemorated their centenaries over the last decade. With these commemorations, the demand to organize and preserve the records of communities organized under colonial sponsorship has grown. Archives in commemorations seem to have acquired a special status as material evidence supporting the symbolic justification of claims of long historical roots as well as the embodiment of collective memory and identity.

5   The American colonial administration of the Philippines identified the island of Culion as a segregation facility in 1901. Construction of the hospital and other facilities began in 1902, but it was only in 1906 that the patients started to be segregated on the island.

6   Leper segregation was justified under the Segregation Law of 1907 entitled An Act Providing for the Apprehension, Detention, Segregation, and Treatment of Lepers in Philippine Islands (Act No. 1711). It is evident that the edict was directed towards subjugating a particular population to a regime of the combined practice of incarceration and cure, precisely expressed in its title: 'apprehension, detention, segregation, and treatment'. At that time, however, no cure for leprosy was known. Thus, treatment was something that the law on its inception could never attain, even if rigorously executed.

7   Senate Committee on Territories and Insular Possessions and House Committee on Insular Affairs, *Leprosy in the Philippine Islands: joint hearings on S. 5434 and H.R. 16618*, 99th Cong., 2nd sess., 15 February 1927, 15. As indicated in the statements made by Capt Gottfried W. Spoerry of the US Army during the US Congressional hearing in 1927: 'Then why not go to Culion? We will go there because it is the largest leper colony in the world, many times over. . . . So that is the reason for choosing Culion, they are there in large numbers – 12,000 in the islands and 5,600 already segregated who would welcome anything that will grant them relief.'

8   This and other subsequent quotes were taken from the transcripts of interviews I conducted on the island and from my field journal made between April 2005 and May 2006.

9   In order to justify America's annexation of the Philippines, US President William McKinley proclaimed on 21 December 1898, 11 days after the signing of the Treaty of Paris, the occupation of the Islands as 'Benevolent Assimilation'. America took upon itself the task of 'civilizing' and 'educating' the Philippines to make the Filipinos become fit for self-governance.

10 For a discussion of the social impact of classification, see G. C. Bowker and S. L. Star (2006) *Sorting Things Out: classification and its consequences*, MIT Press.

11 This is my translation from the original Filipino.

References

Act No. 1711 (1907) An Act Providing for the Apprehension, Detention, Segregation, and Treatment of Lepers in Philippine Islands.

Anderson, W. (2006) *Colonial Pathologies: American tropical medicine, race, and hygiene in the Philippines*, Duke University Press.

Antze, P. and Lambek, M. (1996) Introduction: forecasting memory. In Antze, P. and Lambek, M. (eds), *Tense Past: cultural essays in trauma and memory*, Routledge.

Bastian, J. A. (2003) *Owning Memory: how a Caribbean community lost its archives and found its history*, Libraries Unlimited.

Bastian, J. A. (2006) Reading Colonial Records Through an Archival Lens: the provenance of place, space and creation, *Archival Science*, **6**, 267–84.

Behar, R. (1997) *The Vulnerable Observer: anthropology that breaks your heart*, Beacon Press.

Berlin, I. (2004) American Slavery in History and Memory and the Search for Social Justice, *Journal of American History*, **90** (4), paras. 50–1, www.historycooperative.org.proxy.lib.umich.edu/journals/jah/90.4/berlin.html.

Bowker, G. C. and Star, S. L. (2006) *Sorting Things Out: classification and its consequences*, MIT Press.

Brothman, B. (2001) The Past that Archives Keep: memory, history and the preservation of archival records, *Archivaria*, **51**, 48–80.

Brown, R. H. and Davis-Brown, B. (1998) The Making of Memory: the politics of archives, libraries and museums in the construction of national consciousness, *History of the Human Sciences*, **11** (4), 17–32.

Buckley, L. (2005) Objects of Love and Decay: colonial photographs in a postcolonial archive, *Cultural Anthropology*, **20** (2), 249–70.

Bureau of Health (1911) *Annual Report of the Bureau of Health for the Philippine Islands for the Fiscal Year Ended June 30, 1911*, Manila Bureau of Printing.

Burton, A. (2003) *Dwelling in the Archive: women, writing house, home, and history in late colonial India*, Oxford University Press.

Carpenter, F. G. (1926) *The World's Biggest Leper Colony, through the Philippines and Hawaii*, Carpenter's World Travels, Doubleday, Page & Company.

Craig, B. L. (2002) Selected Themes in the Literature on Memory and Their Pertinence on Archives, *American Archivist*, **65** (1), 276–89.

Douglas, M. (2002 [1966]) *Purity and Danger*, Routledge.

Duff, W. M. and Harris, V. (2002) Stories and Names: archival description as narrating records and constructing meanings, *Archival Science*, **2**, 263–85.

Foote, K. (1990) To Remember and Forget: archives, memory, and culture, *American Archivist*, **53** (Summer), 378–92.

Geertz, G. (1973) *The Interpretation of Cultures*, Basic Books.

Gillett, M. M. (1990) US Army Medical Officers and Public Health in the Philippines in the Wake of the Spanish-American War, 1898–1905, *Bulletin of the History of Medicine*, **64** (4), 567–87.

Harris, V. (2001) On (Archival) Odyssey(s), *Archivaria*, **51** (Spring), 5.

Hedstrom, M. (2002) Archives, Memory and Interfaces with the Past, *Archival Science*, **2**, 21–43.

Heiser, V. G. (1936) *An American Doctor's Odyssey: adventures on forty-five countries*, W. W. Norton & Co.

Jimerson, R. C. (2003) Archives and Memory, *OCLC Systems and Services*, **19** (3), 89–95.

Ketelaar, E. (2005) Sharing: collected memories in communities of records, *Archives and*

Manuscripts, **33** (1), 44–61.

Maus, L. M. (1912) The Sanitary Conquest of the Philippine Islands, *Medical Record: A Weekly Journal of Medicine and Surgery*, **82** (3), 1017.

McIntosh, R. (1998) The Great War, Archives, and Modern Memory, *Archivaria*, **46** (Fall), 1–31.

Millar, L. (2006) Touchstones: considering the relationship between memory and archives, *Archivaria*, **61**, 105–26.

Moran, M. T. (2007) *Colonizing Leprosy: imperialism and the politics of public health in the United States*, University of Carolina Press.

Nesmith, T. (2005) Reopening Archives: bringing new contextualities into archival theory and practice, *Archivaria*, **60** (Fall), 259–74.

Nora, P. (1989) Between Memory and History: les lieux de mémoire, *Representations*, **3** (Spring), 7–25.

O'Toole, J. M. (1993) The Symbolic Significance of Archives, *American Archivist*, **56** (Spring), 234–55.

Papailias, P. (2005) *Genres of Recollection: archival poetics and modern Greece*, Palgrave Macmillan.

Piggott, M. (2005a) Building Collective Memory Archives, *Archives and Manuscripts*, **33** (1), 62–83.

Piggott, M. (2005b) Archives and Memory. In McKemmish, S., Piggott, M., Reed, B. and Upward, F. (eds), *Archives: recordkeeping in society*, Centre for Information Studies.

Rose, N. (1995) Medicine, History and the Present. In Jones, C. and Porter, R. (eds), *Reassessing Foucault: power, medicine and the body*, Routledge.

Rosén, F. I. (2008) Off the Record: outsourcing security and state building of private firms and the question of record keeping, archives, and collective memory, *Archival Science*, **8** (1), 1–14.

Rosenberg, C. E. (1967) *The Cholera Years: the United States in 1832, 1849, and 1866*, University of Chicago Press.

Schwartz, J. and Cook, T. (2002) Archives, Records and Power: the making of modern memory, *Archival Science*, **2**, 1–19.

Senate Committee on Territories and Insular Possessions and House Committee on Insular Affairs (1927) *Leprosy in the Philippine Islands: joint hearings on S. 5434 and H.R. 16618*, 99th Cong., 2nd sess., 15 February.

Stillman, A. K. (2001) Re-Membering the History of the Hawaiian Hula. In Mageo, J. M. (ed.), *Cultural Memory: reconfiguring history and identity in the postcolonial Pacific*, University of Hawaii Press, 187–204.

Stoler, A. L. (2002) Colonial Archives and the Arts of Governance, *Archival Science*, **2**, 87–109.

Stoler, A. L. (2009) *Along the Archival Grain: epistemic anxieties and colonial common sense*, Princeton University Press, 2009.

Strange, C. (2004) Symbiotic Commemoration: the stories of Kaluapapa, *History and*

Memory, **16** (1), 86–117.

Taylor, H. (1982–3) The Collective Memory: archives and libraries as heritage, *Archivaria*, **15** (Winter).

Taylor, H. (1995) 'Heritage' Revisited: documents as artifacts in the context of museums and material culture, *Archivaria*, **40**, 8–20.

Velasco Shaw, A. and Francia, L. H. (eds) (2002) *Vestiges of War: the Philippine-American war and the aftermath of an imperial dream, 1899–1999*, NYU Press.

Yakel, E. (2003) Archival Representation, *Archival Science*, **3**, 1–25.

Zerubavel, Y. (1995) *Recovered Roots: collective memory and the making of Israeli national tradition*, University of Chicago Press, 5–6.

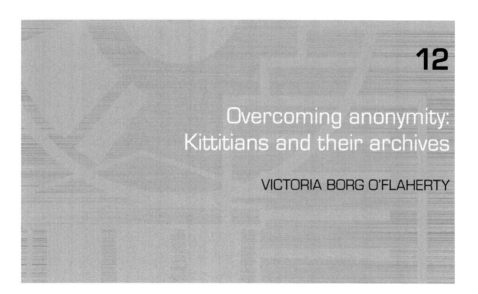

12

Overcoming anonymity: Kittitians and their archives

VICTORIA BORG O'FLAHERTY

Introduction

Many natives of St Kitts have claimed that they do not care about the past because there is nothing in it that is worth remembering. The complexities of the relationship of post-colonial societies and their history have often had an impact on the way archives are viewed. Kittitian researchers approach them with a sense of awe, that something so old has survived while others call them 'white people archives' and refuse to use them. The statement is a rejection of the archives of the colonizer and a yearning for what is not there – an archive of the colonized. Trouillot writes, 'Silences are inherent in history because any single event enters history with some of its constituting parts missing. Something is always left out while something else is recorded' (Trouillot, 1995, 49). Since power and the ability to create archives rested with the island's elite, the records naturally reflect the events they felt were important. As a consequence records are often obstacles that hide and distort significant elements of the history of the colonized (Bastian, 2006, 267). Accounts of visitors to St Kitts and the Caribbean speak of the cheerful singing of the field gangs, but there was nothing enjoyable about the cane fields. The songs, often protests or prayers, were a tool, developed in Africa, to co-ordinate team effort in agricultural activities (Abrahams and Szwed, 1983, 46). By recognizing that the archive was an inherent part of the machinery of colonialism, one becomes conscious of its limitations in contributing to the history of the colonized in a post-colonial community and yet it is still a source of information about them.

For the Kittitian community the 'daily recounting' (Connerton, 1989, 17) or gossip of village life gives rise to a history that is immediate, accessible and appealing to a people whose roots had been severed and who were governed by an alien elite. However in government and in organizations, reliance on memory places severe limitations on decision making. The administration of self-governing St Kitts had to learn the importance of records quickly and almost entirely without assistance. Convincing the rank and file of the civil service to comply with this need required training and the nurturing of a new culture that was inconsistent with what existed in the villages. Without this change, Kittitians stand the risk of silencing themselves.

Record keeping in colonial St Kitts

The written chronicle of St Kitts, a tiny island in the Eastern Caribbean (Figure 12.1), begins with the arrival of the first Europeans who changed the ecology and the demography of the island from one of a tropical rainforest in which the Kalinago subsisted both on what nature provided and on small crops that they grew, to a plantation economy where enslaved Africans and their descendants cultivated one crop for export. The records of the first three hundred years after contact in 1623 were produced by colonists, planters and the imperial state to secure property, maximize profit and protect interests. These are reflected in the sessional papers, official correspondence, court records and legal documents they created, many of which have survived on the island. In these records the enslaved 'intrude abruptly and en masse in

Figure 12.1 Location of St Kitts and Nevis

revolts, mutinies, uprisings, and insurrections, constructed, in an imperial historiography as aberrations and interruptions' (Norton, 1993, 457). This type of political action was usually followed by repression and the re-establishment of the status quo, a process that created the recorded evidence of trials and inquiries as 'officials urgently sought testimonies as mechanisms for defusing a revolt and capturing its organizers' (Dubois, 2006, 294). The planters also created their own business records better known as plantation records. Those that relate to Kittitian plantations are now found in the county record offices and universities of the UK, libraries and collections in the US and at the University of the West Indies, Jamaica. In these records the enslaved were property to be exploited through 'a bondage that dishonoured its subjects as it alienated them from labour and kin in a perpetual and inheritable fashion' (Scarano, 1999, 233). Their necessities were 'provided for' by those who claimed ownership over them but their world was essentially 'temporary rather than one which was preserving and improving a way of life for succeeding generations' (Roberts, 1997, 66).

However, as demands for cheaper produce to feed the European working class grew, the protection that sugar from St Kitts once enjoyed in the mother country disintegrated as did the privileged position of the planters who found themselves to be small parts of a much larger Imperial framework administered from London. Stoler describes the 19th-century colonial state as an 'information hungry machine' and the archive as a 'powerful technology of rule' (Stoler, 2002, 101). This power continuum was predicated on the accumulation of information on the colonized through a detailed mapping of the island,[1] but more often was accomplished through statistical data collected by the colonial civil service, as in the Blue Books and the Register of Slaves, and at times through more intimate knowledge of the community received from informants or law enforcement. This is evident in the police reports on labour activists in the secret files of the Administrator and in the transcripts of visiting Commissions that started arriving in the West Indies in the closing years of the 19th century.[2] Their purpose was 'to scrutinise state practice, reveal bureaucratic mistakes and produce new truths about the workings of the state itself' confirming the state's perceived prerogative to decide what was in the interest of the community (Stoler, 2002, 106).

Most of the enslaved brought to St Kitts were from non-literate cultures but among arriving Africans were Muslim men who were literate in Arabic. In 1682 French Jesuit Jean Mongin noted the presence of Muslim teachers among the enslaved population of St Kitts (Diouf, 1998, 149). One of these literate men may have attempted to record his life experiences. It is therefore possible that other enslaved workers with an oral culture may have been exposed to literacy and personal record keeping within the slave quarters.[3] It would have been these scripts that could have made a 'counter-archive' (Bastian, 2006, 275) a possibility, but slave societies were fraught with suspicion and scripts that were indecipherable could present a danger to their creator. The other enslaved may not have recognized the value of literacy, at least not until they became familiar with the powers that it gave their enslavers. They would have heard their masters read from books and newspapers, carried letters to other households, seen the drafting of documents to be shared or circulated among others of the same class and noticed records kept in desks or locked drawers for safe-keeping. They would have seen plantation accounts, labour registers and punishment books being updated. Those enslaved living on estates run by attorneys would have witnessed the intense scrutiny of the books and letters in preparation for the master's visit. Occasionally the enslaved, especially those who worked close to the planter's family, were afforded the chance to learn to read and write. Some, like Pembroke on the Mills Estate, were trusted enough to receive instructions from their absent master but a fall from grace could come with dire consequences.[4]

The enslaved would have also learned the value of the written document in their own lives. Permits authorizing movement had to be produced on demand (Goveia, 1965, 156). Occasionally a slave would take the risk of leaving the estate without them, resulting in the posting of a notice of reward. All slaves would have been familiar with such notices and with the advertisements of slave auctions as well as with the mental trauma associated with both events even if they could not read the actual announcements.

Acquisition of literacy after a slave was freed was not easy since private tutoring would have been necessary. This did not prevent them from using records to protect their rights. In 1726 John Africa petitioned the Commission for the Sale of the French Lands to be allowed to keep land he had acquired (Journal of Proceeding, n.d., 21). In 1811 Joardine Wells who was freed in her owner's will made a will of her own leaving her property and slaves to her sister and her nephews and nieces (St Christopher Register, n.d.). Dubois comments on the recording activities by former slaves that took place in the period after the two emancipations in the French islands. The right to write a document was a way of securing rights that had previously been denied, a way of solidifying the economic stakes of familial relationships such as inheritance, as well as securing a hold over land and property (Dubois, 2006, 294).

There was one record, they quickly learned, that had to be cared for and kept safe – the manumission (see Figure 12.2). Those who were freed in wills, through gratitude, kinship or purchase knew the value of the document they were given to prove their personal emancipation. This document, although

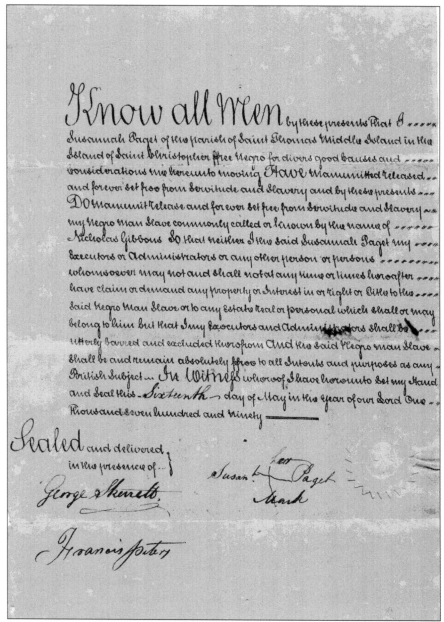

Figure 12.2 Manumission document

recorded in the St Christopher Register along with sales of property, real and
human, was a record they had to be able to produce if they were to remain
free (Goveia, 1965, 221–2; Cox, 1984, 56–8). What this did was enforce the

perception of the written record as an instrument of empowerment. The case of enslaved woman Betto Douglas' claim to freedom, her punishment and her running away were based on records: the letter that was supposed to have set her free, her deposition against the plantation manager, the depositions made against her, the court decision to acquit the manager of wrongdoing, the notice that she had run away (Copies of Despatches, 1826).

These colonial records are 'unintentional witnesses of Afro-Caribbean life as it is reflected in encounters between the colonial administration and the Afro-Caribbean community existing within a plantation society' (Olwig, 1985, 11). They fulfilled the needs of the island's elite for administration and justice and only incidentally recorded the experiences of the enslaved or their descendants. To show what is yet to be uncovered through these records, the National Archives of St Kitts has produced small publications and exhibitions, participated in media programming, presented findings in public lectures, and encouraged potential researchers to visit the facility.

Interest in these pre-20th-century records has come primarily from descendants of planters exploring their family connection with St Kitts and from scholars, both Kittitian and expatriate, doing research at universities abroad. Occasionally members of the St Christopher Heritage Society (SCHS)[5] have visited the National Archives of St Kitts to conduct research in them for projects that the Society was engaged in or in response to queries from abroad. Many Kittitians, however, feel that talking about slavery is dredging up an unpleasant and even humiliating past that they would rather forget. Visitors have stood silently incensed over the Registry of Slaves; others have laid hands on the volumes as if on a loved one, returning with friends and family to see them again. 'My ancestors are in there!' a visitor once declared with pride. The fact that surnames are rare and that the last register is separated from the first civil registration by 25 years seems to be of little importance for those who cling to the hope that the gap can be bridged some day.

Occasionally, there have been persons who have asked to see plantation records because of ruins they noticed in a particular location or because their family had long been associated with a particular estate and they wanted to see if any possible ancestor were on the books or they simply wanted to get a feeling of what life was like in a particular period. These sets of correspondence, punishment books, work books and accounts no longer exist on the island. Plantation owners were often resident in the UK and it was the papers they kept that survived, but several Kittitian researchers have expressed a sense of deprivation at the fact that they cannot see them. Similarly records created by the clergy of the different churches serving on the island are also too far away to be accessed. The National Archives has acquired the *Wingfield Estate Books 1897–99* from the University of the West

Indies, Jamaica, and the *Annual Accounts of a Plantation Belonging to Bertie Greatheed 1781–84* from the Warwickshire County Record Office but other attempts have not had the same success. These records contain valuable information about the daily lives of estate workers that cannot be found in the official proceedings. The problem of their accessibility to those whose stories they documented is dealt with in Bastian's concept of a 'community of records'. She defines it as 'both a record keeping entity and as a memory frame that contextualizes the records it creates' and sees the custodial obligation being fulfilled through access rather than physical control. Bastian maintains that provenance 'suggests the necessity of maintaining the context of record creation' (Bastian, 2003, 13, 111). The plantation records of St Kitts, often considered personal papers, or family archives, are part of 'The multiple layers of actions and interactions between and among the people and institutions within a community. Layers of records parallel the active life of the community itself' (Bastian, 2003, 5).

Due to the nature of the plantation, the records fall into two layers, for, although privately created, the plantation was in many ways until 1838 a substitute for the state with a vast majority dependent on it for their basic needs including housing, food and clothing (Figure 12.3). Although these records too are incomplete, the story of the lives of the majority of Kittitians in the first three hundred years of the island's plantation economy cannot be

Figure 12.3 Estridge Estate, St Kitts

effectively constructed without them and slowly Kittitians are finding that if they want their story told, they have to learn to tell it themselves.

Archives and postcolonial St Kitts

The 20th century brought major changes in the creation of records on St Kitts. For the first half of the century, the trend set earlier continued and records were created as a means of information gathering about the colony. But the constitutional climate of the island was shifting towards a more participatory environment. In 1937 elective representation was introduced admitting men into the Legislative Council who were not part of the planter-merchant class. Workers' rights to organize and to improve working conditions were recognized in the years that followed, strengthening the support base of the elected representatives. Universal suffrage was finally introduced in 1952 and in 1967 an executive consisting solely of elected, black, working-class men was given full responsibility for internal affairs. In 1975 and 1976 the sugar industry was nationalized but by then it was in serious difficulty. Recovery was only temporary and economic diversification had to be initiated. The Federation of St Kitts and Nevis became independent in 1983. The transition to self-determination and self-government was far from easy and often the Kittitians who took charge of the new administration found themselves unprepared to deal with the changing circumstances.

The Leeward Island Federation (imposed in 1871 and consisting of Antigua, the British Virgin Islands, Montserrat, St. Kitts-Nevis-Anguilla and Dominica) was dissolved in 1957 so that each unit could separately join the new West Indies Federation. Government agencies once shared and administered through Antigua had to be recreated in each island. Key positions once held by expatriates became available to Kittitians and Nevisians who were not always trained. Some were able to learn by observation or imitation. A report produced in 1965 found that 'Junior staff – especially new entrants to the service – are not shown thoroughly and systematically what they are required to do and the reason for doing it and for doing it in a particular way'. Training was 'often interpreted as an expense paid visit abroad' which did not reach enough staff to encourage a service oriented machinery (Gardener-Brown, 1965, 12). This was further exacerbated by the 'shortage of men fitted to undertake the work of Permanent Secretary to a Ministry' (Gorsuch, 1960, 6).

In 1957, immediately after the ministerial system was introduced, the Administration published General Orders in an effort to ensure organization. They continued to apply when St Kitts-Nevis-Anguilla became an associated state and after independence although it was felt that they were colonial instructions that should have been revised. The chapter in General Orders dealing with Correspondence and Public Business touched on such matters as who in the service was permitted to write to the Governor, how subjects were to be referenced in correspondence, the use of official stationery, the storage and referencing of confidential and secret correspondence, the production of annual reports and the *Official Gazette*, and finally the disposition of records (General Orders, 1957, 63–5). On this matter General Orders provided for a review of records that were over ten years old to determine disposition. Those to be destroyed had to be recorded and their fate sanctioned by the Administrator. Records could not be destroyed if their preservation was required by law or regulation, if they were 'of historical or other interest', if they related to land, especially Crown Land, or if they were more than 100 years old (General Orders, 1957, 66). However, circulation of General Orders was limited to a couple of permanent secretaries and only a handful of government employees were familiar with their content.[6] Even less had any experience of record appraisal. Financial Instructions were more widely circulated and included specific retention schedules for accounting records but again adherence was rare.

The concept of the maintenance and the archiving of records was not easily absorbed especially in a culture where the oral transmission of information predominated. In many ways record keeping as a whole was part of that alien culture, demanded by foreigners who held positions of power. The lack of public accountability that had infused the colonial service persisted, while the unmanageability of the new records series that were being created in the process of transacting business produced an air of inefficiency. In 1962 E. C. Baker, University of the West Indies Archivist, who had come to the island to make a records inventory, saw first hand the effect that the lack of training was having on the accumulation of records. When he asked why certain records were still in an office, he was told 'I met them there' (Baker, n.d., 4). That same expression and the lack of action, interest or responsibility it implies still persists in the civil service today, even in the senior ranks.

Kittitians who entered the civil service did not come to it with a sense of their nation's worth. They had been taught a history that centred on European colonialism as a civilizing force and considered everything else as primitive: 'England was a place to want to be, unlike those places where savagery still potentially ruled.' The British were seen to be in 'possession of their own history, a narrative that took them from the barbarism of their ancestors to the civilisation of the present' (Hall and Rose, 2007, 36). In these circumstances it was understandable when government officials did not see the same historical value in the heavily used files that they created every day as they did in the impressive volumes inherited from the colonial admin-istration. Since they also had no knowledge of appraisal and disposition, the story of self-governing and independent St Kitts has to be constructed from records that were not deemed worthy of archiving.

It may be, however, that the problem of the lack of interest in record keeping is caused by another factor, one that has its roots in the homes of St Kitts. Until the 1970s, the majority of houses were small, mostly wooden structures, usually consisting of one room partitioned into dining and sleeping areas by a makeshift screen. There was no room for collections unless they were pasted on to the walls of the house. In the Caribbean paper ages quickly and harbours pests. Books were considered valuable but paper was not. When houses received their major cleaning just before Christmas, the old made room for the new with letters and photos rarely surviving more than a few years. If a collection of papers survived this annual ritual, they were often disposed of when their owner passed away, unless they documented property. This behaviour was common to many households and persists even though houses are now larger and built of blocks. It left little room for the internalization of the concept of keeping records or collections.

For example, Union General Secretary, J. N. France was meticulous in his record keeping, recognizing both the utility of records in an industrial dispute and their historical value. He had made effective use of them in a series of articles on labour history that he had published in the Union's newspaper, the *Labour Spokesman*, but soon after France died in 1997, the minutes he had kept were discovered in the street awaiting disposal. Fortunately they were rescued and are now in the National Archives as part of a private collection.[7] Records of benefit societies have not fared so well. Some concerns have also been raised regarding the records of small churches on the island. To minimize the risk of more being lost, their secretariats have been informed that the National Archives will be willing to take their records and keep them safe.

However, when the urge to clean out the old is coupled with a sense of misplaced arrogance there is very little that can be done to save the records at risk. A member of the Carnival Committee spoke of the cleansing that took place when a new committee took over in 1980 following a change in administration. Records were destroyed because the new chairperson felt that his predecessors did not know what they were doing.[8] The National Archives is working with government agencies to convince administrators to use retention schedules and records management procedures to minimize accumulations of records and identify the archives among them before they are destroyed either by negligence or by wilfulness, but the lack of a facility where records selected for preservation can be safely stored and accessed hampers progress.

Conclusion

For most Kittitians, real history started in the 20th century. Most of it falls within memory or at least within that of elders who love to recount how much things have changed. With very little need for encouragement they would gladly tell of how far they had to walk to get to school, the chores they had to do both before and after, the number of Sunday schools they attended. They will talk of the great cricketers who should have made the West Indies side and compare today's politicians, often unfavourably, with Robert Bradshaw[9] and his comrades. Meanwhile a small number of Kittitians are beginning to discover and tell the story of their small island community in books, articles and radio and television programmes. They have a growing audience which is often critical of the fact that these stories had not been part of the curriculum when they were at school. That too is changing gradually. In primary school, children are being taught about the nation's heroes, heritage sites and days of remembrance and in late secondary school they are required to work on small local history projects, which for a brief moment in time allows them to join the ranks of the story tellers. The subjects of these stories are changing, too. Gone is the heroic settler Thomas Warner. It is as an invader, a killer of the Kalinago and a slave owner that he is now remembered. While Brimstone Hill Fortress stands tall as a monument to British engineering, archaeological work is revealing the lives of enslaved men and women who once worked on its construction.[10] On radio, Under Banyan Tree honours the lives of Kittitian performers, teachers, nurses, sportsmen and women, and artists along with legislators and politicians using material gathered from records in the National Archives.

An interest in family history is also growing, primarily among Kittitians resident abroad but it is slowly trickling into the local population. Often these researchers arrive at the National Archive with very little information to work with. Disappointments over relationships gone sour or over misappropriations of funds sent home, high expectations of monetary support, the need to suppress racial origins in order to find acceptance in a new environment all conspired to silence those in the family who could have kept the family connection alive and who would have had information to pass on to the next generation. Because the staff of the National Archives is aware of how important this research is to the person undertaking it, every effort is made to personalize the service offered while attempting to keep expectations within the boundaries of the possible. The indexing of the marriage bonds and some of the birth records has shown what can be achieved but without further work on the vital records the possible solutions to a query are very limited.

There is a growing interest in history in St Kitts. It has been sparked by changes in the economy, political developments and social interactions, all of which have encouraged a demand for local history both in the schools and in the community at large. The vast majority are content to make use of the research of others. For those engaged in this exploration there is a sense of tackling a puzzle, the National Archives being the foundation of their work but having many of its constituent parts hidden in unimaginable locations or scattered in different parts of the world or even lost forever. Among these few there is the determination to find the unwritten story of the island that the rest of the population will eventually make its own.

Notes

1   A new topographical map of the island of St. Christopher in the West Indies, describing all the Plantations with their respective boundaries, the Parishes, Churches, Towns, Rivers, Guts, Highways etc, the whole accurately laid down in the year 1828 by William McMahon, Surveyor of the Island.

2   Judicial reform was the subject of the Fortunato Dwarris investigation, *Third Report of Commissioner of Inquiry into the Administration of Civil and Criminal Justice in the West Indies* (1827) (House of Commons) while poverty and social unrest were the subject of the Norman and the Moyne commissions – Sir H. W. Norman (1898) *Royal Commission on Depression in the Sugar Industry in the W. Indian Colonies*, C. 8655, HMSO, and W. E. Guinness 1st Baron Moyne (1945) *Royal Commission Report*, Cmd 6656, HMSO – just to name a few.

3   This possibility is recognized by novelists trying to overcome the silences in the archives by re-imagining the lives of the enslaved from their perspective. See Dubois (2006), 296–7.

4   I am grateful to Lindon Williams for this information obtained from the transcripts of the Mills Papers at the St Christopher Heritage Society, Basseterre, St Kitts.

5   The SCHS was founded in 1989 by a group of Kittitians who were enthusiastic about the preservation of the culture, environment and history of St Kitts.

6   Conversation with the Hon Tapley Seaton (28 Jan 2008).

7   J. E. Fidel O'Flaherty Collection.

8   This is anecdotal evidence on an issue that many were reluctant to discuss and for which there is no documentation.

9   Bradshaw was leader of the labour movement from 1945 till his death in 1978. He served as the first premier of the state of St Kitts-Nevis-Anguilla and in 1976 had started the process of negotiating the independence. He is recognized as First National Hero.

10   Professor Gerald Schroedl, of the University of Tennessee, heads an archaeological school that comes to the fortress every year in July and August. He has published numerous papers on his work.

References

Abrahams, R. D. and Szwed, J. (1983) After the Myth: studying Afro-American cultural patterns in the plantation literature. In Abrahams, R. D., *The Man-of-Words in the West Indies: performance and emergence of Creole culture*, Johns Hopkins University Press.

Baker, E. C. (n.d.) Problem of Locating and Storing State Archival Material in Caribbean Countries. In *Report of the Caribbean Archives Conference held at the University of the West Indies, Mona, Jamaica, September 20–27, 1965*, University of the West Indies.

Bastian, J. A. (2001) A Question of Custody: the colonial archives of the United States Virgin Islands, *American Archivist*, Spring/Summer, 96–114.

Bastian, J. A. (2003) *Owning Memory: how a Caribbean community lost its archives and found its history*, Libraries Unlimited.

Bastian, J. A. (2006) Reading Colonial Records Through an Archival Lens: the provenance of place, space and creation, *Archival Science*, **6** (3–4), 267–84.

Connerton, P. (1989) *How Societies Remember*, Cambridge University Press.

Copies of Despatches to the Secretary of State Maxwell to Bathurst 9th June 1826 with enclosures.

Cox, E. L. (1984) *Free Coloureds in the Slave Societies of St. Kitts and Grenada, 1763–1833*, University of Tennessee.

Diouf, S. A. (1998) *Servants of Allah: African Muslims enslaved in the Americas*, New York University Press.

Dubois, L. (2006) Maroons in the Archive. In Blouin Jr, F. X. and Rosenberg, W. G. (eds), *Archives, Documentation and Institutions of Social Memory*, University of Michigan Press.

Dwarris, F. (1827) *Third Report of Commissioner of Inquiry into the Administration of Civil and Criminal Justice in the West Indies*, House of Commons.

Gardener-Brown, A. G. H. (1965) *Report of the Commission on the General Structure and Salaries and Conditions of Service of the Civil Service in the Leeward and Windward Islands*, 1965, unpublished.

General Orders for the Civil Service (1957).

Gorsuch, L. (1960) *Report of the Commission on Civil Service Salaries in The Leeward Islands*, unpublished.

Goveia, E. (1965) *Slave Society in the British Leeward Islands at the end of the Eighteenth Century*, Yale University Press.

Hall, C. and Rose, S. O. (2007) *At Home with the Empire: metropolitan culture and the imperial world*, Cambridge University Press.

Journal of Proceeding of the Commissioners for the Disposal of Crown Lands in St. Christopher, Formerly Belonging to the French (n.d.).

Moyne, Baron W. E. G. (1945) *Royal Commission Report*, HMSO, [Cmd. 6656].

Norman, Sir H. W. (1898) *Royal Commission on Depression in the Sugar Industry in the W. Indian Colonies*, C. 8655, HMSO.

Norton, A. (1993) Ruling Memory, *Political Theory*, **21** (3), 453–63.

Olwig, K. F. (1985) *Cultural Adaptation and Resistance on St John: three centuries of Afro-Caribbean life*, University of Florida Press.

Original Register of Slaves (1817).

Roberts, P. A. (1997*) From Oral to Literate Culture: colonial experience in the English West Indies*, University of the West Indies Press.

St Christopher Register (1811) Series 3, Vol. Q, Doc. No. 15381.

Scarano, F. A. (1999) Slavery and Emancipation in Caribbean History. In Higman, B. W. (ed.), *General History of the Caribbean, Vol 6: methodology and historiography of the Caribbean*, UNESCO Publishing, 233–82.

Stoler, A. L. (2002) Colonial Archives and the Arts of Governance, *Archival Science*, **2** (1–2), 87–109.

Trouillot, M.-R. (1995) *Silencing the Past: power and the production of history*, Beacon Press.

13

Always queer, always here: creating the Black Gay and Lesbian Archive in the Schomburg Center for Research in Black Culture

STEVEN G. FULLWOOD

Introduction

In the fall of 2007 a young New York University student named Sarah visited the Schomburg Center for Research in Black Culture to view materials in the Black Gay and Lesbian Archive (BGLA), a project I founded a decade ago to aid in the preservation of Black queer culture and history. As I placed several boxes on the table before her, Sarah's beautiful brown face lit up like sunshine. She was ecstatic about sifting through the stacks of Black queer books of various genres dating from the mid-1970s to the present.

'My brother and I were talking earlier about there being no Black gay culture. That there were only a few Black gay writers like James Baldwin and E. Lynn Harris', she said beaming. Watching as she handled the books, opening and reading parts, her eyes large and smile broad, I shared her enthusiasm. Through Sarah's experience, I recognized myself, small and yearning, recalling that itch for knowledge about Black queerness that became the impetus for the formation and development of the Black Gay and Lesbian Archive.

Behind the archive

Toledo, Ohio, circa 1982. Much like any other black Midwesterner, I was born to working-class people who were products of a post-industrial town in a post-Civil Rights moment. My parents sought to raise children who would live better than they did. Racial equality trumped gay and lesbian rights. The

Black Power and the Black Arts movements dictated the clothes we wore, the way we talked, the movies we saw, and even what we read. Most Black communities dealt primarily with achieving civil rights and upward mobility. By contrast, the reality of gay and lesbian life and culture was complicated. Since everyone knew somebody who was or suspected to be 'that way', homosexuality was tolerated in some sense. There were no specific neighbourhoods for Black queer people because Black people could not afford to, or did not want to, live away from other Black people. Neighbourhoods, schools and churches and anywhere else Black heterosexuals lived, learned or prayed, homosexuals were there, and they too lived, if quietly.

As a teenager, my thirst for a language to describe what I thought I was or at least was becoming ravaged my consciousness. The library became my sanctuary. I regularly perused the shelves for anything Black and homosexual. A friend went to the public library in Cleveland, and discovered *In the Life: a black gay anthology*, edited by Joseph Beam, a book that was a precursor of my future as an archivist. She made photocopies of essays and poems and gave them to me. My heart raced. *Writings by several self-identified Black gay men*. I read those pages repeatedly. These writings expanded my mind about coming out, sexual encounters, homophobia, HIV/AIDS, romance and political activism. I felt less alone in the world. By that time I was collecting books by James Baldwin and continued searching for anything Black and queer. In the ensuing years, I found myself quenching this thirst for knowledge differently, as an archivist.

But it was only after I graduated with a Bachelor's in English and communications that librarianship claimed me. Librarianship revealed itself as a natural choice because it encompassed my love of literature and my interest in managing information in an environment where literacy is celebrated through its collections, exhibitions, programming and public advocacy. After three years of working as a children's librarian, I decided to attend library school at Clark Atlanta University, and earned an MLS. Two years later I was learning to arrange, describe and catalogue collections in the Manuscripts, Archives and Rare Books Division of the Schomburg Center for Research in Black Culture, New York Public Library. New York City effectively changed the way I saw the world and its possibilities. I submerged myself in contemporary Black queer culture.

Arthur Schomburg: invisibility blues and the Schomburg Center

The history of preserving black queer culture at the Schomburg Center is an interesting one, largely because of where the centre now resides, but even more notably for whom it is named. Black bibliophile and scholar Arthur Alfonso Schomburg was a man whose interactions with black queer people indirectly helped to develop and sustain a black queer presence in Harlem, and specifically on dozens of shelves in what is the largest research centre for black resources today. To get a sense of how Schomburg's efforts to preserve black history assisted in what I carefully theorize as a normalization of queerness among black people it is necessary to recognize a confluence of people, location and various events that started with the blues of invisibility and a simple desire to know one's history as experienced by Black bibliophile and scholar Arthur Schomburg.

Schomburg was born in Puerto Rico in 1874 to María Josefa, a freeborn Black midwife from St Croix, and Carlos Féderico Schomburg, a merchant of German heritage. Historians believe that Schomburg was educated at San Juan's Instituto Popular, where he learned commercial printing, and at St Thomas College in the Virgin Islands, where he studied black literature. Biographers speculate on exactly how the young Puerto Rican-born Black thinker became interested in black history (Sinnette, 1989). One story recounts an interview with Schomburg about his involvement with a young people's study group. While all members of the group were social equals, Black and White, the Whites and near Whites had more knowledge of the historical facts of their White forbears than Schomburg. Although Schomburg had studied his Black Puerto Rican heritage, his fellow members were not convinced that Africans or their descendants had contributed anything to the development of the world. This reaction spurred the youngster to extend his research to include Black people in other Caribbean countries including Haiti, Santo Domingo, Cuba and the Virgin Islands. Another story makes the claim that one of Schomburg's teachers told him that 'the Negroes of Puerto Rico have no history', while giving assignments to children of European, Asian and Native Indian (Taino) descent to research the historical achievements of their ancestors. This response both engaged and probably enraged the young scholar thus setting him off on a lifelong quest to discover his African history, and to prove his teacher wrong. It is safe to say that he was unquestionably successful (Urrutia, 1933).

I am less concerned with the origins of either story and more fascinated and inspired by the possible effects each story had on Schomburg directly and indirectly, the communities he subsequently came to represent and serve, and on the thousands of people who now visit and use resources at the Schomburg Center yearly. Most particularly I want to discuss the implications that Schomburg's quest had for Black queer communities, the preservation of their culture and histories.

When Schomburg migrated to the US, it was reported that he immediately immersed himself in black culture. By the 1920s he had amassed what was reportedly the largest collection of Africana materials in the world. In addition to writing about his experiences as a bibliophile and their implications for the community, he also formed personal and professional relationships with a number of historians, artists, politicians and other collectors who would serve his passion for collecting black materials, but who also helped develop the foundation for a black queer presence in the institution that bears his name today.

That Schomburg was in New York and an active participant in the Harlem Renaissance is not only notable; it is critical to the founding of the collection. In 1925, the same year that the 135th Street Branch, Division of Negro History, Literature and Prints was inaugurated and where Schomburg's original collection would be housed the following year, he wrote what would become one of the first theoretical tracts on the value of archives for the displaced African in America, 'The Negro Digs Up His Past'. The essay was published in Alain Locke's seminal text, *The New Negro* and *The Survey Graphic: Harlem mecca of the new negro*. Schomburg speaks emphatically about the role history has had in shaping public discourse about what author Toni Morrison aptly describes as 'a discredited people' (Denard, 2008, 116). History has become less a matter of argument and more a matter of record. There is the definite desire and determination to have a history, well documented, widely known at least within race circles, and administered as a stimulating and inspiring tradition for the coming generations (Schomburg, 1925, 670).

In his essay 'Strange Fruits: rethinking the gay twenties', scholar Mason Stokes offers what he calls a 'preliminary roll call' of queer Harlem: 'Alain Locke, Countee Cullen, Claude McKay, Wallace Thurman, Richard Bruce Nugent, Gladys Bentley, Bessie Smith, Angelina Weld Grimke, Alice Dunbar-Nelson, Richmond Barthe, Augustus Granville Dill, Ma Rainey, Ethel Waters, Alberta Hunter, and, of course, the elusive Langston Hughes' (Stokes, 2002, 56).

During the 1920s Arthur Schomburg socialized with and archived the works of many of these queer writers and artists. Many, including Langston Hughes, Countee Cullen and Claude McKay, gave him autographed copies of their first edition works for his collection. Additionally the collector also corresponded with Hughes and McKay, both of whose archival material is housed at the Schomburg Center today. Artwork by Richmond Barthe is in the art collection.

In 1926 the New York Public Library, with a Carnegie grant, purchased Schomburg's collection, then known as the world's largest collection of black materials and deposited it at the 135th Street Library, the building which now forms part of the Schomburg Center. Schomburg was installed as the curator of the collection in 1932 and served in that capacity until his death in 1938. Two years later the collection was renamed in his honour, and in 1972 the Schomburg Center was designated as one of the four research centres of the New York Public Library.[1]

The beginnings of the Black Gay and Lesbian Archive

When I started working as an archivist at the Schomburg Center, the experience was overwhelming. Far from the one collection I helped to process as a graduate student at the Atlanta University Center, the Schomburg was responsible for maintaining and providing access to the largest collection of Black materials in the world. It was the first repository to collect Black gay and lesbian materials. Not one or two collections, but several. As early as 1977 the papers of Glenn Carrington, which document the personal life of an African-American homosexual from the 1920s to the 1960s, before the advent of the gay pride movement, were donated to the Center. Carrington was noted for his association with figures of the Harlem Renaissance such as Locke, Hughes, Countee Cullen and Harold Jackman, and for his extensive library of first editions by the poets and writers of this movement. Carrington travelled widely in Europe throughout his adult life and developed a broad network of friends, associates and partners.

In addition the Schomburg housed the papers of several men whose work I had read in Ohio or Georgia including Melvin Dixon, author of *Vanishing Rooms*, and other works of fiction and poetry; Assotto Saint, author of *Wishing for Wings*, and editor of *The Road Before Us: one hundred black gay poets*; and, of central significance to me, Joseph Beam, editor of *In the Life: a black gay anthology*. In less than a decade I went from carrying around wrinkled photocopied pages of that book to having access to Beam's papers filled with original submissions, drafts of the manuscript and correspondence with writers such as Barbara Smith and Audre Lorde, founders of Kitchen Table Press, who were inspirations for Beam and scores of other Black queer people. Reading what he read and considering his process of taking an idea to publication resonated with me. Through that seminal publication, he turned on a light in my head as an archivist.

In the introduction, Beam stated that 'visibility is survival', and spoke very clearly about being nourished and inspired by the works of black and Latina lesbian writers, 'I was fed by Audre Lorde's *Zami*, Barbara Smith's *Home Girls*, Cherrie Moraga's *Loving in the War Years*, Barbara Deming's *We Cannot Live Without Our Lives*, June Jordan's *Civil Wars* and Michelle Cliff's *Claiming an Identity I Was Taught to Despise*. Their courage told me that I, too, could be courageous. I, too, could not only live with what I feel, but could draw succor from it, nurture it, and make it visible' (Beam, 1986).

The idea of creating culture and then seeing it preserved would dovetail with another significant experience, processing the records of the Gay Men of African Descent (GMAD). GMAD is a social services organization founded in 1986 by the Reverend Charles Angel. Angel had recognized the need for black gay men in New York City to form coalitions that would address and combat homophobia and racism, as well as HIV/AIDS, and over the years the group evolved from political advocacy into a supportive agency that provides a social space that nurtures black gay men.

My personal involvement with GMAD began soon after I moved to New York City after graduate school. In April 1998 I attended the Friday Night Forum, a programme where topical discussions of the day were presented to a large group of Black gay men. Much like discovering the unique collections of Black queer individuals and organizations at the Schomburg, GMAD offered me the benefit of being in the company of community organizers, writers, artists and professional Black men who identified in a variety of ways: gay, homosexual, same gender loving, or as men who loved men. That particular night I was surrounded by a variety of men, some of whom would later become friends, lovers or colleagues, and would offer their extended social and professional networks thus enabling me to mature and evolve as a writer, thinker and probably most significantly, as an archivist.

In 1999 I approached GMAD about depositing their archives at the Schomburg. Kevin McGruder, the executive director at the time, was interested and helped to develop and execute the project. I was awarded a documentary heritage grant, a programme sponsored by the New York State Archives, which essentially provided a modest stipend to process the papers. The records were moved to the Center, were processed and are now available to the public.

While researching for the grant, I searched for other repositories collecting Black queer materials, both in order to know the territory of queer archives and to develop my grant proposal. The majority of libraries and archival institutions whose stated missions were to collect and preserve Black or queer cultural or historical materials were sadly lacking. What was available in 1999 at many of these institutions were books by mainstream authors like Baldwin, Lorde or Samuel Delany, but less than a handful had Black queer archival records.[2] The Schomburg had (and continues to have) the largest collection of Black queer materials to date.

While I do not recall the exact moment I decided to start an archival initiative to collect the universe of Black queer materials, I do remember feeling that I was in the right place and time to do this work. First, there was location. I was in New York, working as an archivist at the Schomburg Center. Second, I was involved in Black queer cultural and social circles and groups, attending events, and writing for Black queer magazines and journals. Thus I was surrounded by some of the most thoughtful and engaging writers, artists and thinkers of African descent, people who understood instinctively how enormous, complicated and far-reaching their worlds were as Black queer people, and what little representation existed in mainstream media, or was housed in libraries and repositories.

But there's more. Back when I was working as children's librarian in Toledo, Ohio, my feelings about community were constantly evolving. The library I worked at was situated in a lower middle-working class community, where the public schools needed help in educating the community. A legacy of intergenerational poverty was the result of its mis- and under-educated populations. The library became vital to the community and its development, offering free use of its collections, as well as use of computers and public programmes that helped assist community members in need of job training.

It was at this time that I discovered *All Us Come Cross the Water*, by Lucille Clifton, a children's book that celebrates diversity and highlights the importance of acknowledging and empowering individuals to ultimately nourish the community. Clifton captured for me how I wanted to be of use in the community and in the world. Not one of us, not two, but *all* of us come cross the water. It was the first time that I had ever considered that perhaps a healthy community was one where everyone has a role. No one was made invisible. Everyone's gifts were celebrated. I began to consider communities, and how they have typically formed, primarily as ways to develop, define and reify identity. On the surface, it would appear that there are few queer people in Black communities across the US. Where is the evidence in books, magazines, films or businesses? In developing the archive in a very personal way I was proving to myself what I instinctively knew. There are others like me. Hundreds, thousands, perhaps millions. *All Us Come Cross the Water* captures rather succinctly how I feel about my life as a Black queer man, and how the communities I live in – African-American, queer, male, American, citizen of the world – all need to allow misnamed and shunned individuals to come cross the water.

Typically the role of an archivist is not one of active engagement with the community. Usually businesses or organizations close or become burdened with their records, or people retire, achieve a milestone in their careers, or pass away. My approach is to connect with people, organizations and businesses as they are creating these varied histories. But before that I sat down and thought very specifically about what I wanted to do and how to do it.

Conceptualizing the archive

In early 1999 I developed a mission statement for a project that outlined specific goals for the development of a Black queer archive. Although the language has slightly changed over the years, what follows is the original statement:

> The Black Gay and Lesbian Archive (BGLA) is a five-year project (2000–5) created to aid in the documentation and preservation of cultural materials produced by and about black lesbian, gay, bisexual, transgender, Same Gender Loving, queer, questioning and in the life people (LGBT/SGL/Q/Q/inthelife). The project was divided into two phases. The first phase of the project was to gather materials for five years to create a collection that would span the gamut of documented black LGBT/SGL/Q/Q/in the life culture and history. The second phase focused on identifying a repository to donate the materials for the expressed purpose of preservation and access to the public.

I spent about ten years collecting materials before formerly instituting the BGLA in 2000. The collection was housed at my apartment. Inspired by the lack of documentation of non-heterosexual black life in libraries and repositories nationally, the genesis of the project began with my collection of books, magazines, flyers, programmes, conference materials and other ephemera. For five years I travelled extensively in the US and abroad, attending readings, conferences and other cultural events seeking and collecting materials created by and about activists, writers, filmmakers, organizations, businesses and other artists in the US, Europe and Africa. Materials in the collection, as well as photographic collections and artefacts, reflect those efforts. Currently the BGLA contains information dating from the mid-1950s to the present, documenting the experiences of non-heterosexual men and women of African descent primarily in the US, London and several countries in Africa. Consisting of dozens of small collections of one to five folders, these miscellaneous collections form the bulk of the paper-based, non-photographic materials that I acquired through donation or purchase in an effort to bring to light the culture and history of Black LGBT/SGL/Q/Q/in the life people.

Subject areas in the collections will be familiar to members and students of Black queer culture and history including files for writers such as Audre Lorde and Essex Hemphill, but there is also information on lesser known individuals and organizations such as filmmaker Michelle Parkerson,[3] the Los Angeles-based Association of Black Gays[4] and IRUWA! Minnesota Coalition of Black Gays.[5] The collection spans the mid-20th century to the present including a focus on information about underdocumented individuals, organizations and subjects in the 1980s when many organizations formed in response to the HIV/AIDS crisis.

Types of materials in the collection include printed matter (reviews and feature articles, programmes, flyers and broadsides, newsletters), letters, including correspondence generated by me with donors and individuals documented in the collection, CVs and other biographical information, scripts, academic papers and speeches. In some cases, files contain scant information. Additionally, the administrative files contain information about the structure and development of the project and its deposit in the Schomburg Center.

Building the archive

At the beginning I was not completely certain how to collect the universe of Black queer culture and history. As I have mentioned, the nucleus of the archive was the material I had been collecting for years: books I was fortunate to get my hands on, magazines and newsletters I had written for, flyers and brochures for conferences, events and programmes I had attended in New York, Atlanta, Washington, DC, Detroit and my hometown, Toledo. These things were in boxes in my bedroom. It was a start.

But as I said I was in the right place at the right time. As an archivist and an active member of the Black queer community, I had a certain vantage point. My curator Diana Lachatanere,[6] who serves as my unofficial mentor for the project, helps to shape my consciousness about archiving cultures, ways to think about Black queer history and what types of materials are being generated, shares advice on working with donors, and offers feedback on the project's brochures and press releases. With her assistance, I strategized about how to approach the various communities. I sent e-mails to listservs and to my networks announcing the project and wrote articles about the BGLA, attended dozens of Black queer events, walking directly up to people to ask for books and materials for the archive. In this way I became visible to people who did not know about the archive. The relationship between the Black queer and Black communities was nurtured through literature (my writing), the press (online and print) and through my visibility. My complementary roles as archivist, writer and later as a publisher[7] (in 2004), enabled me to reach various communities of people – information specialists, readers, writers, and community organizers – and nurture those relationships over the years by sharing information about the archive and Black queer culture and history in general. The community has responded with overwhelming support. Fortunately a great deal of those relationships resulted in donations to the archives.

I sent letters and e-mails to writers, publishers, filmmakers, photographers and activists. One of the first donors to the BGLA was Herukhuti, sexologist, academic and author of *Conjuring Black Funk: notes on culture, sexuality and spirituality*, vol. 1. He notes that his own work has been supported by his association with the archive, primarily as inspiration for his groundbreaking work. In an e-mail he wrote:

> The BGLA has provided me with a certain level of legitimacy as an independent scholar because of my institutional affiliation with it. It has also helped me by contributing to the way I consider the historical nature of my work. When I am visioning, strategizing, and designing my work, I have in my mind the fact that my work will be included in the BGLA and therefore available to future scholars and researchers. I am conscious of the fact that my actions are contributing to history. I think that has a positive impact upon me as a scholar and researcher. It provides a longer view to what I do.

Other significant donors include Jewelle Gomez, author of the science fiction novel *The Gilda Stories*, who sent copies of all of her books, essays, articles and personal photographs from her collection (her main collection is housed at the James C. Hormel Gay and Lesbian Collection at the San Francisco Public Library). Alan Bell, pioneering publisher and activist, donated an entire run of *BLK*, the first news magazine focused on Black lesbian, gay, Black and transgender (LGBT) news and culture, along with copies of his other publications, *Blackfire*, *Black Lace* and *Kuumba*. Cornelius Moore, director of African Cinema at California Newsreel, contributed copies of *MOJA = Black + Gay*, the first black gay and lesbian oriented newspaper, as well as a copy of the late Marlon Riggs' last film *Black Is . . . Black Ain't*. Lisa C. Moore, founder and editor of RedBone Press, donated copies of her groundbreaking first title, *Does Your Mama Know: an anthology of Black lesbian coming out stories* and *The Bull Jean Stories*, by Sharon Bridgforth, in book and CD format, in addition to donating bags full of books, magazines, newspapers and clippings by and about black LGBT life. Moore believes that the BGLA affects her as a publisher. She writes,

> I want to see my titles preserved for the long-term, as physical books are more and more becoming ephemeral products. . . . Society is pushing publishers to move toward electronic books, which reduces the efficacy of the reading experience. Reading requires many senses, not just vision, and a physical book, I would say, is necessary to the focus and concentration required to read and to think critically – skills that are basic to a civilized society. Additionally, archival preservation of the materials (notes, working files) of the process of publishing will help future generations understand the nuts and bolts of book publishing. That the BGLA is

specific to black LGBT records is fantastic; who else is doing that kind of work in the United States?[8]

Reginald Harris, writer and a librarian at Enoch Pratt Library in Baltimore, Maryland, is a staunch supporter of the BGLA, regularly donating materials from his own collection. When asked about his thoughts about the BGLA, he responded thoughtfully:

> Oddly enough, having you [at the Schomburg Center] does make me feel better in that I'm not the only one saving/collecting things. As you know I had a lot of stuff I just saved/kept over the years, with no real 'reason' or 'purpose' behind it other than the vague idea that some one should be hanging on to, say, SBC Magazine, or flyers/cards from various parties. . . . And I did it even before becoming a librarian. . . . So much is gone, so much that is formative and important to individuals and our community as a whole is 'ephemeral' and easily lost and forgotten. The [BGLA] gives us a place where Our Memory can be stored.

Support for the BGLA has not been limited to the US. London-based photographer and activist Ajamu X donated copies of his own photographs, as well as items from his own burgeoning archive project, 'Family Treasures'. In his own words, 'Family Treasures' is 'a living archive edu-bition' which covers the whole gamut of the UK Black queer experience, from club flyers, films and love objects to posters, radio interviews, workshops and video booths. The archive is overseen by rukus, a Black queer arts organization,[9] aimed at celebrating and showcasing the work of Black lesbian, gay, bisexual and transgender and other practitioners who are at the cutting edge of their practice. rukus was founded by Ajamu and filmmaker Topher Campbell. Additional items include newsletters from the Black Lesbian and Gay Centre, the magazine Bullers and Wickers, and flyers and items from the Breakfast Club, a men's group of all sexual preferences engaging in dialogue, and the Black Perverts Network, an all-male sex party. Dirg Aab Richards, poet and London-based activist donated copies of *The Voice*, Britain's Black newspaper, and *Capital Gay*, both of which featured stories about the pioneering work of Black Lesbians and Gays Against Media Homophobia (BLGAMH) in the early 1990s. There are also files for organizations, articles and events concerning black gay and lesbian life and homophobia in various parts of Africa primarily West Africa and South Africa.

This is satisfying work. Through the Black Gay and Lesbian Archive I have met dozens of writers, academics, activists, publishers, organizers and regular folk, some of whom have become good friends, helping me to find people who have donated materials and serve as advocates for the project, and recommending to others that they donate their materials. I have received scores of letters, e-mails and phone calls asking about the archive, about doing research, inquiring about how to contribute to the project, or simply visiting the library to see the collection. People cleaning out their closets, attics and basements want to know if I am collecting this book or that magazine. Some writers and graduate students have volunteered. I am grateful that these and many other women and men decided to make contributions to the archive project. Their assistance continues to fortify my life's work. Indeed the work that Black queer people have created over the last century has helped shaped more than one activist, artist, organizer, performer, publisher, politician or scholar. Certainly it helps me to build and shape my vision for the archive.

Since 1999 the archive has been written about in a number of publications, and in 2004 the project was featured in *In the Life TV*, a gay and lesbian news magazine. Articles have appeared in library and information resources such as *Library Journal* and the *Archivist of Color Newsletter*, a bulletin of the Society of American Archivists; Black gay publications such as *Arise Magazine*, *Venus Magazine* and *BLACKlines Magazine*; Black publications such as *Africana.com*; and gay publications such as the *New York Blade* and *Between the News*. I have presented papers and given workshops on the archive at professional conferences such as the American Library Association and the Black Caucus of the American Library Association, and at various colleges and universities in the US and abroad.

My work in the community at prides, readings and other functions has offered me visibility and put me in conversation with individuals of varied interests. People have often introduced themselves at these events, and more often than not the Archive gains a donation or I am able to add another advocate to call upon when searching for the whereabouts of a particular individual, organization, book, magazine or other piece of ephemera particular to Black queer culture.

Locating the archive

Although the BGLA has always been partially available to the public for research, in 2004 I donated the archive to the Schomburg and was better able to serve researchers who requested access by appointment.[10] Engaging scholars has been beneficial. Their research interests have helped me think about current trends in the academy and consequently the archive. Over the years scholars and researchers of all walks of life have come to the Center to research the collection to complete theses, dissertations, articles and documentaries, or simply to look at the variety of materials. Although the benefits of having the presence of the archive travel through cultural productions is gratifying and often brings other researchers to the BGLA, it is the casual researcher looking for evidence of queer life among people of African descent that is just as valid, if not more a reason to do this generative work.

That said, there are challenges in managing this collection. One lies in the name itself, Black Gay and Lesbian Archive, which does not cover the scope and range of the project. Indeed, it goes against what the archive stands for: to collect a variety of non-heterosexual cultures and histories created by and about people of African descent. As the project continues to be processed, I have consulted with a number of people who are helping to find an appropriate name for this project that will acknowledge but not change due to the evolving sensibilities of current and future non-heterosexual *self-defining* women and men of African descent. Challenges also include properly archiving emerging technologies such as websites, blogs, MP3s and even text messages, in an environment that is constantly changing forms and modalities. What is perhaps most challenging, however, is to continue publicizing the existence of the archive so that the public knows what it is, how to use the materials, and by association lets others know it lives at the Schomburg Center.

Conclusion

A decade has passed since my initial idea to start the archive. The archive has afforded me the benefit of being a part of a worldwide sensibility about collecting and preserving underdocumented cultures. In doing so, the Black queer community, which is the archive's primary audience, has offered its unyielding support for its development and maintenance. Much of what I have heard over the years in the form of thank yous is the budding consciousness to save and sometimes rescue the evidence of being, living and sometimes thriving in the Black queer community. There is something to be said about the enduring presence of a largely misunderstood and often ridiculed community of people persecuted because of their sexuality by Black people, and because of their race among the larger white community in the US and abroad. This absence is unmistakably measurable by the lack of evidence in libraries and archival institutions, in the curriculum at schools, colleges and university, in the media, and in public discourse.

The Black Gay and Lesbian Archive was created to address these issues, create public dialogues and share in the responsibility of bringing progressive change to every aspect of everyday living. The intention is to transfer culture so that we, as people, have the benefit of looking at ourselves in a variety of ways. Without the contributions of the Black queer community, the archive would cease to be.

Several donors over the past years have been extremely supportive of the work I do because, from various vantage points, they understand what having such an archive can do for the community and its history and culture; and its vitality, through having the privilege of seeing the road travelled by others, before. Records of those individuals who created culture and organizations, and were out in ways unimaginable to most, can be gratifying, and in some crucial ways life-sustaining.

Notes

1   Schomburg Center for Research in Black Culture, www.schomburgcenter.org.

2   These few collections include The James C. Hormel Gay & Lesbian Center at the San Francisco Public Library, which housed the Jewelle Gomez Papers and the Gary Fisher Papers, and there was a small collection of materials at the Auburn Avenue Research Center on African American Culture and History, Atlanta/Fulton Public Library.

3   Michelle Parkerson is a writer, filmmaker, university lecturer and performance artist currently based in Washington DC. Among her award-winning films are *But Then, She's Betty Carter* and *A Litany for Survival: The Life and Work of Audre Lorde*. See www.wmm.com/filmCatalog/makers/fm289.shtml.

4   Association of Black Gays (ABG) is one of the first Black queer organizations to form in Los Angeles in 1975. ABG organized out of a need to develop a political, social and economic voice for Black gays and lesbians in the larger gay and Black communities. ABG's newsletter, *Rafiki: The Journal of the Association of Black Gays*, features a variety of articles on current events, and editorials about the state of Black queer rights in fall 1976.

5   IRUWA! Minnesota Coalition of Black Gays was a chapter of the National Coalition of Black Gays founded in 1978. It worked against racism, sexism, ageism and classism with Black communities and Gay Communities. IRUWA! means 'high God' in Masai.

6   Diana Lachatanere is the Curator of Rare Books and Manuscripts at the New York Public Library.

7   Vintage Entity Press, vepress.com.

8   Lisa C. Moore and Steven G. Fullwood, e-mail correspondence, 2009.

9   rukus! Federation is a ground-breaking cutting-edge organization dedicated to celebrating and showcasing the best in challenging, provocative works by Black lesbians, gay, bisexual and trans artists nationally and internationally. See www.rukus.co.uk/.

10   There were two phases of the project that helped found the BGLA. The first phase was the gathering of materials; the second was to place materials in a reputable repository for the express purpose of preservation and access to the public for research.

References

Beam, J. (ed.) (1986) *In the Life: a black gay anthology*, Alyson Publications.

Clifton, L. (1973) *All Us Come Cross the Water*, Henry Holt.

Denard, C. C. (ed.) (2008) *Conversations with Toni Morrison*, University of Mississippi Press.

Hunter, M. B. (ed.) (1993) *Sojourner: Black gay voices in the age of AIDS*, Other Countries Press.

Schomburg, A. (1925) The Negro Digs Up His Past, *Survey Graphic*, **6**, 670-2.

Sinnette, E. D. V. (1989) *Arthur Alfonso Schomburg: Black bibliophile and collector*, Wayne State University Press.

Stokes, M. (2002) Strange Fruits: rethinking the gay twenties, *Transition*, **12** (92), 56-79.

Urrutia, G. E. (1933) 'Schomburg' Diario de la Marina, Havana, Cuba, 2 November, 1933. Arthur A. Schomburg Papers, Schomburg Center for Research in Black Culture, New York Public Library; two conversations with Toni Morrison, interview with Charles Ruas, 113.

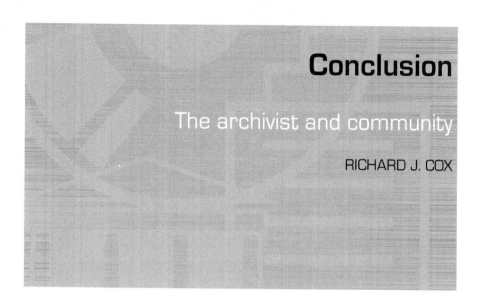

Conclusion

The archivist and community

RICHARD J. COX

Introduction: feeling good

Invoking the notion of community as part of our professional mandate is another way we can feel good about what we do. We feel good if we can say we build or connect to community, even if we are not altogether sure about what it means. Indeed, community may have as many definitions as information. Social pundits invoke it to urge citizens to take control of improving the quality of their lives and to understand a broader public good. Real estate agents carefully describe it to market and sell a house, affirming that location is everything. Historians study its meaning, or use it as a means of focusing their investigations. Sociologists use it as a way of investigating social, political, economic and other trends in society. Journalists and others in the media use the term for their investigative reporting.

Community is seen by many to be an asset; to not belong to a community is a problem, a detriment to living out life to its fullest. The point here is that being part of some sort of community is deemed to be a normal part of humanity, and it is seen as an essential objective if one seems disconnected from a community. Professions, such as are represented by archivy, are also communities, and archivists usually feel just as good when they commune with each other at conferences, workshops and other venues.

The current interest in community may be the result of so many thinking it is endangered in the digital era. Before a few hundred years ago, humanity lived in local communities, and they often could do so in some degree of isolation. The rise of commercial networks, the broadening intellectual

Enlightenment, the emergence of telecommunications, the demands of the Industrial Revolution for raw materials, and the electronic computer revolution all brought with them threats to how we conceived community. Another way of looking at this is to understand the shift from agrarian to mechanical to virtual time, where we see a transition from very natural to extremely artificial notions of timing our daily routines. The earliest notions of community were delineated by how far one could walk to beat out a living and back again, and that distance kept expanding from feet to horse or animal power to steam, then automotive and, finally, air power. Notions of community changed from groups banded together around streams and lakes to nearby roads and railways to proximity to airports. Local became regional then national and finally global community. Cultural institutions – such as libraries, museums and, of course, archives – often served to ground us into the community, and, in the case of some, particularly archives, were often the focus of professional mission and agenda (Cox, 1996).

Communication, and especially more recent modes of telecommunications, ought to remind us about the role of recorded information in the creation, or erosion, of community. Once upon a time community was completely associated with place, that is, it was shaped by topography and natural resources. Technology enabled us to overcome all that, and geography was replaced by networks (some could now work from anywhere). At one time we needed to be close to sources of power generation, and soon even that was not completely necessary. We began to associate geographic place with virtual place (cyberspace), or, maybe a better explanation is that we began to assign characteristics of the old place with the new space virtually taking over. We used to be limited by walking to communicate with one another, but then we could use various faster routes, some natural like rivers and others artificial such as rail, to send letters. The postal age was then overcome by the digital age, the handwritten letter and postage became the dinosaur and the information highway became the meteorite hurtling toward earth and potentially bringing with it the extinction of one era and the birth of another. In all this, we can see how records have always played a role in the creation or sustenance of community, although, as many who have studied communication, information or knowledge historically have reminded us, we need to be careful not to over emphasize the role of how information has functioned or the importance it has played (McNeely and Wolverton, 2008) while at the same time acknowledging how communication networks, enabling the regular exchange of letters and specimens, were essential to the creation of new kinds of scientific and disciplinary communities (Parrish, 2006).

We often tend to discuss community softly, as a kind of feel-good term.

When we get down to specifics, real cases involving archival, archaeological and other assets documenting the past, the issues can be more complex than we thought and quite unsettling for scholars, curators and custodians of material culture and documentary evidence. Sarah Tarlow, considering archaeological ethics, provides a glimpse into such complexities, when she raises the thorny issues of what, if any, responsibilities we have towards the people of the past: 'Because modern people through their acts of scholarship and imagination give existence to past people, those past people should not be regarded as dead or static but, as social beings, capable of being affected by action or discourse in the present' (Tarlow, 2006, 202). In building her case she cites the Australian National Statement on Ethical Conduct in Research Involving Humans, a statement asserting 'that non-Western traditions as well as more recent developments in social science research practice have often emphasized the importance of community values. Members of societies see value in collective activities well beyond the value of each person's individual share of the benefits' (quoted in Tarlow, 2006, 210). These different cultural perspectives may explain why some Westerners see the looting (or acquisition) of antiquities very differently from non-Westerners (compare Cuno, 2008, with Brodie et al., 2006).

Archival sources and community characteristics

We can discern the notion of community in the linkage of documents (the ideas of provenance and the evidence of context are often associated with community). We can see this in correspondence, the creation of an interior world between two letter writers, and sometimes deliberately read by others and purposefully saved for later generations. We see this in diaries, mostly written to be read by others, to shape a particular life's remembrance and to function as a memory device. We can even see this in government and organizational records, where records compiled (and piled) get read and reread over time, generating a sense of belonging and purpose among workers and building varieties of corporate memories. Sometimes we find in the most routine letters glimpses of the individual rather than the organization peering out, seeking to connect with us. This is not altogether unlike why we see people blog and participate in listserves, often being more visible via virtual means than interpersonal face-to-face forms of interaction. They seek to connect, to be heard and, yes, to build a community (real and virtual) around themselves. While some criticize the negative aspects of digital communication on society, and especially community, we can also sense that for some individuals and groups life would be worse off without the digital networks.

It is because of the attributes, roles and values of documents, especially after they have become archival (and whether that means that they have been physically placed in an archival repository or preserved in some other fashion is something that is changing because of the shift in the technologies used to create and use records as well as our deepening understanding of the forces creating records), that the relationship between archives and community seems so vital, both practically and potentially. We learn in the essays in this book that archival records (and the archival repositories established to deal with them) perform complicated roles of commemoration, celebration and communication that establish or strengthen communities. We also learn that records, especially as they morph into ones with archival value, serve interesting and complicated roles related to the power of particular groups in any society or culture within that society.

We even learn that archives, sometimes because they are not understood completely by various segments of society, assume interesting and also complex symbolic aspects that can shape (or imagine) the communities constituting any society. The fact that a group may resist placing documentary materials into established archival repositories, opting to create their own, enhances our understanding of the role of power and authority emanating from the acts of creating and preserving documents. However, the fact that the establishment of an archives suggests critical things about a community achieving certain aspects of identity, pride, cohesion and so forth also brings into play other factors that we need to comprehend as we, the archivists, scan the societal horizon and the documentary heritage society leaves behind. It is not just about feeling good about ourselves.

One of the important points emerging from these essays is that the traditional Western orientation to archives as textual records, created in the course of ordinary business and other human activity, is not sufficient for all cultures or places. Former European colonies cannot be understood merely through such records, especially since the primary portion of these documents were created by those doing the colonizing, but we have to take into account other forms of expression, such as song, dance and oral tradition. This has proved difficult at times, as one scholar suggests, when we understand that 'For the administrations of the Western world, a life without files, without any recording, a life *off the record*, is simply unthinkable' (Vismann, 2008, xii). And, the idea of how such sources, broadly defined, are managed, must be reconsidered; old notions of ownership, control and even preservation must be carefully re-evaluated in light of how some peoples view records and how they might be used. Some documents possess religious significance or reveal ceremony not meant to be viewed by those outside a community; the idea that these records and their evidence and information are there to be used by anyone at any time can be seen as anathema or sacrilege by those who originally generated the records. Scholars examining the relationship between archives and community tend to perceive the greater complexity of sources making up what can become the documentary heritage. As Galloway notes, from the perspective of ethnography, all cultures construct information systems combining both textual and oral sources.

Archives, community and truth-telling

One of the most discussed aspects of archival sources in the past generation has been the relationship of records and record keeping to truth or, put in another way, the veracity of evidence these records contain. Such issues have especially emerged as archivists have begun, although *just* begun is the better way to put this, to deal with the greater complications of working with communities such as indigenous peoples or those that have been pushed to the fringe of society. For example, in dealing with claims, from property ownership to intellectual property, the emphasis has been on textual records, such as those created by legal and government processes. However, for many groups there are other sources, performance and story, that carry equal weight for them and, in many instances, command more power and influence as a means for community stability and meaning. Oral history, and its parallel, oral tradition is often seen as part of an 'activist practice', an attribute also often suggesting that oral sources are often assigned lower authority than traditional textual sources (see Hamilton and Shopes, 2008). This is but one reason why many communities have opted to form their own archives, operating under their own rules and principles, rather than work with the older, established archival repositories.

The critical analysis of documentary sources has led to a bewildering array of postmodern and other discourses about the notion of socially constructed truth and the role of power in the generation of documentary sources and their control once deposited behind the walls of archives or hidden by complicated legal and policy frameworks. Exemplary of this, the past several decades have also witnessed *new* kinds of archives built as part of truth commissions. Often these commissions have led to the establishment of archives apart from the official government archives and different forms of commentary on the effectiveness of those other public archives (see, for example, Grandin and Klubock, 2007). Whether we believe in truth or not, or see the complicated nature of what truth means in any kind of documentary form, society and its inhabitants still need or desire truth.

As some have pointed out, as does Ketelaar in this volume, the notion of truth has more to do with victims being able to tell their stories in a manner that brings healing to them, their families, and their communities than it does with some verifiable, pure idea of being able to reconstruct past events in an absolute way. Considering such issues moves us into the murky, but always interesting, realm of memory and what public or collective memory does to challenge more objective notions of the past or historical evidence. If we follow the idea that public memory is often more powerful an idea for community identities, then we can also acknowledge that sometimes it is the mere existence of a memory institution – museum, library, historic site and archives – that is crucial and not what any of these repositories might actually hold or how their holdings might be used. The many stories found in archival repositories becomes, just as importantly, the idea of *many memories* found there; if nothing else, this suggests a competition between the memories and the sustenance of many communities.

Archives, connected to truth commissions, establish a relationship between archives, memory, justice and accountability. These are complicated relationships. Archives, used for social justice, can seem to politicize the archival function, muddling the old objective of archivists functioning as neutral observers and participants (see Ridener, 2008). And accountability, even when called upon within the archival community when the utility of the archival codes of ethics is debated, is not yet a universally agreed upon part of the archival mission. Professional archival associations often employ rhetoric about matters of government transparency, broad access to archival documentation from democratic governments to private corporations, and the necessity of archival records in an open society, but the unresolved tensions about the utility of ethical codes even threaten the sense of archival community. Once again, this may be the result of power issues, although here it is the power coming with professional associations (rather than government agencies or corporate entities). Professional associations have power in how they choose (or not) to enforce ethical practice or, just as important, in how they deal with requests such as those made within the scope of the Protocols for Native American Archives.

The notion of truth, a topic that will always be associated with archives and the documents they hold, will also always be a compelling one for reflection, debate and dissent. Mary Lefkowitz, the classicist who took on the Afro-centrists (arguing that the Greeks stole their philosophy and other knowledge from Africa), worries that 'Telling the truth, instead of being our first responsibility, had suddenly become less important than achieving social goals' (Lefkowitz, 2008, 2); others might argue that there are issues of Western power, colonial power structures, and even the ignorance of other sources outside the traditional ones. The point here is that when we, the archivists, reach out into under-represented and supposedly under-documented communities, we need to expect different kinds of questions, comments and discussions. Are we ready for this?

Archives and the mythology of impartiality

Archives are not neutral, benign, static institutions (although we have a long tradition of pretending that this is the case). They are also not just devices to create community, add self-respect or pride, and improve identity of particular societal groups. In fact, if we are doing our job well, we often will hold archival materials challenging the identity or role or even value of other groups. We want the records of both the National Association for the Advancement of Colored People and the Ku Klux Klan. We want to document both the gay and lesbian community, as well as groups who are opposed to the rights and role of this community. We want the records of groups supporting the war in Iraq and Afghanistan as well as those opposing this war. These are all bellwether issues for our society, and if our objective is to leave for future generations a reasonable documentation of what our society represents, we need to be deliberate and public about efforts to encompass a wide range of perspectives, activities, organizations and institutions.

This is why it is sometimes difficult to not have mixed reactions to stimulating presentations about archival programmes getting out into the community to motivate various societal sectors to care for their documentary heritage. Archives and archivists working on projects involving school children, working with community institutions such as churches, and reaching out to under-represented groups such as those who are economically disadvantaged or who have been the victim of discrimination often couch their projects in terms of enhancing community cohesion, building pride and improving education. Given that one of the purposes of this volume is to demonstrate how non-traditional sources can be viewed as archival materials – as Bastian argues, performances, celebrations and commemorations can be shown to be kinds of records – it is also necessary to realize that expanding our definition of archives can lead to a cacophony of voices and conflicting interpretations that can set one community against another. If government agencies restrict the kinds of public demonstrations allowable in order to keep the public order, what kinds of restrictions will archivists have to impose?

Reaching into the community seems like a logical activity, but it is not one that should be undertaken without some careful thought. Acquiring the records of one group might offend other groups. Providing identity, meaning and authority to one group often must challenge or undermine the same qualities of another group. Such concerns are readily obvious in any grassroots efforts that have developed to fill in gaps in the dominant, traditional archival programmes, such as the acquiring and preserving of home movies. Patricia Zimmerman describes how 'home movies constitute an imaginary archives that is never completed, always fragmentary, vast, infinite' (Zimmerman in Ishizuka and Zimmerman, 2008, 18); for her, archives are not 'depositories of old, dead cultural artifacts' they are 'never inert, as they are always in the process of addition of new arenas and unknown objects. The archive, then is not simply a depository, which implies stasis, but is, rather, a retrieval machine defined by its revision, expansion, addition, and change' (Zimmerman in Ishizuka and Zimmerman, 2008, 19). We can assert, quite logically and confidently, that new and more energetic efforts to engage new and different communities is part of the change in archival work in the early 21st century.

Such issues may mean that other kinds of repositories (some physical, some virtual) do need to be established. Some of the commentators in this volume write about the challenges of building trust and positive relationships with certain groups who have felt left out by the mainstream archival community. It will be hard, indeed, to convince a particular community that their records and other archival materials should be placed within a repository that is also accessioning the records of groups opposed to them or that seem to hate them. This, however, challenges archivists about how to convey their mission in an increasingly complicated society that is pluralistic, divided and contentious. It reminds us that records are seen in different ways by different groups at different times. In playing with the notion of the colonial archive, for example, Bronwen Masemann concludes,

> whether colonial archives are understood as nodes in communication networks, as property transferred between sovereign nations, as storehouses for the memories and voices of the past, or as catalysts for the ideological and political controversies of the present, it is clear that they are not dusty, forgotten collections of papers, but dynamic and relevant institutions that will continue to be discussed and re-evaluated far into the future.   Masemann, 2009, 12

Hey, it's not always positive

Let's consider some instances where the process of creating records or establishing archives can be seen as resisting community identity, memory and status. In a popular, but powerful, book about efforts to restore an African-American cemetery in East Texas, China Galland uses local government records to examine the history and ownership of the cemetery, fighting her way through crowds of people searching land records for mineral rights, the very purpose of which threatens the cemetery. First, she recognizes the limitations of these records with their 'silences, the omissions, the gaps', recognizing that the 'records . . . were the victor's story. They were elaborate lists of who ended up with the title, not whether they had gained the title legally or ethically. That information was not recorded' (Galland, 2008, 168). Then she recognizes that the process of even generating records in her research conjures up issues of power and submission for the African-American community, observing that the courthouse records 'had shown me how white people made the rules, kept the records, and wrote the history. There was power in being someone who knew how to use that system. I could see that. Now I was beginning to see the lens of whiteness that I was wearing, beginning to feel the glasses on my own nose, becoming aware of this distortion' (Galland, 2008, 185–6). The kinds of personal revelations Galland experienced await every archivist walking beyond their repository walls into the community.

Power and mistrust often tend to jinx our efforts when we discuss matters such as community outreach and building new grassroots projects. Commentators about archives from the outside, such as Ann Stoler, have emphasized the elements of power expressed in records and record keeping. Although many archivists acquire, describe and provide access to their documents without much reflection about what the evidence and information in these sources promise, Stoler's study reminds us that an archival document brings into play issues of power, control, memory, forgery and fabrication, and other such aspects. Records are not just neutral testaments of evidence waiting to be mined by a researcher, but they generate fiction and fact, story and testimony, all rolled up into bureaucratic and societal conventions of recording and remembering. Stoler uses terms such as 'uncertainty and doubt', 'confused assessments', and 'contradictory testimonies' as a normal part of record creation (Stoler, 2009, 4, 23). In records we find contests over power, efforts to find belonging and community, sentiment, explorations into faith, visions of the future, revisions of the past, and rumours shaped into facts.

In such assessments, we see why communities who feel disenfranchised avoid established archives and seek to establish their own archives, but one act of power expressed in establishing such archives also can be seen as an act of power against another group. Where does it end? Can attributes like identity and self-esteem be driving forces in helping communities if we understand that there may be many communities, with polar opposite agendas and perspectives, represented in our archives or that seek our assistance in forming one, independent archives? And, to be sure, why should we think that what communities do might be all that different, or necessarily better, than what older archival programmes have been doing for decades or centuries?

Behind great walls

When we think about archivists out in the community, we can conjure up visions of the new paradigm that this might represent. For sure, we know that old-school archives were designed to suggest fortresses or palaces, places where the archives were safe, locked away and reflecting the power holders in any particular society. In W. Ralph Eubanks' essay about the Mississippi State Sovereignty Commission, we learn that there were many sources needed to tell the complete story, with archives only being *one* part of understanding how his 'parents ended up in the Sovereignty Commission files' (Eubanks, 2008, 113). Eubanks' experience suggests how citizens get motivated to go to the archives. Another commentator, Malea Powell, considers what physical repositories such as the Newberry suggest about archives, seeing them as 'textual spaces designed to intimidate. I believe they do so as a way to negate their own temporality and impermanence. . . . [T]hese large Gilded Age buildings . . . manage the physical place upon which the imperial society they represent has engaged in empire into a space of argument for the value of Western culture' (Powell, 2008, 120). It is why citizens are sometimes hesitant even to make the effort to go into the archives. Craig Robertson's account of his entrance into Archive II (the National Archives building in College Park, Maryland) is instructive, prompting this researcher to declare, 'The staff here, like all workers in documentary archives, knows the power of the printed and written word' (Robertson, 2005, 68). Such assessments suggest that archivists desire to keep the community out, or, at least, at arm's length.

We might also wonder if the aforementioned concerns about archives and truth have not kept researchers away from the repositories, prompting them to use an array of other sources from those found on the web to those held by community groups, individuals and other places *outside* traditional archival repositories. If anything can assist us in re-creating the past, why worry so much about *official* archives? Even some of the most intrepid users of archives, such as historians, have had some difficulties in how they relate to the documents held by archives. Some historians, seasoned about the challenges of doing historical research in archives because of the many questions raised about the veracity of these sources, now see an opportunity for a new emphasis on archival research. Hoffer provides a sense of what, why and how archives represent the past in his book about history and historical research, noting how little documentation most of us leave behind, although after a generation or so of historians and other scholars arguing about the flaws and bias in archival records, Hoffer suggests that it is safe *now* to go back to these sources:

> What is the philosophy of history for our time? It is that it is safe to go back into the archives, safe to return to the classroom and the lecture hall, safe to sit at the

word processor or to lift the pen over the yellow pad, safe to go to the library and take out a history book or buy one on Amazon.com. It is safe to teach and write and read and listen to history. Something happened out there, long ago, and we have the ability, if we have the faith, to learn what that something is.

Hoffer, 2008, 181

As archivists, we certainly must possess this kind of faith, and we have to wonder what this implies in terms of our efforts to work with disparate groups and documentary evidence that has not often come into archival repositories.

Conclusion: breaking down walls and embracing community

This new, emerging emphasis by archivists on building and interacting with community is, perhaps, partly reflective of the kinds of opportunities represented by the many new social computing technologies available to everyone. Andrew Flinn, a contributor here, also writes elsewhere, 'It is clear that involvement with both digital archives and with community or otherwise marginal or transitory campaigning groups fundamentally challenge the notion that the archivist can afford to be merely a passive recipient of these records.' Flinn emphasizes how these groups are using 'relatively fixed and well-understood digital forms such as e-mail, websites and word-processed documents but also via dynamic and evolving media such as instant messaging, social networking sites, wikis, blogs and other virtual, participatory and collaborative mediums. The skills and expertise required by the archivist working with groups to capture and understand these interactions will have to be significantly enhanced' (Flinn, 2008, 123). In other words, there are many societal changes and transforming expectations that suggest that archivists must engage with a range of communities in order, first, to be able to guarantee the survival of certain forms of documentary evidence and, second, to be relevant.

What I have tried to reflect on in this essay are the challenges posed by archivists striving to be more proactive in adopting a more inclusive, community-based agenda. The mantra of pride, identity, memory and other such concepts are certainly important, but each is burdened with problems that require some careful reflection and weighing of the plusses and minuses of what might be encountered when archivists take to the streets. In order to conclude thinking about this, all we need to remind ourselves about is the powerful symbolic value of archives and their holdings. If books are targets for destruction as symbols, so then are archival documents. Báez partly attributes humankind's destruction of these cultural materials to 'behavior originating in the depths of personality, in a search for the restitution of an archetype of equilibrium, power, or transcendence. . . . The destructive ritual, like the constructive ritual applied to the building of temples, houses, or any work, fixes patterns that return the individual to the community, to shelter, or to the vertigo of purity' (Báez, 2008, 9). He understands that 'books are not destroyed as physical objects but as links to memory, that is, as one of the axes of identity of a person or a community' (Báez, 2008, 12), stressing that the destruction of books is an 'attempt to annihilate a memory considered to be a direct or indirect threat to another memory thought superior' (Báez, 2008, 14). All of these characteristics extend to archives, of course, and they suggest that, as we work with one community to empower them with the preservation of the sources of their past, we may suggest to another community that we are not interested in them, or worse, that we are more inclined to threaten them with a relegation of their identity and culture to oblivion.

All I am trying to say here is that archivists must enter into new relationships with communities with their eyes wide open, especially as moving in this direction might open up new challenges to how their professional mission (one that has vestiges of exclusivity, Western notions of power and authority, assumptions about evidence and objectivity, and additional baggage connected with it) has been defined and implemented. There is much to be gained from more aggressive partnerships with the diversity of the communities constituting society. However, these efforts need to be made carefully and with sensitivity. As we work with one community, we risk losing or offending another. We need to make sure that our involvement with these communities does not allow notions of pride, identity, image and other positive attributes to overwhelm the essential significance of records and record keeping for evidence (warts and all), accountability (often with its unpleasant aspects), and memory (just as often contested as not).

References

Báez, F. (2008) *A Universal History of the Destruction of Books: from ancient Sumer to modern Iraq*, trans. A. MacAdam, Atlas and Co.

Brodie, N., Kersel, M. M., Luke, C. and Tubb, K. W. (eds) (2006) *Archaeology, Cultural Heritage, and the Antiquities Trade*, University Press of Florida.

Burton, A. (ed.) (2005) *Archive Stories: facts, fictions, and the writing of history*, Duke University Press.

Cox, R. J. (1996) *Documenting Localities: a practical model for American archivists and manuscript curators*, Society of American Archivists and Scarecrow Press, Inc.

Craven, L. (ed.) (2008) *What Are Archives? Cultural and theoretical perspectives: a reader*,

Ashgate Publishing Co.

Cuno, J. (2008) *Who Owns Antiquity? Museums and the battle over our ancient heritage,* Princeton University Press.

Eubanks, W. R. (2008) Mississippi On My Mind. In Kirsch, G. E. and Rohan, L. (eds), *Beyond the Archives: research as a lived process,* Southern Illinois University Press, 107–14.

Flinn, A. (2008) Other Ways of Thinking, Other Ways of Being: documenting the margins and the transitory; what to preserve, how to collect. In Craven, L. (ed.), *What Are Archives? Cultural and theoretical perspectives: a reader,* Ashgate Publishing Co, 109–28.

Galland, C. (2008) *Love Cemetery: unburying the secret history of slaves,* HarperOne.

Grandin, G. and Klubock, T. M. (eds) (2007) Truth Commissions: state terror, history, and memory, *Radical History Review,* **97**.

Hamilton, P. and Shopes, L. (eds) (2008) *Oral History and Public Memories,* Temple University Press.

Hoffer, P. C. H. (2008) *The Historian's Paradox: the study of history in our time,* New York University Press.

Ishizuka, K. L. and Zimmerman, P. R. (eds) (2008) *Mining the Home Movie: excavations in histories and memories,* University of California Press.

Kirsch, G. E. and Rohan, L. (eds) (2008) *Beyond the Archives: research as a lived process,* Southern Illinois University Press.

Lefkowitz, M. (2008) *History Lesson: a race odyssey,* Yale University Press.

Masemann, B. (2009) Power, Possession and Post-Modernism: contemporary readings of the colonial archive, *Faculty of Information Quarterly,* January, http://fiq.ischool.utoronto.ca/index.php/fiq/article/view/24/68.

McNeely, I. F. with Wolverton, L. (2008) *Reinventing Knowledge: from Alexandria to the internet,* W. W. Norton and Co.

Native American Archival Materials, Protocols for, (2007), April, www2.nau.edu/libnap-p/protocols.html.

Parrish, S. S. (2006) *American Curiosity: cultures of natural history in the colonial British Atlantic world,* published for the Omohundro Institute of Early American History and Culture by University of North Carolina Press.

Powell, M. (2008) Dreaming Charles Eastman: cultural memory, autobiography, and geography in indigenous rhetorical histories. In Kirsch, G. E. and Rohan, L. (eds), *Beyond the Archives: research as a lived process,* Southern Illinois University Press, 115–27.

Ridener, J. (2008) *From Polders to Postmodernism: a concise history of archival theory,* Litwin Books.

Robertson, C. (2005) Mechanisms of Exclusion: historicizing the archive and the passport. In Burton, A. (ed.), *Archive Stories: facts, fictions, and the writing of history,* Duke University Press, 68–86.

Stoler, A. L. (2009) *Along the Archival Grain: epistemic anxieties and colonial common sense,* Princeton University Press.

Tarlow, S. (2006) Archaeological Ethics and the People of the Past. In Scarre, C. and Scarre, G. (eds), *The Ethics of Archaeology: philosophical perspectives on archaeological practice*, Cambridge University Press, 199–216.

Vismann, C. (2008) *Files: law and media technology*, trans. G. Winthrop-Young, Stanford University Press.

Zimmerman, P. (2008) Introduction: the home movie movement; excavations, artifacts, minings. In Ishizuka, K. L. and Zimmerman, P. R. (eds), *Mining the Home Movie: excavations in histories and memories*, University of California Press, 1–28.

Bibliography

Abrahams, R. D. (1983) *The Man-of-Words in the West Indies: performance and emergence of Creole culture,* Johns Hopkins University Press.

Adami, T. A. and Hunt, M. (2005) Genocidal Archives: the African context – genocide in Rwanda, *Journal of the Society of Archivists,* **26**, 105–21.

Adler, N., Leydesdorff, S., Chamberlain, M. and Neyzi, L. (eds) (2009) *Memories of Mass Repression: narrating life stories in the aftermath of atrocity,* Transaction Publishers.

Akhavan, P. (1998) Justice in The Hague, Peace in the Former Yugoslavia? A commentary on the United Nations war crimes tribunal, *Human Rights Quarterly,* **20**, 737–816.

Allcock, J. B. (ed.) (n.d.) *The International Criminal Tribunal for the Former Yugoslavia,* Research Group 10, report by the Scholars' Initiative, www.cla.purdue.edu/academic/history/facstaff/ingrao/si/scholars.htm.

Alleyne, B. (2002) *Radicals Against Race: black activism and cultural politics,* Berg.

Alleyne, B. (2002) An Idea of Community and its Discontents: towards a more reflexive sense of belonging in multicultural Britain, *Ethnic and Racial Studies,* **25** (4), 607–727.

Ander, E. (2007) *Black and Minority Ethnic Community Archives in London,* MLA London, www.mlalondon.org.uk/uploads/documents/Black_and_Ethnic_Minority_Community_Archives_in_London_final.doc.

Anderson, W. (2006) *Colonial Pathologies: American tropical medicine, race, and hygiene in the Philippines,* Duke University Press.

Antze, P. and Lambek, M. (eds) (1996) *Tense Past: cultural essays in trauma and memory,* Routledge.

Arendt, H. (1977) *Between Past and Future: eight exercises in political thought*, Penguin Books.

Ashmore, R. D., Deaux, K. and McLauglin-Volpe, T. (2004) An Organizing Framework for Collective Identity: articulation and significance of multidimensionality, *Psychological Bulletin*, **130** (1), 80–114.

Atwood, B. and Magowan, F. (eds) (2001) *Telling Stories: indigenous history and memory in Australia and New Zealand*, Allen & Unwin Academic.

Báez, F. (2008) *A Universal History of the Destruction of Books: from ancient Sumer to modern Iraq*, trans. A. MacAdam, Atlas and Co.

Bass, G. J. (2000) *Stay the Hand of Vengeance: the politics of war crimes tribunals*, Princeton University Press.

Basso, K. H. (1996) *Wisdom Sits in Places: landscape and language among the western Apache*, University of New Mexico Press.

Bastian, J. A. (2001) A Question of Custody: the colonial archives of the United States Virgin Islands, *American Archivist*, (Spring/Summer), 96–114.

Bastian, J. A. (2003) *Owning Memory: how a Caribbean community lost its archives and found its history,* Libraries Unlimited.

Bastian, J. A. (2006) Reading Colonial Records Through an Archival Lens: the provenance of place, space and creation, *Archival Science*, **6** (3–4), 267–84.

Bates, D. (1966) *The Passing of the Aborigines: a lifetime spent among the natives of Australia*, Heinemann.

Bates, D. (1985) *The Native Tribes of Western Australia*, edited by I. White, National Library of Australia.

Bates, D. (1992) *Aboriginal Perth and Bibbulmun biographies and legends*, edited by P. J. Bridge, Hesperian Press.

Behar, R. (1997) *The Vulnerable Observer: anthropology that breaks your heart*, Beacon Press.

Bell, D. (ed.) (2006) *Memory, Trauma and World Politics: reflections on the relationship between past and present*, Palgrave Macmillan.

Bellos, L. (2006) Black v Asian?, *Catalyst*, 25 May, http://83.137.212.42/siteArchive/catalystmagazine/Default.aspx.LocID-0hgnew0ex.RefLocID-0hg01b001006009.Lang-EN.htm.

Berlin, I. (2004) American Slavery in History and Memory and the Search for Social Justice, *Journal of American History*, **90** (4), 1251–68.

Berndt, R. M. and Berndt, C. H. (eds) (1979) *Aborigines of the West*, University of Western Australia Press.

Bevernage, B. (2008) Time, Presence, and Historical Injustice, *History and Theory*, **47** (May), 149–67.

Blanton, T. S. (2008) Recovering the Memory of the Cold War: forensic history and Latin America. In Joseph, G. M. and Spenser, D. (eds), *In From the Cold: Latin America's new encounter with the Cold War*, Duke University Press.

Blouin Jr, F. X. and Rosenberg, W. G. (eds) (2007) *Archives, Documentation and*

Institutions of Social Memory: essays from the Sawyer Seminar, University of Michigan Press.

Booms, H. (1987) Society and the Formation of a Documentary Heritage: issues in the appraisal of archival sources, *Archivaria*, **24** (Summer), 69–107.

Booth, W. J. (2006) *Communities of Memory: on witness, identity, and justice*, Cornell University Press.

Borer, T. A. (ed.) (2006) *Telling the truths: truth telling and peace building in post-conflict societies*, University of Notre Dame Press.

Bourne, J. (2008) IRR: the story continues, *Race and Class*, **50** (2), 31–9.

Bowker, G. C. and Star, S. L. (2006) *Sorting Things Out: classification and its consequences*, MIT Press.

Briggs, B. (1977) What is Oral Tradition? In Vatu, S. (ed.), *Talking About Oral Tradition*, University of the South Pacific.

Brightman, C. (1998) *Sweet Chaos: the Grateful Dead's American adventure*, Pocket Books.

Brij, V. L. (1992) *Broken Waves: a history of the Fiji Islands in the twentieth century*, University of Hawaii Press.

Brodie, N., Kersel, M. M., Luke, C. and Tubb, K. W. (eds) (2006) *Archaeology, Cultural Heritage, and the Antiquities Trade*, University Press of Florida.

Brothman, B. (2001) The Past that Archives Keep: memory, history and the preservation of archival records, *Archivaria*, **51**, 48–80.

Brown, S. (1973) *Men from Under the Sky: the arrival of westerners in Fiji*, Charles E. Turtle Company.

Brown, R. H. and Davis-Brown, B. (1998) The Making of Memory: the politics of archives, libraries and museums in the construction of national consciousness, *History of the Human Sciences*, **11** (4), 17–32.

Brubaker, R. and Cooper, F. (2000) Beyond 'Identity', *Theory and Society*, **29** (1), 1–47.

Buckley, L. (2005) Objects of Love and Decay: colonial photographs in a postcolonial archive, *Cultural Anthropology*, **20** (2), 249–70.

Burton, A. (ed.) (2005) *Archive Stories: facts, fictions, and the writing of history*, Duke University Press.

Carbery, G. (1995) Australian Lesbian & Gay Archives, *Archives and Manuscripts*, **23** (1), 30–7.

Carpenter, F. G. (1926) *The World's Biggest Leper Colony, through the Philippines and Hawaii*, Carpenter's World Travels, Doubleday, Page & Company.

Chapman, A. R. and Ball, P. (2001) The Truth of Truth Commissions: comparative lessons from Haiti, South Africa, and Guatemala, *Human Rights Quarterly*, **23**, 1–43.

Christodoulidis, E. A. (2000) Truth and Reconciliation as Risks, *Social Legal Studies*, **9**, 179–204.

Comisión Nacional de Verdad y Reconciliación [Chile] (1993) *Report of the Chilean National Commission on Truth and Reconciliation*, translated by Phillip E. Berryman, Notre Dame Press.

Comisión para el Esclarecimiento Histórico [Guatemala] (1999) *Guatemala: memoria del silencio*, Guatemala, CEH.

Connerton, P. (1989) *How Societies Remember*, Cambridge University Press.

Constable, P. and Valenzuela, A. (1991) *A Nation of Enemies: Chile under Pinochet*, W. W. Norton & Company.

Cook, T. (2001) Archival Science and Postmodernism: new formulations for old concepts, *Archival Science*, **1**, 3–24.

Cox, E. L. (1984) *Free Coloureds in the Slave Societies of St. Kitts and Grenada, 1763–1833*, University of Tennessee.

Cox, R. J. (1996) *Documenting Localities: a practical model for American archivists and manuscript curators*, Society of American Archivists and Scarecrow Press.

Cox, R. J. (2004) *No Innocent Deposits: forming archives by rethinking appraisal*, Scarecrow Press.

Craig, B. L. (2002) Selected Themes in the Literature on Memory and Their Pertinence on Archives, *American Archivist*, **65** (1), 276–89.

Craven, L. (ed.) (2008) *What Are Archives? Cultural and theoretical perspectives: a reader*, Ashgate Publishing.

Crooke, E. (2007) *Museums and Community: ideas, issues and challenges*, Routledge.

Cuno, J. (2008) *Who Owns Antiquity? Museums and the battle over our ancient heritage*, Princeton University Press.

Derrick, R. A. (1946) *A History of Fiji*, Printing Department, Suva Fiji.

Diouf, S. A. (1998) *Servants of Allah: African Muslims enslaved in the Americas*, New York University Press.

Dodd, D. G. and Spaulding, D. (eds) (2000) *The Grateful Dead Reader*, Oxford University Press.

Douglas, M. (2002 [1966]) *Purity and Danger*, Routledge.

Duff, W. M. and Harris, V. (2002) Stories and Names: archival description as narrating records and constructing meanings, *Archival Science*, **2** (3–4), 263–85.

Edkins, J. (2003) *Trauma and the Memory of Politics*, Cambridge University Press.

Ehrenreich, B. (2005) *Dancing in the Streets: a history of collective joy*, Metropolitan and Henry Holt and Company.

Etherton, J. (2006) The Role of Archives in the Perception of Self, *Journal of the Society of Archivists*, **27** (2), 227–46.

Evans, M. (2007) Archives of the People, by the People, for the People, *American Archivist*, **70** (2), 387–400.

Flinn, A. (2007) Community histories, community archives: some opportunities and challenges, *Journal of the Society of Archivists*, **28** (2), 151–76.

Foote, K. (1990) To Remember and Forget: archives, memory, and culture, *American Archivist*, **53** (Summer), 378–92.

Fraser, J. A. and Averill, H. A. (1983) *Organizing an Archives: the Canadian Gay Archives experience*, Canadian Gay Archives.

Freeman, M. (2006) *Truth Commissions and Procedural Fairness*, Cambridge University Press.

Frisch, M. (1991) *A Shared Authority: essays on the craft and meaning of oral and public history*, SUNY Press.

From History to Her Story, www.historytoherstory.org.uk/.

Fuhrer, U. (2004) *Cultivating Minds: identity as meaning making practice*, Routledge.

Galland, C. (2008) *Love Cemetery: unburying the secret history of slaves*, HarperOne.

Gans, D. (2002) *Conversations with the Dead: the Grateful Dead interview book*, Da Capo.

Garretón, M. A. (2003) Memoria y Proyecto de País, *Revista de Ciencia Política*, **23** (2), 215–30.

Garrison, L. (1994) The Black Historical past in British Education. In Stone, P. G. and MacKenzie, R. (eds), *The Excluded Past: archaeology and education*, 2nd edn, Routledge, 231–44.

Geertz, C. (1973) *The Interpretation of Cultures*, Basic Books.

Giddens, A. (1986) *The Constitution of Society: outline of the theory of structuration*, Polity Press.

Gilroy, P. (1995) *There Ain't No Black in the Union Jack*, Routledge.

Goveia, E. (1965) *Slave Society in the British Leeward Islands at the end of the Eighteenth Century*, Yale University Press.

Grandin, G. (2005) The Instruction of Great Catastrophe: truth commissions, national history, and state formation in Argentina, Chile, and Guatemala, *American Historical Review*, **110** (1), 46–7.

Grandin, G. and Klubock, T. M. (eds) (2007) Truth Commissions: state terror, history, and memory, *Radical History Review*, **97**.

Green, N. (1979) *Nyungar – The People: Aboriginal custom in the southwest of Australia*, Creative Research.

Grossberg, L. (1996) Identity and Cultural Studies: is that all there is? In Hall, S. and Du Gay, P. (eds), *Questions of Cultural Identity*, Sage.

Hackman, L. J. and Warnow-Blewett, J. (1987) The Documentation Strategy Process: a model and a case study, *American Archivist*, **50** (Winter), 12–47.

Haebich, A. and Delroy, A. (1999) *The Stolen Generations: separation of Aboriginal children from their families in Western Australia*, Western Australian Museum.

Hagan, J. (2003) *Justice in the Balkans: prosecuting war crimes in the Hague tribunal*, University of Chicago Press.

Halbwachs, M. (1992) *On Collective Memory*, edited by L. Coser, University of Chicago Press.

Hall, C. and Rose, S. O. (2007) *At Home with the Empire: metropolitan culture and the imperial world*, Cambridge University Press.

Hall, S. (1998) Cultural Identity and Diaspora. In Rutherford, J. (ed.), *Identity: community, culture, difference*, Lawrence & Wishart.

Hall, S. (2001) Constituting an Archive, *Third Text*, **54**, 89–92.

Hall, S. (2005) Whose Heritage? Un-settling 'The Heritage', re-imagining the post-nation. In Littler, J. and Naidoo, R. (eds), *The Politics of Heritage: the legacies of 'race'*, Routledge, 23–35.

Ham, G. (1975) The Archival Edge, *American Archivist*, **38** (January), 5–13.

Hamilton, C., Harris, V., Pickover, M. and Reid, G. (eds) (2002) *Refiguring the Archive*, Kluwer Academic.

Hamilton, P. and Shopes, L. (eds) (2008) *Oral History and Public Memories*, Temple University Press.

Harris, V. (2000) Exploring Archives: an introduction to archival ideas and practice in South Africa, 2nd ed., *National Archives of South Africa*.

Harris, V. (2001) On (Archival) Odyssey(s), *Archivaria*, **51** (Spring), 2–14.

Harris, V. (2007) *Archives and Justice: a South African perspective*, Society of American Archivists.

Hayner, P. B. (2001) *Unspeakable Truths: confronting state terror and atrocity*, Routledge.

Hedstrom, M. (2002) Archives, Memory and Interfaces with the Past, *Archival Science*, **2**, 21–43.

Helsinki Watch (1993) *War Crimes in Bosnia-Hercegovina*, vol. 2, Human Rights Watch.

Higman, B. W. (ed.) (1999) *General History of the Caribbean*, vol 6, Methodology and Historiography of the Caribbean, Macmillan Caribbean.

Hoffer, P. C. (2008) *The Historian's Paradox: the study of history in our time*, New York University Press.

Hooper-Greenhill, E. (ed.) (1996) *Cultural Diversity: developing museum audiences in Britain*, Leicester University Press.

Hopkins, I. (2008) Places From Which To Speak, *Journal of the Society of Archivists*, **29** (1), 83–109.

Hunter, M. B. (ed.) (1993) *Sojourner: Black gay voices in the age of AIDS*, Other Countries Press.

Huyssen, A. (2000) Present Pasts: media, politics, amnesia, *Public Culture*, **12** (1), 21–38.

Illich, I. (1991) A Plea for Research on Lay Literacy. In Olson, D. R. and Torrance, N. (eds), *Literacy and Orality*, Cambridge University Press, 28–46.

Ishizuka, K. L. and Zimmerman, P. R. (eds) (2008) *Mining the Home Movie: excavations in histories and memories*, University of California Press.

Jelin, E. (2003) *State Repression and the Labors of Memory*, University of Minnesota Press.

Jimerson, R. C. (2003) Archives and Memory, *OCLC Systems and Services*, **19** (3), 89–95.

Josipovici, G. (1998) Rethinking Memory: too much/too little, *Judaism: A Quarterly Journal of Jewish Life and Thought*, **47** (2), 232–40.

Kansteiner, W. (2002) Finding Meaning in Memory: a methodological critique of collective memory studies, *History and Theory*, (May), 179–97.

Kaplan, E. (2000) We Are What We Collect, We Collect What We Are: archives and the construction of identity, *American Archivist*, **63** (1), 126–51.

Kester, N. G. (ed.) (1997) *Liberating Minds – the stories and professional lives of gay, lesbian, and bisexual librarians and their advocates*, McFarland.

Ketelaar, E. (2001) Tacit Narratives: the meanings of archives, *Archival Science*, **1**, 143–55.

Ketelaar, E. (2002) Archival Temples, Archival Prisons: modes of power and protection, *Archival Science*, **2** (3–4), 221–38.

Ketelaar, E. (2005) Sharing: collected memories in communities of records, *Archives & Manuscripts*, **33**, 44–61.

Kinsman, G. (1987) *The Regulation of Desire – sexuality in Canada*, Black Rose.

Kinsman, G. (1996) *The Regulation of Desire – homo and hetero sexualities*, Black Rose.

Kirsch, G. and Rohan, L. (eds) (2008) *Beyond the Archives: research as a lived process*, Southern Illinois University Press.

Kornbluh, P. (2003) *The Pinochet File: a declassified dossier on atrocity and accountability*, The New Press.

Krause, M. and Yakel, E. (2007) Interaction in Virtual Archives: the Polar Bear Expedition digital collections next generation finding aid, *American Archivist*, **70** (2), 282–314.

Kritz, N. J. (ed.) (1995) *Transitional Justice: how emerging democracies reckon with former regimes*, US Institute of Peace Press.

Kugelmass, J. and Boyarin, J. (eds) (1998) *From a Ruined Garden: the memorial books of Polish Jewry*, Indiana University Press.

Lazzara, M. J. (2006) *Chile in Transition: the poetics and politics of memory*, University Press of Florida.

Lefkowitz, M. (2008) *History Lesson: a race odyssey*, Yale University Press.

Lesh, P. (2005) *Searching for the Sound: my life with the Grateful Dead*, Little, Brown.

Lewis, B. (1975) *History: remembered, recovered, invented*, Princeton University Press.

Light, M. and Hyry, T. (2002) Colophons and Annotations: new directions for the finding aid, *American Archivist*, **65** (2), 216–30.

Lord, A. B. (1960) *The Singer of Tales*, Harvard University Press.

Lowenthal, D. (1998) *The Heritage Crusade and the Spoils of History*, Cambridge University Press.

Manzi, J. et al. (2003) El Pasado que nos Pesa: la memoria colectiva del 11 de septiembre de 1973, *Revista de Ciencia Política*, **23** (2), 177–214.

Marshall, L. (2003) For and Against the Record Industry: an introduction to bootleg collectors and tape traders, *Popular Music*, **22** (1), 57–72.

Masemann, B. (2009) Power, Possession and Post-Modernism: contemporary readings of the colonial archive, *Faculty of Information Quarterly*, January, http://fiq.ischool.utoronto.ca/index.php/fiq/article/view/24/68.

McIntosh, R. (1998) The Great War, Archives, and Modern Memory, *Archivaria*, **46** (Fall), 1–31.

McKemmish, S., Piggott, M., Reed, B. and Upward, F. (eds) (2005) *Archives: recordkeeping in society*, Centre for Information Studies.

McNally, D. (2002) *Long Strange Trip: the inside history of the Grateful Dead*, Broadway Books.

McNeely, I. F. with Wolverton, L. (2008) *Reinventing Knowledge: from Alexandria to the internet*, W. W. Norton.

Menne-Haritz, A. (2001) Access – the reformulation of an archival paradigm, *Archival Science*, **1**, 57–82.

Millar, L. (2006) Touchstones: considering the relationship between memory and archives, *Archivaria*, **61**, 105–26.

Miller, P. B. (2006) Contested Memories: the Bosnian genocide in Serb and Muslim minds, *Journal of Genocide Research*, **8**, 311–24.

Minow, M. (1998) *Between Vengeance and Forgiveness: facing history after genocide and mass violence*, Beacon Press.

MLA London (2006) *Exploring Archives: the George Padmore Institute*, MLA London.

Moran, M. T. (2007) *Colonizing Leprosy: imperialism and the politics of public health in the United States*, University of North Carolina Press.

Morley, D. and Robins, K. (1995) *Spaces of Identity: global media, electronic landscapes, and cultural boundaries*, Routledge.

Morrison, T. G. (ed.) (2004) *Eclectic Views on Gay Male Pornography: pornucopia*, Haworth.

Mould, T. (2003) *Choctaw Prophecy: a legacy of the future*, University of Alabama Press.

Moulian, T. (1998) A Time of Forgetting the Myths of the Chilean Transition, *NACLA Report on the Americas*, **32** (2), 16–21.

Muir, R. (2007) *The New Identity Politics*, Institute for Public Policy Research.

Mulvaney, J. and Green, N. (eds) (1992) *Commandant of Solitude: the journals of Captain Collett Barker 1828–1831*, University of Melbourne Press.

The National Directory of Community Archives in the UK (2007) http://communityarchives.org.uk/.

Neisser, U. (1982) Memory: what are the important questions? In Neisser, U. (ed.), *Memory Observed: remembering in natural contexts*, W. H. Freeman, 3–19.

Nesmith, T. (2005) Reopening Archives: bringing new contextualities into archival theory and practice, *Archivaria*, **60** (Fall), 259–74.

Nestle, J. (1990) The Will To Remember: the Lesbian Herstory Archives of New York, *Feminist Review*, **34**, 86–94.

Neumann, M. and Simpson, T. A. (1997) Smuggled Sound: bootleg recording and the pursuit of popular memory, *Symbolic Memory*, **20** (4), 319–41.

Nora, P. (1989) Between Memory and History: les lieux de mémoire, *Representations*, **6** (Spring), 7–24.

Norton, A. (1993) Ruling Memory, *Political Theory*, **21** (3), 453–63.

O'Donnell, G. and Schmitter, P. C. (1986) *Transitions from Authoritarian Rule: tentative conclusions about uncertain democracies*, Johns Hopkins University Press.

Olick, J. K. (2007) *The Politics of Regret: on collective memory and historical responsibility*, Routledge.

Olson, D. R. and Torrance, N. (eds) (1991) *Literacy and Orality*, Cambridge University Press.

Olwig, K. F. (1985) *Cultural Adaptation and Resistance on St. John: three centuries of Afro-Caribbean life*, University of Florida Press.

Ong, W. (1991) *Orality and Literacy: the technologizing of the word*, Routledge.

Osiel, M. (1997) *Mass Atrocity, Collective Memory, and the Law*, Transaction Publishers.

O'Toole, J. (2000) The Symbolic Significance of Archives. In Jimerson, R. C. (ed.), *Archival Studies: readings in theory and practice*, Society of American Archivists.

Papailias, P. (2005) *Genres of Recollection: archival poetics and modern Greece*, Palgrave Macmillan.

Parrish, S. S. (2006) *American Curiosity: cultures of natural history in the colonial British Atlantic world*, published for the Omohundro Institute of Early American History and Culture by University of North Carolina Press.

Pennebaker, J. W., Paez, D. and Rimé, B. (eds) (1997) *Collective Memory of Political Events: social psychological perspectives*, Lawrence Erlbaum.

Peterson, T. H. (2005) *Final Acts: a guide to preserving the records of truth commissions*, Woodrow Wilson Center Press, Johns Hopkins University Press, www.wilsoncenter.org/press/peterson_finalacts.pdf.

Peterson, T. H. (2006) *Temporary Courts, Permanent Records*, www.usip.org/pubs/specialreports/sr170.html.

Phelps, T. G. (2004) *Shattered Voices: language, violence, and the work of truth commissions*, University of Pennsylvania Press.

Piggott, M. (2005) Building Collective Memory Archives, *Archives and Manuscripts*, **33** (1), 62–83.

Reginbogin, H. R. and Safferling, C. J. M. (eds) (2006) *The Nuremberg Trials: international criminal law since 1945*, Saur.

Rheingold, H. (1994) A Slice of Life in My Virtual Community. In Harasim, L. M. (ed.), *Global Networks: computers and international communication*, MIT Press.

Ridener, J. (2008) *From Polders to Postmodernism: a concise history of archival theory*, Litwin Books.

Riedlmayer, A. (2001) Convivencia under Fire: book-burning and genocide in Bosnia. In Rose, J. (ed.), *The Holocaust and the Book: destruction and preservation*, University of Massachusetts Press, 266–91.

Riedlmayer, A. J. (2007) Crimes of War, Crimes of Peace: destruction of libraries during and after the Balkan wars of the 1990s, *Library Trends*, **56**, 107–32.

Ritzer, J. (2000) Deadheads and Dichotomies: mediated and negotiated readings. In Adams, R. G. and Sardiello, R. (eds), *Deadhead Social Science: you ain't gonna learn what you don't want to know*, Altamira Press.

Roberts, P. A. (1997) *From Oral to Literate Culture: colonial experience in the English West Indies*, University of the West Indies Press.

Robertson, G. (2006) *Crimes Against Humanity: the struggle for global justice*, 3rd edn, The New Press.

Roht-Arriaza, N. (2005) *The Pinochet Effect: transitional justice in the age of human rights*, University of Pennsylvania Press.

Roht-Arriaza, N. and Mariezcurrena, J. (2006) *Transitional Justice in the Twenty-first Century: beyond truth versus justice*, Cambridge University Press.

Rose, N. (1995) Medicine, History and the Present. In Jones, C. and Porter, R. (eds), *Reassessing Foucault: power, medicine and the body*, Routledge.

Rosén, F. I. (2008) Off the Record: outsourcing security and state building of private firms and the question of record keeping, archives, and collective memory, *Archival Science*, **8** (1), 1–14.

Rosenberg, C. E. (1967) *The Cholera Years: the United States in 1832, 1849, and 1866*, University of Chicago Press.

Sachs, A. (2006) Archives, Truth, and Reconciliation, *Archivaria*, **62**, 1–14.

Salter, E.(1971) *Daisy Bates: 'the great white queen of the never never'*, Angus and Robertson.

Samuels, H. W. (1998) *Varsity Letters: documenting modern colleges and universities*, Scarecrow Press.

Scarre, C. and Scarre, G. (eds) *The Ethics of Archaeology: philosophical perspectives on archaeological practice*, Cambridge University Press.

Schomburg, A. (1925) The Negro Digs Up His Past, *Survey Graphic*, **6**, 670–2.

Schwartz, J. and Cook, T. (2002) Archives, Records and Power: the making of modern memory, *Archival Science*, **2** (1–2), 1–19.

Sen, A. (2006) *Identity and Violence: the illusion of destiny*, Allen Lane.

Sinnette, E. D. V. (1989) *Arthur Alfonso Schomburg: Black bibliophile and collector*, Wayne State University Press.

Sivanandan, A. (1981 [2008]) *Catching History on the Wing: race, culture and globalisation*, Pluto Books.

Sivanandan, A. (2008) Race and Resistance: the IRR story, *Race and Class*, **50** (2), 31–9.

Slyomovics, S. (1998) *The Object of Memory: Arab and Jew narrate the Palestinian village*, University of Pennsylvania Press.

Stern, S. J. (2004) *Remembering Pinochet's Chile: on the eve of London, 1998*, Duke University Press.

Stern, S. J. (2006) *Battling for Hearts and Minds: memory struggles in Pinochet's Chile, 1973–1988*, Duke University Press.

Stillman, A. K. (2001) Re-Membering the History of the Hawaiian Hula. In Mageo, J. M. (ed.), *Cultural Memory: reconfiguring history and identity in the postcolonial Pacific*, University of Hawaii Press, 187–204.

Stokes, M. (2002) Strange Fruits: rethinking the gay twenties, *Transition*, **12** (92), 56–79.

Stoler, A. L. (2002) Colonial Archives and the Arts of Governance, *Archival Science*, **2** (1–2), 87–109.

Stoler, A. L. (2009) *Along the Archival Grain: epistemic anxieties and colonial common sense*,

Princeton University Press.

Stover, E. and Weinstein, H. M. (eds) (2004) *My Neighbor, My Enemy: justice and community in the aftermath of atrocity*, Cambridge University Press.

Strange, C. (2004) Symbiotic Commemoration: the stories of Kaluapapa, *History and Memory*, **16** (1), 86–117.

Sullivan, A. (ed.) (2004*) Same-Sex Marriage Pro & Con: a reader*, Vintage.

Sullivan, N. (2003) *A Critical Introduction to Queer Theory*, NYU Press.

Taylor, H. (1982–3) The Collective Memory: archives and libraries as heritage, *Archivaria*, **15** (Winter), 118–30.

Taylor, H. (1995) 'Heritage' Revisited: documents as artifacts in the context of museums and material culture, *Archivaria*, **40**, 8–20.

Teitel, R. G. (2000) *Transitional Justice*, Oxford University Press.

Terracciano, A. (2006) Mainstreaming African, Asian and Caribbean Theatre: the experiments of the Black Theatre Forum. In Godiwala, D. (ed.), *Alternatives within the Mainstream*, Scholars Press, 22–60.

Trager, O. (1997) *The American Book of the Dead: the definitive Grateful Dead encyclopedia*, Fireside.

Trouillot, M.-R. (1995*) Silencing the Past: power and the production of history*, Beacon Press.

Turner, T. (1991) Representing, Resisting, Rethinking: transformations of Kayapo culture and anthropological consciousness. In Stocking Jr, G. W. (ed.), *Colonial Situations: essays on the contextualization of ethnographic knowledge*, University of Wisconsin Press, 285–313.

Velasco Shaw, A. and Francia, L. H. (eds) (2002) *Vestiges of War: the Philippine-American war and the aftermath of an imperial dream, 1899–1999*, NYU Press.

Vismann, C. (2008) *Files: law and media technology*, trans. G. Winthrop-Young, Stanford University Press.

Wesselingh, I. and Vaulerin, A.(2005) *Prijedor: laboratory of ethnic cleansing*, Saqi Books.

Wieviorka, A. (2006) *The Era of the Witness*, transl. by J. Stark, Cornell University Press.

Wilde, A. (1999) Irruptions of Memory: expressive politics in Chile's transition to democracy, *Journal of Latin American Studies*, **31** (2), 473–500.

Williams, P. (2007) *Memorial Museums: the global rush to commemorate atrocities*, Berg.

Wilson, R. (2001) *The Politics of Truth and Reconciliation in South Africa: legitimizing the post-apartheid state*, Cambridge University Press.

Wright, P. (1985) *On Living in an Old Country: the national past in contemporary Britain*, Verso.

Woods, J. M. (1998) Reconciling Reconciliation, *UCLA Journal of International Law and Foreign Affairs*, **81**, 81–127.

Yakel, E. (2003) Archival Representation, *Archival Science*, **3**, 1–25.

Yerushalmi, Y. H. (1996) *Zakhor: Jewish history and Jewish memory*, University of Washington Press.

Zalaquett, J. (1992) Balancing Ethical Imperatives and Political Constraints: the dilemma of new democracies confronting past human rights violations, *Hastings Law Journal*, **43**, 1425–38.

Zalaquett, J. (2006) La Comisión de Chile y su Misión Moral e Histórica, *Hechos del Callejón*, (November), 26–30.

Zerubavel, Y. (1995) *Recovered Roots: collective memory and the making of Israeli national tradition*, University of Chicago Press.

Index

Preserving Archives
Helen Forde

Access to archival material is dependent on the survival of fragile materials: paper, parchment, photographic materials, audiovisual materials and, most recently, magnetic and optical formats. The primary importance of such survival is widely acknowledged but sometimes overlooked in a rush to provide ever better means of access.

Archivists in all types of organizations face questions of how to plan a preservation strategy in less than perfect circumstances, or deal with a sudden emergency. This practical book considers the causes of threats to the basic material, outlines the preservation options available and offers flexible solutions applicable in a variety of situations. Benefiting from the author's contact with international specialists as Head of Preservation Services at The National Archives of the UK, it offers a wide range of case studies and examples. Key topics are:

- standards and policies of archive preservation
- preservation assessment
- understanding archive materials and their characteristics
- managing digital preservation
- archive buildings and their characteristics
- managing archival storage
- managing risks and avoiding disaster
- setting up a conservation workshop
- handling and moving records
- exhibiting archives
- managing a pest control programme
- using and creating surrogates.

This is a vital handbook for professional archivists, but also for the many librarians, curators and enthusiasts, trained and untrained, in museums, local studies centres and voluntary societies in need of good clear advice.

SERIES **Principles and Practice in Records Management and Archives**
Series editor Geoffrey Yeo

2006; 224pp; hardback; 978-1-85604-577-3; £44.95

Digital Preservation
Edited by Marilyn Deegan and Simon Tanner

Digital preservation is an issue of huge importance to the library and information profession right now. With the widescale adoption of the internet and the rise of the world wide web, the world has been overwhelmed by digital information. Digital data is being produced on a massive scale by individuals and institutions: some of it is born, lives and dies only in digital form, and it is the potential death of this data, with its impact on the preservation of culture, that is the concern of this book.

So how can information professionals try to remedy this? Digital preservation is a complex issue involving many different aspects and views, and each chapter of this edited collection is written by an international expert on the topic. Many case studies and examples are used to ground the ideas and theories in real concerns and practice. The book will arm the information professional with the knowledge they need about these important and pressing issues, and give examples of best practice to help find solutions. Chapters cover:

* Key issues in digital preservation
* Strategies for digital preservation
* The status of preservation metadata in the digital library community
* Web archiving
* The costs of digital preservation
* It's money that matters in long-term preservation
* European approaches to digital preservation
* Digital preservation projects: case studies.

This is an indispensable guide for information managers, librarians and archivists worldwide. Others in the information and culture world, such as museum curators, media professionals and web content providers, will also find it essential reading, as will students of digital culture on library and information studies courses and within other disciplines.

 Digital Futures
Series editors Marilyn Deegan and Simon Tanner

2006; 288pp; hardback; 978-1-85604-485-1; £39.95

Preservation Management for Libraries, Archives and Museums
Edited by G. E. Gorman and Sydney J. Shep

This forward-looking collection charts the diversity of preservation management in the contemporary information landscape, and offers guidance on preservation methods for the sustainability of collections from a range of international experts. The authors are connected to a wide international network of professional associations and NGOs, and have been selected not only for their specific expertise, but for the contribution they are making to the future of preservation management. The chapters cover:

- managing the documentary heritage: issues for the present and future
- preservation policy and planning
- intangible heritage: museums and preservation
- surrogacy and the artefact
- moving with the times in search of permanence
- a valuation model for paper conservation research
- preservation of audiovisual media: traditional to interactive formats
- challenges of managing the digitally born artefact
- preserving cultural heritage in times of conflict
- access and the social contract in memory institutions
- redefining 'the collection' in the 21st century.

An informed guide to managing preservation for anyone working in the library, archives, museum and heritage sectors.

2006; 224 pp; hardback; ISBN 978-1-85604-574-2; £44.95